WILLIAM WALLACE:
BRAVE HEART

Other titles by the same author:

Burns: A Biography of Robert Burns
Vagabond of Verse: A Biography of Robert Service

WILLIAM WALLACE

BRAVE HEART

JAMES MACKAY

MAINSTREAM
PUBLISHING
EDINBURGH AND LONDON

MAINSTREAM PUBLISHING COMPANY (EDINBURGH) LTD
7 Albany Street
Edinburgh EH1 3UG

First published in 1995 (reprinted three times)
This edition 1996 (reprinted six times)
Reprinted 1997 (twice)
Reprinted 1998
Reprinted 1999
Reprinted 2000
Reprinted 2002
Reprinted 2003

ISBN 1 85158 823 X

A CIP catalogue record for this book is available from the British Library

Subsidised by THE SCOTTISH ARTS COUNCIL

Typeset in Palatino by Saxon Graphics Ltd, Derby
Printed and bound in Great Britain by Butler & Tanner Ltd, Frome

For Willy and Muriel

CONTENTS

INTRODUCTION

No national hero has ever excited greater admiration than William Wallace. No hero has remained such a shadowy figure, his life and actions beset by myths and contradictions. When Scotland's fortunes were at their lowest, when the Scots were oppressed and their nation virtually obliterated, Wallace emerged from obscurity like some bright meteor in the night sky. He gained a spectacular victory over the English in one pitched battle and sustained a crushing defeat in a second. He disappeared from recorded history just as swiftly as he had come, emerging only briefly seven years later when he was betrayed to the English, brought to London, subjected to a mockery of a trial and then done to death in a most hideous and barbaric manner.

If we confine ourselves to the facts recorded in contemporary and near-contemporary chronicles, Wallace's appearance, disappearance and ultimate fate are about equally mysterious. What is even more extraordinary, in such a view of his career, is the fact that this man became, and has remained in popular belief, *the* undoubted, undisputed hero of the Scottish Wars of Independence, so that the highest ideal of Scottish patriotism has ever since been associated with his name.

The enigma of Wallace, the landless younger son of a minor nobleman, who, without power, privilege or patronage, rose meteorically to become the political leader of his country and its most skilful general when scarcely out of his teens, has excited the imagination for centuries, from the epic poem of Blind Harry to the celluloid exploits of Mel Gibson. The admiration and gratitude of the generations which immediately followed, intensified by national sentiment, led his countrymen to exaggerate many of Wallace's deeds and to imbue him with personal qualities belonging rather to the realms of romance than of reality. At the same time, however, his character was vilified by English propagandists (not only the monkish chroniclers of his own time but many historians nearer the present day). On one side he was a patriot, a hero and a martyr; on the other a brigand, a traitor and a bloodthirsty outlaw.

In an era when the natural leaders — the earls, barons and great magnates and prelates of Scotland — betrayed their country for their own selfish ends, William Wallace shines forth as the one man who never swerved for an instant in his devotion to Scotland and its liberty. Almost miraculously he was to lead the common people in a struggle against the finest army in Europe, and defeat it. Such a hero must be endowed with personal prowess, physical and moral courage, a lofty devotion to duty and spiritual qualities far exceeding those which fall to ordinary mortals. His exploits during life assumed the character of the prodigious; his death and dismemberment came to be regarded as the sacrifice required to redeem his country and secure its salvation; and his spirit continued to haunt every spot that could, however remotely, be associated with his memory.

Such uncritical adulation inevitably led to reappraisal. Exaggeration of his valorous deeds laid them wide open to sober criticism. Sceptics pared away the layers of myth until it seemed as if the lineaments of the popular hero would disappear altogether. Even nowadays there is a school of thought which rejects everything of popular tradition that cannot be corroborated by contemporary records. Nevertheless, historical research over the past century and a half has gone far to confirm many things connected with Wallace's life which for a long time were treated as imaginary; and the real features of the man are found, although not perhaps corresponding exactly with the popular image, to be of an even nobler type.

The aspect of the traditional portrait of Wallace with which critics and detractors had the least forbearance concerned his physical attributes — his unusual stature, his extraordinary strength and stamina, his powers of endurance, his dauntless courage, his martial accomplishments and feats of prowess. But when we consider the circumstances in which he was placed, and the times in which he lived, we can see that these attributes were really essential to a leader of men, who had nothing but these very attributes to commend him. War, as conducted in the late thirteenth century, was not a matter of science or technology, but mostly of brute strength, individual courage and dexterity in the use of the dirk and broadsword, the spear and the battle-axe.

Significantly the longbow, one of the first weapons which enabled men to kill each other at a distance, was only just coming into use; hitherto regarded with loathing and even outlawed by the international conventions of warfare, it was to revolutionise strategy just as the introduction of gunpowder and firearms would a century later. But in Wallace's time battles were fought and wars were won by relatively small bodies of men engaged in bloody hand-to-hand, close-quarter combat.

The struggle begun by William Wallace was eventually completed by Robert Bruce. The latter possessed immense advantages of wealth, land, feudal power, royal connections and international influence. Yet he would have failed to achieve his goals had he not been, quite simply, a strong man, capable of facing any personal danger, an accomplished warrior on foot and horseback, skilled in the use of the weapons of the period. How much more so must it have been with Wallace who, lacking every one of Bruce's material and hereditary advantages, emerged in 1297 as the leader of a well-disciplined force capable of taking on and defeating the most formidable military array in all Europe, commanded by a seasoned veteran of many campaigns in Wales and the Continent.

In trying to explain the enigma that was William Wallace I have carefully re-examined the poetic chronicle of Wyntoun and the saga compiled by Blind Harry the Minstrel. Unless we are to believe that these authors, without any motive, asserted deliberate falsehoods, capable at the time of instant refutation, there did exist in their day numerous 'gestis and deedis', the popular accounts, both oral and written, concerning Wallace's exploits. It seems that Harry also had access to a Latin manuscript compiled by Wallace's chaplain, Master John Blair, and those portions of his poem possessing a wealth of circumstantial detail appear to have been derived from this long-lost source.

Unfortunately, interwoven in the saga is a mass of oral tradition which ranges from the possible to the frankly improbable, with a cavalier disregard for chronology or dates. Ludicrous passages describing the great Battle of Biggar which never took place or the state of Scotland on the eve of Wallace's betrayal have tended to blind scholars to the essential veracity of Harry and the value of his poem as an historical record. I have analysed the episodes related in this poem, sifting the wheat from the chaff, and comparing them with primary source material ranging from the contemporary English chronicles to the charters, writs and other documents which have survived from this period.

In the course of my research I have made use of the facilities of many libraries at both national and local level. I am indebted as ever to the unfailing courtesy of the staff of the British Library, London; the Bodleian Library, Oxford; the National Library of Scotland, Edinburgh; the university libraries of Edinburgh and Glasgow and the Mitchell Library in Glasgow. For help in tracking down monuments and memorials, many of them all but forgotten in our mundane age, I must record my thanks to councillors and employees in Strathclyde Region, Central Region, Kilmarnock and Loudoun District, Cunninghame District, Inverclyde District and Clydesdale District. A number of individuals have given me information or assistance with this project and I should like to take this opportunity to convey my heartfelt thanks to Andrew Boyle, Sheena and William Frew, Dr Helen Henley, John Holman and Norman Shead. Finally, I would like to thank John Fleck for reading the proofs and making a number of helpful suggestions and constructive criticisms.

James Mackay
Glasgow, 1995

1

ORIGINS AND
BOYHOOD

Of Scotland born, my richt name is Wallace.

BLIND HARRY

Wilhelmus Waleis, Scotus, et de Scotia ortus (William Wallace, a
Scot and of Scottish birth).

INDICTMENT, WESTMINSTER, 23 AUGUST 1305

FEW national heroes have had such an obscure and contradictory background as William Wallace. The year of his birth
has been variously stated as anywhere between 1260 and 1278,
his father's name was Malcolm, Andrew or William, his mother's name is given as Jean, Joan or Margaret or not stated at all,
her surname being Crawford, Craufurd, Crawfoord or some
other variant. But most glaring of all is the mistaken assumption
that Wallace was born in Renfrewshire. This error can be traced
back no further than the early eighteenth century but has been
blindly followed by every writer since that time.

It derives from the fact that William Wallace was styled 'of
Ellerslie', from the land held by his father Sir Malcolm Wallace,
who was styled of Auchenbothie and Ellerslie. As Auchenbothie
is in Renfrewshire (near Kilmacolm) it has invariably been
understood that Ellerslie referred to the Renfrewshire town of
Elderslie, and this view has, not surprisingly, been reinforced by
the town itself which, in the course of the nineteenth century,

created the myth of his birth and boyhood there. A small castellated house, the oldest edifice in the village, was habitually pointed out to visitors as the birthplace of the Wallace. No matter that this structure could not be dated earlier than the sixteenth century, the belief arose that it must have been erected on the spot where the patriot was born.

Likewise a venerable yew in the garden, popularly known as Wallace's Yew and still standing, is associated with the myth although it could not have been planted till centuries later. There was also a gnarled oak nearby which, from its great age, was regarded as somehow connected with Wallace. Indeed, a local legend, not supported by any reference in Blind Harry's poem, let alone historical record, has it that this great oak once gave shelter not only to the patriot but also to three hundred of his followers, when they were being hard pressed by the English. An eighteenth-century description of this ancient oak states that it had a girth of 21 feet, stood 67 feet tall and its branches covered almost five hundred square yards. In the early nineteenth century, however, the relic-mongers got to work and by mid-century only a blackened trunk remained, and even that perished in the great storm of February 1856.

To this day Elderslie proudly boasts its connection with Scotland's greatest hero, not only in the road signs at the boundaries of the town, but in the Wallace Tavern whose Ring o' Bells sign perpetuates one of the many myths and legends surrounding the local hero. The ancient yew and the foundations of the castellated house have been preserved in a public park alongside an ornate monument, erected as recently as 1970 and now the town's chief landmark.

Much of the history of William Wallace is derived, directly or indirectly, from the epic poem composed by Blind Harry in the fifteenth century, more than a century and a half after Wallace met his death in 1305. Harry claimed — and, indeed, made frequent references to his source — that his poem was based on a prose manuscript compiled by John Blair in Latin and submitted to Pope Boniface but apparently no longer extant. Blair was a friend of Wallace from their schooldays and subsequently his chaplain. As Blair's manuscript has never been found, it is a matter of speculation how closely Harry followed it. While it is unlikely that the minstrel was blind from birth (as was claimed by the sixteenth-century historian John Major) or, indeed, the uneducated man which, self-deprecatingly, he claimed to be, he was certainly steeped in the oral traditions of his time and doubtless grafted on numerous anecdotes which had circulated during and since the time of Wallace.

The lengthy passages of the poem dealing with Wallace's early career and rise to fame have an air of verisimilitude and a wealth of circumstantial detail which, confirmed by those shreds of documentary evidence still extant, lead me to suppose that this part at least of the minstrel's epic is a useful guide, despite some very obvious discrepancies in chronology. By contrast, there are glaring errors in the later sections, such as the great Battle of Biggar (which never took place) and the assertion that, on the eve of his betrayal, Wallace had virtually cleared Scotland of the hated Southron, when in fact he was a fugitive, on the run with no more than a handful of men. This points to the fact of John Blair's lost account having terminated some time after 1298 but probably by 1303, the minstrel then filling in later detail from popular myths compounded by his own imagination.

Such glaring errors tended to blind scholars to the general usefulness of the poem, and it was vilified and neglected by turns. This trend was set by Lord Hailes, towards the close of the eighteenth century, questioning the value of Blind Harry's poem as an historical record and echoing the doubts expressed by John Major centuries earlier. Perhaps this was a case of familiarity breeding contempt for Major, born two hundred years after Wallace, was a boy at the time when Blind Harry was writing his poem and tended to be rather dismissive of the exploits set out in that saga. Major fell into the trap of rejecting out of hand stories which he could not corroborate from independent sources; but research by later scholars showed Major to be wrong and Harry right. For a time the exploits recounted in the poem were accepted without question, but then the pendulum swung back again at the end of the eighteenth century and historians since that time have tended to ignore or overlook Harry, seeking the truth elsewhere. It is only within quite recent years that Harry's statements have been re-examined and tested against historical evidence, but a thorough analysis of the poem is still awaited.

Blind Harry mentions Ellerslie without actually saying where this place was, but all of the other details concerning the antecedents of Wallace, together with his exploits before he became a national figure, are placed fairly and squarely in Ayrshire, and more particularly that portion of the county known as Kyle. Moreover, John Major himself stated that 'This William was one of a family of only inferior nobility in the district of Kyle, in which the surname is common.'[1] The confusion arose because Elderslie in Renfrewshire developed into a place of some importance, whereas the place from which the hero's family took their title was a small and quite obscure estate near Kilmarnock. It featured on commercial maps as recently as 1946 but has since all but vanished, confined to the large-scale Ordnance Survey sheets, and it was not of sufficient importance to merit an entry in the six-volume Gazetteer of Scotland, published in the 1880s. Ellerslie or Elderslie are variants of the same name and both spellings have, at some time or another, been used in maps and documents to denote both the Ayrshire and Renfrewshire places. Today the Ayrshire place has adopted the more modern spelling of Elderslie, but throughout this book I have retained the original spelling merely to distinguish it from the Renfrewshire town.

Ellerslie, Ayrshire, was, until the Second World War, a hamlet which developed around a colliery and brickworks. All have now vanished, but the name is perpetuated in Elderslie, a large house which was formerly the home of the colliery manager and is now the residence of Sheena and William Frew, directors of Annandale Engineering, a company specialising in architectural and ornamental ironwork. Ironically, while the name Ellerslie has virtually disappeared, this part of Kilmarnock and Loudoun district is now known as Annandale — not to be confused with the historic district of that name in Dumfriesshire, the heartland of the Bruce family.

When the myth of the Renfrewshire origin developed in the nineteenth century a counter-claim was raised by the Wallace Club in Ayrshire. Even this overlooked the likeliest birthplace (at Ellerslie itelf) and maintained that Wallace was born at Riccarton Castle. This ancient edifice had long since disappeared but a plaque was erected on the wall of a building in Fleming Street, Kilmarnock, occupying the site of the castle. During road-widening in the 1980s, however, this building was demolished and the plaque was consigned to the oblivion of a district council repository. It has now been re-erected — on the wall of Kilmarnock Fire Station — and its existence must be one of Ayrshire's best-kept secrets.

Even the surname Wallace has given rise to confusion. The medieval names Walays, Waleys or Wallensis (from which are derived the modern surnames of Wallace, Wallis, Welsh and Vallance) merely denoted a Welshman in the language of the English-speaking peoples in both England and Scotland, just as people surnamed Inglis were Scots of English descent, and the Scotts were Borderers from the Scottish side. The surname or rather epithet Waleys or Wallensis is widespread in charters, writs and other documents of the twelfth and thirteenth centuries in both England and Wales. From this arose the notion that the Wallaces had come to Scotland from Wales, which Blind Harry, alluding to the father of the hero, expressed thus:

> The secund O he was of great Wallace,
> The which Wallas full worthily that wrought
> When Walter hyr of Waillis from Warrayn socht.

'The secund O' in this context means great-grandson. These lines refer to Walter, the Steward and progenitor of the Stuart dynasty, who was a Warren or Warenne of Shropshire. There is an ancient tradition in the Welsh Marches that Walter Warenne courted a Welsh lady to whom he was vaguely related, and that the go-between in the affair was one Richard the Welshman, the great-grandfather of Sir Malcolm Wallace, father of William. This tradition is confirmed by the fact that Ricardus Wallensis held lands in Kyle, the northern part of Ayrshire, under Walter the Steward. Walter was the son of Alan, himself the son of Flaald, a Norman mercenary who had obtained considerable lands in Shropshire from William the Conqueror. Alan married a daughter of Warin, Sheriff of Shropshire, from whom the surname of his son was derived. Walter Warenne was one of that Norman military élite recruited by King David I (1124–53) to come north and assist him in subduing the diverse Celtic and Anglo-Saxon peoples under his rule, and welding them into a nation. King David introduced the feudal system and made grants of land to these Norman knights and barons. Thus the feudal bailieries of Cunninghame, Kyle and Carrick came into being. The River Irvine, running due west to the sea, formed the boundary between Cunninghame and Kyle.

In the thirteenth century Cunninghame was governed from the port of Irvine by Hugh de Morville, the Great Constable of Scotland, while Kyle came under the control of Walter Fitzalan. Richard Wallace may have been one of those retainers who settled in Kyle as a vassal of Walter whom the King appointed as his Steward. On the other hand, the story of a Welsh origin may be entirely fanciful, for Wallensis applied just as well to the people of the south-west of Scotland of ancient Cymric stock, the descendants of the Britons of Strathclyde, ethnically and linguistically akin to the Cumbrians and the Cambrians.

At any rate, Richard Wallace acquired lands in the vicinity of Kilmarnock and gave his name to the village and parish of Ricard-tun, or Riccarton. Richard was a witness to a charter of Walter the Steward, granted to the Abbey of Paisley some time before 1174. The Steward held lands of the King in both Renfrewshire and Ayrshire and it would not be surprising for members of the Wallace family to hold lands of the Steward in either or both counties.

According to one account, Richard Wallace had a son and grandson of the same name, contemporaries of the next three Stewards. The third Richard, styled Walense alias Waleys, lived in the time of Walter II and his son Alexander the Steward. He held the estate of Auchencrowe or Auchencruive on the River Ayr, as well as the original Riccarton estate. To fit the nineteenth-century notion of Elderslie in Renfrewshire as the birthplace of the hero, a pedigree was concocted which traced William's ancestry to one Henry Walense who held lands in that county from Walter, the first Steward of that name. Henry was believed to be a younger brother of Richard the first Wallace; furthermore, it was conjectured that he had a son named Adam who was the grandfather of William. Improbably, after the judicial murder of William in 1305, his Renfrewshire estates were alleged to have passed some time later to the Wallaces of Riccarton. The source of this story was George Crawfurd who compiled a history of Renfrewshire, published in 1710. Crawfurd asserted that 'the lands of Eldersly returned to the family of Craigie, a younger son of that ancient family obtaining them in patrimony about the beginning of the reign of King Robert III', which would place this transaction no earlier than the closing years of the fourteenth century.

Even in this regard, however, there is nothing to connect the Wallaces of Renfrewshire with the Wallaces of Craigie. A John Wallace of Elderslie is recorded as appending his seal to a resignation of the lands of Fultoun to the monks of Paisley in 1409 and he may be the same *Johannes Wallace de Eldersly, Scutifer* (shield-bearing) mentioned in a chartulary of the Monastery of Paisley in 1432; but a landowner in Ayrshire would be just as likely to have a connection with Paisley Abbey (the greatest monastic foundation in the west of Scotland) as one from Renfrewshire, or Lanarkshire for that matter. There were certainly people named Wallace holding land in Renfrewshire by the mid-fifteenth century and this reinforced the myth, but unfortunately there is nothing which definitely connects them with the Wallaces of Craigie. The last of the Renfrewshire line was Helen Wallace who married Archibald Campbell of Succoth and sold her estate to Alexander Speirs in 1769. To confuse the matter even further, it should be noted that the land which she disposed of, and which was called Elderslie, was not actually in the village of that name, but located some miles away, in the parish of Renfrew. Miss Wallace and her family had merely assumed the title 'of Elderslie' on the assumption that they were somehow descended from, or at least connected with, the famous medieval hero. On this land the Speirs family built a mansion called Elderslie in 1777–82 and over the ensuing century acquired a number of relics allegedly associated with William Wallace, which they installed in their house. These relics (including one of the many two-handed broadswords which, to this day, masquerade as Wallace's weapon) were of doubtful provenance to say the least, but were accepted unquestioningly, just as the assumption that William Wallace had hailed from Elderslie, Renfrewshire, was taken for granted. By Victorian times, therefore, the myth itself had acquired considerable antiquity.

In another account, however, the son of the first Richard was Adam Wallace, referred to in a document of the second Walter as *miles noster* (our knight). He is said to have been the father of two sons, Sir Richard, who succeeded him in the Kyle estates, and Malcolm. Within the parish of Riccarton was the five-pound land of Ellerslie, which was held by Malcolm 'in portion-natural, holding by ward and relief of the family of Richardton'.[2] Ellerslie, to the south-east of Crosshouse and west of Annanhill, was about a mile west of the medieval town of Kilmarnock and a little over a mile north-west of Riccarton village.

According to the Craigie Wallace genealogy, however, Malcolm married Jean Craufoord, daughter of Sir Ranald (sometimes shown as Ronald or Reginald) Craufoord of Corsbie in Ayrshire, the Sheriff of that county. From other sources, however, it appears more likely that the lady's name was Margaret de Craufurd. The archaic name Corsbie vanished long ago but, translated into modern English, it survives as Crosshouse, on the road between Kilmarnock and Irvine and about a mile north-west of Ellerslie. The issue of this marriage included three sons, Sir Malcolm the eldest, William and John, as well as at least two daughters who were much older than their famous brother for each had a son, respectively Tom Halliday and Edward Little, who, though nephews of William, were his faithful companions in arms. Blind Harry is, however, the sole source for these details. He refers to Edward Little as Wallace's sister's son and Tom Halliday as 'sib sister's son to Good Wallace'.

In the *Scotichronicon*,[3] compiled about 1442 and thus predating Blind Harry by some thirty years, the reference to the origins of William Wallace is tantalisingly brief, the *Anglicorum malleus* (hammer of the English) being described simply as *filius nobilis militis* {   }. In the manuscript preserved in Corpus Christi College, Cambridge, the Latin reference to the 'noble son of a knight' is followed by about half a line which had been left blank for the name of William's father to be inserted subsequently, when the compiler had ascertained this detail. In the copy of the manuscript now in the National Library of Scotland, *Malcolm Vales* was inserted in a much later hand, while the earliest printed version inserted the words *eiusdem nominis* (of the same name, i.e. William). But the Harleian manuscript in the British Library, another version of the *Scotichronicon*, has an entirely different insertion: *domini Andree Vallace domini Kragge* (Lord Andrew Wallace, Lord of Craigie).[4] This variant has, at least, the merit of being more substantial and specific than the others, which suggests that someone took great pains to ascertain the truth.

The family of Craufurd, to use the Ayrshire spelling, traced its ancestry back to Thorlongus, an Anglo-Danish chief who was expelled from Northumberland by William the Conqueror and who obtained lands in the Merse from King Edgar of Scotland around the beginning of the twelfth century. A hundred years later, a Sir Ragnald or Reginald de Craufurd married the heiress of Loudoun at the head of the Irvine Valley, and was created first hereditary Sheriff of Ayr. His grandson, Sir Ranald, was the father-in-law of Sir Malcolm Wallace and thus the grandfather of William. In turn, he was succeeded in both the title and the sheriffdom by his eldest son, also Sir Ranald, the brother of Margaret de Craufurd and uncle of William Wallace. This is an important point, for those who take the view that the Scottish hero was a very young man cite as evidence the fact that his grandfather Sir Ranald was still alive in 1307.[5] In fact William's grandfather was dead by 1297 and the Sir Ranald who was alive ten years later was the hero's uncle.

The Morville family declined in power in the course of the twelfth century and their lands in Cunninghame passed to the Craufurds in 1189. The Craufurds of Craufurdland Castle continued to be major landowners in the district until within living memory. Another family to which the Wallaces were attached by ties of blood were the Boyds of Kilmarnock, who had their seat at Dean Castle about a mile north of the medieval town. A witness to a charter of 1205 between Bryce de Eglingstoun (Eglinton) and the town of Irvine was one *Dominus Robertus Boyd, miles* (Lord Robert Boyd, knight). There is a tradition that this surname was derived from the Gaelic word *buidhe* (yellow-haired) but it may equally have been of Norman origin. The son of this knight, also Sir Robert, distinguished himself at the Battle of Largs in 1263. A local tradition maintains that in the mopping-up operations after Haakon's defeat, Sir Robert Boyd and his companions routed a Norse army at a place called Goldberry Hill. The words Gold Berry were later adopted as the motto of the Boyds of Kilmarnock in commemoration of this feat of arms. The son of the victor of Goldberry, another Robert Boyd, was one of Wallace's ablest lieutenants throughout the early campaigns of the Wars of Independence and subsequently gave his staunch support to Robert Bruce.

Apart from the families to which he was related, the majority of the incidents in the early part of William's military career took place in the Irvine Valley, so that the tradition of a connection with Elderslie in Renfrewshire is no longer tenable.

The matter of William's birthplace is more easily resolved than the date of his birth. In this regard Blind Harry is contradictory, stating that he was forty-five years of age when he was betrayed to the English.[6] Some authorities have regarded this as a clerical error for thirty-five, which would place his birth in 1270 rather than 1260, but the same lines conveyed that Master John Blair and Sir Thomas Gray (the parson of Libberton in Lanarkshire) had known Wallace from the age of sixteen 'until other nine and twenty had passed'. This is flatly contradicted by Harry elsewhere, when he states unequivocally that William was only eighteen at the time of the Selby incident in Dundee. This, in turn, raises the question of when this fracas took place. Some scholars have suggested the end of 1296 or the beginning of 1297, which would put William's date of birth in 1278; but this would make him no more than nineteen years of age when he defeated the English at Stirling Bridge — which is preposterous. Alexander Brunton (1881), on no good ground, assumed that the Selby incident took place in 1294 and from this computed the date of Wallace's birth as January 1276, making him twenty-one at the time of his greatest victory and twenty-nine years and seven months old at the time of his execution. It seems more probable that the Selby incident took place in December 1291, as will be shown in Chapter Two, and this would therefore place William's birth in 1272 or 1273. Various nineteenth-century writers have suggested a date *circa* 1270, while the Marquess of Bute[7] made a plausible case in favour of 1274, which had a certain attraction, for it implied that Wallace was the same age as Robert Bruce who succeeded where he had failed. Aeneas Mackay[8] cautiously suggested ?1272, which is probably not far out.

The Scotland into which William was born about 1272–73 was prosperous and at peace. Alexander III had been on the throne since 1249 and his comparatively long reign was to last another fourteen years. He continued the policies of his predecessors, relying heavily on a baronage which was Norman in origin and French in tongue to administer his diverse dominions.

The native inhabitants of Scotland had only been under the rule of the one monarch for about four generations and local loyalties were as yet stronger than any notion of national patriotism. The term Scotia, previously used to designate the land north of the Clyde and Forth isthmus, was only applied to the whole of the kingdom in the reign of Alexander III. Orkney and Shetland were still part of the Scandinavian empire, while the Inner and Outer Hebrides had only been under Alexander's sovereignty since 1266. Caithness and Sutherland were still largely Norse, while large tracts of the north and west, as well as Galloway in the extreme south-west, were Celtic; even in the Lowland counties of Ayr and Lanark was Gaelic still commonly spoken. Paradoxically, the Scottish language, which would eventually dominate the Lowlands, was originally confined to the southeast, around Edinburgh and the Lothians, although in the course of the twelfth century it spread all over the Forth and Clyde basins, then south to the Solway and west to Kyle. In the time of Alexander III it was spreading up the east coast north of the Forth.

The largest and most prosperous town in the kingdom was Berwick, situated at the mouth of the River Tweed and the centre of Scotland's thriving trade with the Low Countries and the Baltic. It was described by one English chronicler of the thirteenth century as 'a city so populous and of such trade that it might justly be called another Alexandria, whose riches were the sea and the waters its walls'. It was, indeed, one of the most important ports anywhere in the British Isles, producing a customs revenue estimated as equal to a quarter of England's as a whole. Significantly, the bulk of its trade was with the Low Countries, northern Germany and Scandinavia, and relatively little with England. Edinburgh, the capital city, was almost as large, whereas Glasgow was relatively unimportant but for its cathedral. The population of Scotland was less than half a million — about a quarter that of its southern neighbour.

Relations with England were better than they had been for generations. Because the border between the two countries had never been precisely delineated, the Scottish kings long nurtured an ambition to annex Cumbria and Westmorland which had at one time formed the southern part of the kingdom of Strathclyde, and also portions of the old kingdom of

23

Northumbria. It was to resist Scottish expansionism under Malcolm III Canmore that William the Conqueror had founded Newcastle upon Tyne in 1079 and his son William Rufus had fortified Carlisle in 1091.

The frontier effectively lay in a straight line from the Solway to the Tyne. Ironically, the claim to Northumberland rested on the marriage of David I to the granddaughter of Earl Siward of Northumbria. King Henry I would not recognise David's claim to this powerful northern earldom, but readily acknowledged the Scottish king as Earl of Huntingdon whose title and estates also came to him as a result of his marriage. It was this ambiguous position, of Scottish kings who were also English magnates, which was to bedevil Anglo-Scottish relations at the end of the thirteenth century.

David's marriage might have won him a valuable English estate and a prestigious title, but it was to embroil him in English politics and create problems a century later. During the wars between Stephen and Matilda for succession to the English throne (1135–54), King David used the chaotic situation to further his own ends. The Empress Matilda was David's niece — as was the wife of Stephen who granted Northumberland as an English fief to Prince Henry, son of King David and heir to the Scottish throne. David died in 1153 and Prince Henry predeceased him, so his successor Malcolm IV (1153–65), derisively known as 'the Maiden', was forced to surrender David's territorial gains. Malcolm was succeeded by William the Lion (1165–1214), a man of sterner stuff as his epithet implies. When the English king, Henry II, was confronted by an uprising in 1173, King William invaded northern England in support of the rebels. His capture, near Alnwick, in July 1174 not only put paid to his territorial ambitions but resulted in the temporary loss of Scottish sovereignty.

Since the tenth-century alliances against the Danes, in which the English ruler had been styled as 'father and lord' of the king of Scots, the position of Scotland in relation to England had been open to various interpretations. Since the time of William the Conqueror the Scottish kings had held English fiefs and had done homage for them. The exact nature of this homage had never been defined and the meaning of the act of homage had been left deliberately ambiguous.

The act of homage was a ceremony used in the granting of land, and indicated the submission of a vassal to his lord. It could only be received by the suzerain in person. The vassal would uncover his head, lay aside his sword and spurs, and kneel before his lord. He would stretch out his hands, which the lord would grasp in his, and then say: 'I become your man from this day forth, of life and limb, and will hold faith to you for the lands I hold.' The oath of fealty followed the act of homage, and then came the ceremony of investiture, either directly on the ground or by the delivering of a turf or a handful of earth. The obligations involved in the act of homage were often general and varied in nature, but they provided a strong moral sanction for more specific engagements.

So far as the position of the kingdom of Scotland in relation to the King of England, the matter was clarified by the Treaty of Falaise (1174); William the Lion was only released from captivity on condition that he did homage to Henry for the Scottish crown. The terms of this treaty, however, were cancelled fifteen years later when Richard the Lionheart sold the rights acquired by his father for a large sum of money which was used to finance Richard's adventures in the Holy Land. This bargain merely annulled the Treaty of Falaise and left the question of homage exactly where it had been before 1174.

William the Lion continued to hope for the annexation of Northumberland and in 1194 offered to purchase it from the ever impecunious Richard, but the deal fell through when Richard insisted that William would have no right to fortify castles in this territory. Furthermore, William the Lion meekly gave way to Richard's successor King John, to whom he conceded the right to choose a bride for his son Alexander, the English princess Joanna (sister of Henry III). Alexander II (1214–49) tried to seize Northumberland while King John was otherwise preoccupied by his rebellious barons at the time of Magna Carta; but in 1236 he was forced to give up his claims to Northumberland in exchange for a grant of land in the north of England.

Ever since the time of Malcolm Canmore in the eleventh century, the Scottish kings had chosen English princesses as their brides — or had them foisted on them. When Joanna of England, first wife of Alexander II, died childless, he broke with tradition and defied his brother-in-law Henry III by choosing a bride for himself. Marie de Couci was the great-great-granddaughter of Louis VI of France. Alexander III, who ascended the Scottish throne at the age of eight, was therefore half French. The years of his minority were marked by a bitter struggle between two powerful Norman factions led by Walter Comyn, Earl of Menteith, and Alan Durward, Justiciar of Scotland. In 1251 he was manœuvred into marriage with his cousin Princess Margaret of England, and Henry III seized the opportunity to demand from his son-in-law homage for the kingdom of Scotland, homage which Alexander firmly but politely refused. Otherwise Alexander's relations with Henry III who was his uncle as well as his father-in-law, and Edward I, his brother-in-law, were superficially very cordial.

The marriage of Alexander's daughter Margaret to Eirik of Norway, son of King Magnus and grandson of that old adversary Haakon, cemented the treaty by which the Norwegian king had relinquished the Western Isles. Alexander was well satisfied with the political marriages which seemed to safeguard Scotland from external threats, and in the latter years of his long reign he concentrated on consolidating his kingdom. Alexander's equanimity was marred only by a succession of domestic tragedies. His younger son David died unmarried in 1281. Alexander, the elder son and heir to the throne, died three years later; although married to the daughter of the Count of Flanders, he had produced no heir. In 1283 his sister Margaret of Norway died in childbirth, leaving as heir to the Scottish and Norwegian thrones a girl baptised Margaret but better known to posterity as the Maid of Norway. After Prince Alexander's death the sorrowing king took steps to have his baby granddaughter acknowledged by the magnates of Scotland as his successor. The following year, in 1285, he remarried, and the hopes of Scotland were pinned on his beautiful young French bride, Joleta (Yolande) of Dreux, presenting him with a sturdy son who would ensure the continuation of the dynasty. Joleta was another descendant of Louis VI, and in these Franco-Scottish marriages lay the seeds of the Auld Alliance which flourished between Scotland and France in the fifteenth and sixteenth centuries. The untimely death of Alexander, however, brought this incipient French influence to an abrupt end.

The Scotland of the 1280s was a comparatively wealthy country, far removed from the beggarly nation which English propagandists were to satirise in succeeding generations. One has only to consider the splendid religious houses of the period, the great cathedrals from Glasgow in the south to Dornoch in the north, the magnificent abbeys and monasteries at Arbroath, Scone, Dunfermline and Cambuskenneth north of the Forth, as well as Paisley, Kilwinning, Crossraguel, New Abbey and Dundrennan in the south-west, and Holyrood, Kelso, Jedburgh, Dryburgh and Melrose in the south-east. These majestic buildings could only have been erected in a country possessed of considerable resources. Secular development matched this religious might and the country was studded by hundreds of castles, regal, baronial and knightly, the fortified homes of the landed classes. It was an age in which a prosperous bourgeoisie emerged, and many of the cities and towns of the present day date their burghal charters from this period. The wealth and status of Berwick has already been mentioned, but it was by no means the only great port in Scotland. Inverness, for example, was the centre of a shipbuilding industry that attracted orders from the Baltic and France. When the Count of Blois accompanied St Louis to the crusades in 1249 the largest ship in his fleet was built specially for him at Inverness.

Documentary evidence for the way people lived in thirteenth-century Scotland is meagre, but archaeological operations in very recent years are beginning to reveal much more about how people lived and worked, about what they ate and wore, and how they spent their time. Later generations would look back on the reign of Alexander III as a golden age. Recent evidence reveals that Scottish agriculture was more prosperous than its English counterpart. Scottish wool exports amounted to 20 per cent of those for the whole of England, while a buoyant export trade in hides reflects the highly successful cattle industry. Significantly, it was a period of abundant silver coinage of a good quality. Taxation was low and trade flourished. The inhabitants of the new towns enjoyed a varied diet, they wore homespun woollens and good leather boots. Houses were still largely wattle and daub but in Perth, Aberdeen and Berwick there were many stone houses with cellars.

From the documents of the period some idea of the scale and

diversity of Scotland's exports and imports can be gained. There was a thriving export trade in fish, timber, wool and hides to the Low Countries, Germany and Scandinavia as well as to northern England and Ireland. Economically, socially and culturally, Scotland was orientated towards the mainland of northern Europe rather than towards her more powerful southern neighbour. After the treaty of 1266 relations between Scotland and the Norse countries improved rapidly — a fact which is often overlooked.

Significantly, serfdom was abolished in Scotland by the end of the fourteenth century, long before slavery ceased to exist in England. Successive Scottish kings were wealthy enough not to require 'voluntary aids' and similar imposts at times of unusual expenditure. When Marjory, the sister of Alexander II, married the Earl of Pembroke, the King gave her a dowry of ten thousand marks out of his own pocket. Similarly, the four thousand marks for the purchase of the Western Isles in 1266 were paid by Alexander III personally. By contrast, Henry III of England was forced to seek extensions of time in making payments towards the dowry of his daughter Margaret, first wife of Alexander III, because he was chronically short of money. Perhaps the most telling evidence of the relative prosperity of Scotland in this golden age was the attention to the infrastructure. Scotland has often been portrayed as a wilderness of trackless wastes or, at best, a land where the few tracks through the vast forests could only be traversed by men on foot or horseback. More recent research, however, has revealed that this was a period when a network of good roads, capable of taking wheeled carts and wagons, was established. More importantly, the erection of bridges requires a great deal of money and expertise; in the course of Alexander's reign bridges were built over the Tay at Perth, over the Esk at Brechin and Marykirk, over the Dee at Kincardine o'Neil, Durris and Glenmuick, and over the Spey at Orkill. Many of these roads and bridges were destroyed during the Wars of Independence and not replaced till long afterwards, reflecting the poverty and destitution which came in the wake of Scotland's struggle to regain its freedom.

Young William Wallace, growing up at Ellerslie, would probably have been quite unaware of such matters. He grew up in a time of peace and plenty, when trade flourished and law and justice prevailed. About the time of his birth King Henry III of England died and was succeeded by the man who would one day become William's deadliest adversary. England, like Scotland, was free from external threat and so stable domestically that Edward (who was in Sicily when he got the news of his father's death) took his time about returning home. After a leisurely journey through Italy and France, where he did homage to his cousin Philip III, he went to Gascony where he stayed for almost a year. He landed at Dover on 2 August 1274 and was crowned at Westminster sixteen days later. He was thirty-five years of age, tall, well proportioned and handsome. Considerably above average height, he certainly deserved his nickname of Longshanks.

William Wallace, perhaps inheriting something from his Danish ancestry, also developed into a sturdy youth and when fully grown attained a height of two metres — six foot seven inches — with proportionately large hands and feet, and a muscular physique. In an age when the average height of a fully grown man was not much over five feet, to judge by the clothing and armour surviving from the period, William was truly a giant of a man. Blind Harry's physical description is probably not far removed from the truth:

> Wallace's stature, in largeness and in height,
> Was judged thus, by such as saw him right
> Both in his armour dight and in undress:
> Nine quarters large he was in length — no less;
> Third part his length in shoulders broad was he,
> Right seemly, strong, and handsome for to see;
> His limbs were great, with stalwart pace and sound;
> His brows were hard, his arms were great and round;
> His hands right like a palmer's did appear,
> Of manly make, with nails both great and clear;
> Proportioned long and fair was his visage;
> Right grave of speech, and able in courage;
> Broad breast and high, with sturdy neck and great,
> Lips round, his nose square and proportionate;
> Brown wavy hair, on brows and eyebrows light,
> Eyes clear and piercing, like to diamonds bright.
> On the left side was seen below the chin,

By hurt, a wen; his colour was sanguine.
Wounds, too, he had in many a diverse place,
But fair and well preserved was aye his face.
Of riches for himself he kept no thing;
Gave as he won, like Alexander the King.
In time of peace, meek as a maid was he;
When war approached, the right Hector was he.
To Scots men ever credence great he gave;
Known enemies could never him deceive.
These qualities of his were known in France,
Where people held him in good remembrance.[9]

And the *Scotichronicon*, compiled closer to his own time, confirms this:

He was a tall man with the body of a giant, cheerful in appearance with agreeable features, broad-shouldered and big-boned, with belly in proportion and lengthy flanks, pleasing in appearance but with a wild look, broad in the hips, with strong arms and legs, a most spirited fighting-man, with all his limbs very strong and firm. Moreover the Most High had distinguished him and his changing features with a certain good humour, had so blessed his words and deeds with a certain heavenly gift, that by his appearance alone he won over to himself the grace and favour of the hearts of all loyal Scots. And this is not surprising, for he was most liberal in all his gifts, very fair in his judgments, most compassionate in comforting the sad, a most skilful counsellor, very patient when suffering, a distinguished speaker, who above all hunted down falsehood and deceit and detested treachery; for this reason the Lord was with him, and with His help he was a man successful in everything; with veneration for the church and respect for the clergy, he helped the poor and widows, and worked for the restoration of wards and orphans bringing relief to the oppressed. He lay in wait for thieves and robbers, inflicting rigorous justice on them without any reward. Because God was very greatly pleased with works of justice of this kind, He in consequence guided all his activities.[10]

Some nineteenth-century historians tended to scoff at these

descriptions, without offering any alternative explanation of Wallace's extraordinary physical and mental powers. Burton (1897), for example, derided 'the later romancers and minstrels who have profusely trumpeted Wallace's personal prowess and superhuman strength'. This overlooks the plain fact that Wallace came to maturity in an era when strength, stamina, endurance, courage and, above all, skill in handling sword and dagger were of paramount importance in the emergence of leaders, when warlike renown depended so essentially on personal deeds of derring-do. In view of this, it would have been astonishing — indeed, well-nigh incredible — had Wallace not been a man of pre-eminent physical strength and considerable manual dexterity. By what other means could the second son of an obscure knight, a mere youth just out of his teens, without the support or patronage of a single great magnate, have maintained himself, attracted followers, impressed the enemy, secured the enduring hatred of Edward Plantagenet, and become the hero of a nation, if he did not possess quite exceptional physical strength and prowess?

Apart from his physical attributes, Wallace was endowed with considerable mental faculties. He had the conventional upbringing of a boy of his class and time. The younger son of a minor laird, he received the rudiments of his education at home, probably at his mother's knee. Various writers, mindful of the supposed boyhood at Elderslie, have suggested that he would have received a formal secular and religious education from the monks of Paisley Abbey. While this cannot be ruled out — William's father was also laird of Auchenbothie, and Paisley lay within the fiefdom of his feudal superior, the Steward of Scotland — it would be unwise to stress this possibility as a probability. At any rate Paisley Abbey would have offered the best centre of learning in the south-west of Scotland at that time, whether the Wallaces were closely connected with Renfrewshire or not. Evidence of William's early religious education is provided by the psalter which he habitually carried on his campaigns, and his attachment to the Psalms of David was noted by the eyewitnesses of his execution. There is less ground for supposing that William was the fine all-round scholar which the Marquess of Bute made him out to be:

I conceive that there can be no doubt that his mental culture
was at least as great as would be that of a person in a corresponding position at the present day . . . Sir William Wallace at
least knew how to read and write three languages — namely,
his own, and Latin and French; and it appears also that he
knew Gaelic. He knew the ancient and modern history, and the
common simpler mathematics and science of his own day.[11]

Although he could read and write, probably more attention
was paid to the acquisition of horsemanship and martial skills,
sparring with his elder brother Malcolm and learning to fight
with the dirk and the claymore. The latter was to become
William's favourite weapon. With a five-foot double-edged
blade and a handle almost a foot in length, it was taller than
most men. It was worn in a scabbard strapped to the back, and
unsheathed by reaching over the shoulder. This was a two-
handed weapon, relying on the reach and the strength of the
man wielding it for deadly effect, rather than the agility and skill
required of lighter swords; but in the hands of a swordsman like
Wallace its whirling movement could hack and slash with a
velocity and force which even the armour of the period could
not withstand.

William would have been about ten or eleven years old
when Edward Longshanks completed his six-year conquest of
Wales, in 1283. Three years later, some thoughts as to a future
career for young William were being expressed at a time when
momentous events were taking place. In 1285 Philip III of France
had died; in the summer of 1286 Edward crossed the Channel
and made his way to Paris where he did homage to the new
King, Philip the Fair, in respect of his fiefdoms in France. It is
ironic that this act of homage should not have been construed as
affecting the sovereignty of England in any way; yet Edward
and his predecessors had tried to use the homage of the Scottish
kings in respect of their English estates to assert their paramountcy over Scotland. Things were so settled in England that
Edward felt secure enough to remain abroad for three years.
During that time he was preoccupied with the administration of
Gascony and repeatedly trying to mediate in the long-running
struggle between the houses of Anjou and Aragon. His long
absence, however, threw the government of England into con-

fusion. On his return, in 1289, he was obliged to dismiss most of his judges and ministers for corruption. Finally, Edward's answer to political discontent and economic unrest at home was to seek a scapegoat; on 18 July 1290 he ordained the expulsion of all Jews from his kingdom. Some 16,000 men, women and children were expelled, often in circumstances of great brutality, and set a precedent soon followed by other countries in western Europe.

Restless and ambitious, Edward now turned his attention to Scotland. William Wallace was probably in his fourteenth year when disaster struck, and Scotland was plunged into a sequence of events that changed the course of history utterly. Monday, 18 March 1286, was a wild, stormy day in the east of Scotland, with more than a hint of snow in the air and equinoctial gales raging round the coast. It was a day beset by evil omens and strange rumours that it would be the Day of Judgment. People remembered the gloomy death-bed prophecy of Prince Alexander and spoke of coming woes in hushed tones. Others remembered the wedding feast of the King and Joleta at Jedburgh the previous summer, when a mummer, dressed as a skeleton, had upset the wedding masque and terrified the superstitious onlookers. In hindsight they took this as a portent of the King's imminent death.

Alexander himself seems to have shrugged aside the forebodings of his courtiers. When a soothsayer warned the King that his horse would be the death of him he robustly solved the problem by having the unfortunate steed put to death. Later a story gained credence that it was the sight of this beast's decomposing remains which had frightened the King's new mount into rearing up and throwing its hapless rider over the cliffs.

On 19 March the King held a council in Edinburgh Castle, then relaxed over a good meal and fine wines with his barons. When the banquet broke up the hour was late and another storm was brewing. The King's advisers urged him to remain in the Castle that night, but Alexander ignored their counsel and decided, on the spur of the moment, to return to his residence at Kinghorn on the other side of the Firth of Forth. He was forty-four years old, in the prime of life, fearless, wilful and apparently anxious to return to the voluptuous young wife half his age.

He set out from Edinburgh that stormy night, accompanied

by his squires, and braved the perilous crossing of the Firth from Dalmeny to Inverkeithing. There he was met by Alexander le Saucier, master of the royal sauce-kitchen and a bailie of the burgh. The Saucier bluntly asked the King, 'My Lord, what are you doing out in such weather and darkness? How many times have I tried to persuade you that midnight travelling will bring you no good?' The last remark seems to imply that the King was in the habit of commuting nocturnally between Edinburgh and his royal manor. At any rate, Alexander turned down the offer of hospitality and ignored the warning, and with an escort of three esquires and two local guides, set off for his house at Kinghorn. Eleven miles of indescribably bad road lay between Inverkeithing and Kinghorn. Not far from their destination Alexander became separated from his companions in the teeth of a howling gale and a pitch-black night, took a wrong turning and ended up on the cliffs of Pettycur. The exact manner of his death will never be known, but his body, the neck broken, was found the following day among the rocks at the foot of the cliffs. Joleta had not conceived, and a few weeks later the youthful widow returned to her father's house at Dreux.

The King's death, so sudden and unexpected, spread consternation throughout the country. Fordun's eulogy and lament for Alexander doubtless summed up the general feeling of loss: 'O! Scotland, truly unhappy when bereft of so great a leader and pilot.'[12] Two weeks after Easter that year, or little more than a month after the King's tragic death, the magnates and prelates of Scotland met at Scone near Perth and took the oath of fealty to their sovereign lady, Alexander's granddaughter Margaret of Norway, and solemnly swore to protect and uphold the peace of the land. That done, they set up a form of provisional government, appointing six *custodes pacis* (Guardians of the Peace) as regents.

The Guardians consisted of two earls, Alexander Comyn of Buchan and Duncan of Fife; two barons, James the Steward and John Comyn of Badenoch; and two bishops, Robert Wishart of Glasgow and William Fraser of St Andrews. The earls and Bishop Fraser had special responsibility for Scotland north of the Forth, the barons and Bishop Wishart for the southern districts. The ethnic composition of the Guardians was not so finely balanced: the Comyns hailed from Picardy and the Steward from

Normandy, while the Frasers or Frasiers were a Norman family which settled in Tweeddale in the late twelfth century; the other two were of mixed Anglo-Saxon or Celtic blood, but even Earl Duncan had a Norman mother.[13] The earls of Buchan and Fife were the most powerful landowners in the north of Scotland, while Comyn of Badenoch, despite his title, had extensive lands in the Border counties. The most significant factor about the choice of Guardians was the omission of anyone who might be regarded as a serious contender for the throne.

On the face of it, Scotland continued much as before: 'for three years in peace the realm stood desolate' were Harry's picturesque words. But before the year was out powerful factions were beginning to emerge. Like the Guardians, the leaders of these groups were of Norman origin, from Bailleul and Brix respectively; interestingly, though, both had strong Celtic connections. Devorgilla, heiress of Galloway, was the mother of John Balliol, while Marjorie, Countess of Carrick in her own right, was the daughter-in-law of the Competitor Bruce, wife of the Earl of Carrick and mother of Robert Bruce the future king. In the south Balliol, Lord of Galloway, and Bruce, Lord of Annandale, mustered their adherents; in the north Comyn of Badenoch also cast covetous eyes on the empty throne. Meanwhile the Guardians thought it courteous, if not exactly prudent, to keep King Edward informed of developments, even to the extent of despatching an embassy to Gascony. The aim of this mission was well intentioned, to seek Edward's friendly assistance and advice; later, however, it was to be interpreted as an acknowledgment of his overlordship.

In the dangerous political vacuum created by the death of King Alexander and the minority of his distant granddaughter, the Guardians were at pains to emphasise that they had been elected by common counsel of the community of the realm. Within three months, trouble erupted in the south when Robert Bruce, Lord of Annandale, together with his eldest son, the Earl of Carrick, raised an army and invaded Galloway, seizing the Balliol stronghold of Buittle and the royal castles of Dumfries and Wigtown. The exact reason for this assault is obscure, but in the context of the period it was clear enough. Possession of Dumfries Castle gave the Bruces control over the route through Nithsdale to their lands in Carrick and, by the same token, contained the Balliols in Galloway. Later, John Balliol would refer to this outrage in his own Pleas for the Crown:

> The aforesaid Sir Robert de Brus and the Earl of Karrick, his son, dared to take by force of arms with banners displayed the aforesaid Lady of Scotland's castle of Dumfries, against her peace. And thence the aforesaid Sir Robert advanced to the castle of Botil, and there he caused one Patrick McCuffok within the Bailey of the same castle to proclaim that all the —— [*illegible*] should immediately depart from the land. The Earl of Karrick with the assent and power of his father took the aforesaid Lady's Castle of Wigton in Galloway, and killed many of her men there.

On 20 September 1286 a group of noblemen which included one of the Guardians, James the Steward, as well as the Bruces father and son and the Lord of Islay, met at the seat of the Earl of Carrick and entered into a band or sworn agreement to give aid to Thomas de Clare and the Earl of Ulster, Richard de Burgh, against their enemies. The Turnberry Band may have been occasioned by no more than some vague Norman-Irish adventure, although many historians have asserted (on the flimsiest of evidence) that the Band upheld Bruce's claims to the throne. In fact the conspirators took an oath saving the fealty of all parties to the king of England and 'to whoever shall be king of Scotland by reason of the blood of the late King Alexander' — which seems to have been an allusion to a hypothetical son of the supposedly pregnant Joleta.

The Guardians issued a writ to sheriffs and other royal officers to mobilise knights, freemen and others who owed military service to the royal dignity for the defence of the realm, and there is some evidence to suggest that levies were in fact called out in the spring of 1287. In all probability, therefore, Sir Malcolm Wallace and his eldest son would have been called up, and it is not impossible that young William, now fourteen or fifteen and already a well set-up lad, would have had his first taste of military action at this time, serving as page or esquire to his father. By the time the forces of law and order had been mobilised, however, the revolt of the Turnberry Band — if it was indeed a revolt — had fizzled out and the south-west of

Scotland was restored to its former tranquillity. Nevertheless, the meeting of September 1286 left an ugly taste in the mouth; the Guardians lacked solidarity, and powerful magnates like the Bruces could flout the law with impunity whenever it suited their purpose.

Even when Scotland had a lawful king on the throne, the great magnates had had a tendency to treat the crown as their plaything. In the reign of Alexander III the chief troublemaker had been Alan Durward. In 1254, acting in concert with the earls of March, Strathearn and Carrick, Robert de Brus and Alexander the Steward, he had kidnapped the King and Queen Margaret and held them incommunicado at Kelso Abbey. King Henry III had retaliated by mounting an expedition to rescue his daughter and son-in-law, but in the aftermath of this incident Alexander III had been compelled to acknowledge Henry as his superior and virtual master of Scotland. Only three years later the Comyns seized the King and Queen and confined them in Stirling Castle. The matter was only resolved in 1259 when the Anglo-Norman earls of Hereford and Albemarle met with the Scoto-Norman John Balliol at Melrose and negotiated peace terms.

Thereafter there was an uneasy peace that lasted about three years. In 1289 Alexander Comyn died of old age, but in September that year Duncan of Fife, whom the Lanercost Chronicle describes as cruel and greedy above the average, was murdered by his own family. The earls were thus left unrepresented in the collective Guardianship. In their place, however, were co-opted Matthew Crambeth, Bishop of Dunkeld, and Sir Andrew de Moray or Murray of Petty. The latter, although only a knight, was a powerful magnate with important holdings not only in the north of the country but also in Lanarkshire, including the strategic stronghold of Bothwell to the south of Glasgow. More significantly, the composition of the Guardianship had subtly changed, diminishing the importance of the Norman element. Despite his name, Sir Andrew was the descendant of a Flemish mercenary who married into the Celtic nobility.

It was probably during this ominous period, in the lull before the storm, that William Wallace spent some time at Dunipace in east Stirlingshire where he lodged with an uncle, a younger brother of his father, who was the cleric there, at a chapelry of Cambuskenneth Abbey. By now William had shown by his intellect that he might make a career in the Church, the traditional role for landless younger sons. Blind Harry describes the parson of Dunipace as 'a man of great riches', a 'mighty parson' and 'a full kind man'. William was about sixteen or seventeen by this time, and his education now proceeded in a more mature manner. In particular, his uncle inculcated in him moral maxims compactly framed in Latin, and referred frequently to the great classical authors. This priest is given the credit for instilling in William's soul that passionate love of liberty which was to be the keynote of his elevated character and his glorious career. The very formula employed to imprint the memorable injunction has been preserved down the centuries:

> *Dico tibi verum, libertas optima rerum;*
> *Nunquam servili sub nexu vivito, fili.*

> My son, I tell thee soothfastlie,
> No gift is like to libertie;
> Then never live in slaverie.

This was a precept which remained firmly implanted in William's mind till the end of his days.

Meanwhile, protracted negotiations were taking place to arrange the marriage of the Maid of Norway and the five-year-old Lord Edward, son of King Edward I and a year her junior. Eirik II, himself a mere youth, bowed to the inevitable and acquiesced in Edward's plans. The negotiations culminated in the Treaty of Birgham on 18 July 1290, ratified by King Edward at Northampton a month later. From the Scottish viewpoint, this marriage was to be the union of two individuals, and in the terms of the treaty the Guardians emphasised that, while Edward and Margaret might be one flesh, Scotland must remain quite separate from England.

Previously, the Guardians had sent four emissaries (Bishops Wishart and Fraser, John Comyn of Badenoch and Bruce of Annandale) to treat with commissioners of Norway and England regarding the entry of the little Queen into her realm. The three groups of commissioners reached an amicable arrangement and presented their report to King Edward at Salisbury on 9 November 1289. Margaret was to come over to

England or Scotland on All Saints Day (1 November) 1290. She was to come free of any prior marriage contract, but Edward I was to be given assurances that she would not be married except by his ordinance, will and counsel, and that Scotland was in a safe and peaceful condition, so that Margaret might live there willingly 'as its true lady, queen and heir'. The Scots reserved the right, however, to remove any unsuitable guardians or servants supplied by Norway and replace them by Scots who were to be approved by men of both countries and by King Edward's agents. In these and other matters the arbitration of Edward was sought as a matter of course.[14]

At the same time, Pope Nicholas IV issued a bull granting dispensation for the marriage of the two cousins, King Edward having advanced the plea that it was a matter of political necessity that Margaret should be married to his son. From the correspondence in March 1290 it was clear that the Scots, on their side, welcomed the marriage. At this time they wrote to Eirik II formally asking his acceptance of the match, and at the same time they wrote to Prince Edward referring to 'the joyous tidings of which many people speak' — an allusion to the papal dispensation.

On the English side, the chief architect of the Treaty of Birgham was Antony Bek, Bishop of Durham, a leading prelate and a powerful magnate. The son of Walter, Baron of Eresby in Lincolnshire, he had come to the notice of King Edward while still a young man and had been nominated by him to the bishopric of Durham. The monks of Durham were then at loggerheads with the Archbishop of York and elected Bek unanimously. Immediately after his consecration at York in January 1285 he was asked by Archbishop Romanus to excommunicate the rebellious monks, but this he flatly refused. This was only the first of several incidents in which Bek asserted his independence of his Archbishop. He soon emerged as a prelate of the secular and political type. He was one of the most magnificent lords in all England, always surrounded by a large retinue of barons and knights. Personally extravagant, he was nevertheless to die a rich man. Paradoxically he had simple, not to say austere, tastes and was famed for his chastity; it was said that he had never even looked a woman in the face. He was the very epitome of the Church militant, a mighty hunter delighting in horses, hawks and hounds, more at home in armour and chain-mail than in the vestments of his high office. This then was the man who was King Edward's chief agent in his dealings with the Scots. In February 1290 King Edward appointed him custodian of the Scottish monarch's estates in Penrith and Tynedale in the north of England, but the following June he was empowered to admit to the King's peace the men of the Scottish Islands 'who were in war and discord'. In August, when the marriage of the royal children was arranged, Bishop Bek was foisted on the Guardians as Lieutenant for Margaret and her would-be husband and they were instructed to defer to him in all matters 'which are required for the governance and peaceful state of the realm'. This appointment, however, came to nothing when the Maid of Norway died.[15]

The terms of the Treaty of Birgham explicitly preserved the independence of Scotland 'separate, free and without subjection'. Tenants-in-chief were required to do homage in Scotland alone, no court outside the kingdom could have jurisdiction over persons in Scotland, nor could York or Canterbury interfere in the elections of the Scottish clergy. The legal framework of Scotland was to be preserved intact and no writ of common law or letter of special favour could be issued other than by the normal process of the 'King's chapel' and of the Scottish realm. Other clauses limited the rights of any parliament other than that of Scotland to legislate for, or impose taxes on, the Scots. The treaty was a canny document; the Guardians did their utmost to protect their country's interests both for the present and, as far as they could foresee, for the future. It is clear that the purely or mainly Scottish element had prevailed at this point. The Norman magnates had nothing to lose, and everything to gain, by seeing Scotland firmly under English control, for they had lands in both countries. For the moment it seemed as if the integrity of Scotland was to be maintained, although, in truth, King Edward was only biding his time and sooner or later the marriage between the Queen of Scots and the heir to the English throne would inevitably lead to a merger of the two kingdoms.

A portent of things to come, however, occurred in June 1290 when King Edward quietly installed Walter Huntercombe as governor of the Isle of Man. The island had been ceded by Norway to Scotland in 1266 but now it effectively became an

English protectorate. Cynically, soon after this coup, the Manxmen were induced to petition Edward saying that they needed his protection. This illegal act seemed oddly at variance with Edward's apparent reasonableness towards the Scots and Scotland at this time. Nevertheless, he had, in effect, seized an important part of the Scottish realm — an island which was strategically important to England and Ireland as well as Scotland.

The English occupation of the Isle of Man was overlooked in the general flurry of preparations being made to welcome the Maid of Norway to her kingdom. Edward himself fitted out a ship for the express purpose of bringing the girl-queen over from Norway. The victualling of the ship was meticulous, including sweetmeats, fruit and 28 pounds of gingerbread. The vessel arrived in Norway in May 1290 but returned to England a month later, empty-handed. Eirik decided to send his daughter to Scotland via the northern isles which then formed a part of his kingdom, and it was at Kirkwall in Orkney that envoys of the Scottish community were to meet their sovereign at the beginning of October. Meanwhile, the magnates of Scotland assembled at Perth to meet the Prince-Bishop of Durham, together with John de Warenne, Earl of Surrey, and the Dean of York.

Warenne, one of the wealthiest and most powerful magnates in England, had married Alice of Lusignan, half-sister of Henry III, and was thus very close to the English throne. Born in 1231, he was a veteran of many campaigns in Gascony and Wales and one of King Edward's most trusted advisers. As early as September 1285 he had been sent on a mission to Scotland,[16] and between September and November 1289 he was one of the commissioners engaged in negotiating the Treaty of Salisbury with the Scots, whereby the Maid of Norway was to come to Scotland and subsequently marry Prince Edward.[17] On 14 February 1290 he went back to Scotland as Edward's envoy and on 20 June he was appointed, with Bek, to treat with the Scottish Guardians, assisting the Bishop in concluding the Treaty of Birgham on 18 July. On 28 August he was nominated Proctor for Prince Edward on the occasion of his intended marriage, and the following day was appointed to head the embassy sent to treat with Eirik II in Norway.

Subsequently the English mission, accompanied by Bishop Fraser of St Andrews, made the arduous journey north to Orkney. On 9 October Bishop Fraser wrote to King Edward from Leuchars, even before setting out from Fife, saying that he had just heard a disquieting rumour that the Queen had died. He feared that civil war would erupt as a result, unless Edward took steps to prevent it. The letter went on to hint that John Balliol might go to Edward, and Fraser urged the King to handle him carefully 'so that your honour and advantage may be preserved'. The closing remarks of this letter made the worthy Bishop's views clear. He urged Edward to come up to the Borders, to be ready to install the rightful heir 'if so be he will follow your counsel'.

The generally accepted story is that Queen Margaret turned ill on the voyage from Norway to Orkney and died soon after landing there, on 26 September. Her little corpse was returned to her sorrowing father at Bergen — and thus the ancient Scottish dynasty finally and tragically came to an end.

2

EARLY MANHOOD

Dico tibi verum, libertas optima rerum;
Nunquam servili sub nexu vivito, fili.

My son, I tell thee soothfastlie,
No gift is like to libertie;
Then never live in slaverie.

LATIN PRECEPT OF WALLACE'S UNCLE, THE PRIEST OF DUNIPACE.

SCOTLAND'S problem, following the death of the Maid of Norway, was not the lack of an heir to the throne, but too many heirs. In all, thirteen candidates came forward, most of them basing their claims on descent, legitimately or illegitimately, from the Scottish royal house. Eirik II claimed the Scottish throne in right of his late wife and daughter. Had his wife lived after Alexander III he would have had a strong claim *de jure uxoris*, but her untimely decease made his candidature frivolous. John of Badenoch, the Black Comyn, advanced a claim based on descent from Donald Ban, younger brother of Malcolm Canmore. Despite his tenuous link with the royal family, the Black Comyn could back up his claim with the fact that he was one of the most powerful men in the land, a Guardian of Scotland and closely connected to the earls of Buchan and Mar. Seven of the claimants were descended from royal bastards, one the illegitimate offspring of Alexander II, five from the prolific William the Lion and one from Henry of Scotland, son of David

I. As illegitimacy was regarded, even then, as a strong bar to inheritance, none of these claims could be seriously entertained. In view of the extremely tenuous nature of some of the claims it is a wonder that Edward I did not put himself forward as a candidate. After all he, too, was a direct descendant of Malcolm Canmore, whose daughter Matilda or Maud had married Henry I and become the mother of the English royal family.

It was singularly unfortunate that the descendants of Malcolm Canmore were not very fecund on the right side of the blanket. Malcolm IV died without issue, his brother Alexander II was succeeded by his only son Alexander III, whose sole surviving heir was the sickly infant Margaret. As a result of her death the direct line died out and it became necessary to go back to a common ancestor and ascertain who, among his descendants, had the strongest claim to the throne. David I, son of Malcolm Canmore, was that common ancestor.

Of the five legitimate descendants of David I, one did not bother to enter a claim. John II, Duke of Brittany, was a great-great-grandson of Margaret, younger sister of David, Earl of Huntingdon, by her marriage to Conan of Brittany. At best it would have been a weak claim, but in an age when the laws of primogeniture were by no means clearly defined, it was a claim worth making. Incidentally, John's son Arthur II subsequently married Joleta of Dreux, the young widow of Alexander III.

Prince Henry, Earl of Carlisle, the only son and heir of King David I (1124–53), predeceased his father, dying in 1152. In turn, the Scottish throne passed to Henry's sons, Malcolm IV (1153–65) and William the Lion (1165–1214). Their sister Ada married Florence III, Count of Holland. Ada's great-great-grandson, Florence V, was one of the four legitimate claimants.

The other three were the descendants of David, Earl of Huntingdon (younger brother of Malcolm IV and William the Lion), who had died in 1219. Earl David had one son, known as John of Scotland or the Earl of Chester and Huntingdon, who had died without issue in 1237, and three daughters. These ladies married the scions of noble houses in Scotland and England and from them were descended the three other major claimants to the throne. John Balliol was the grandson of the eldest daughter Margaret, Robert Bruce of Annandale was the eldest son of the second daughter Isobel, and John Hastings,

Lord of Abergavenny, was the grandson of the youngest daughter Ada. It should also be noted that Devorgilla, mother of John Balliol and founder of Balliol College, Oxford, was the youngest daughter of Margaret.

In addition, the eldest daughter of Margaret was Elena, whose own daughter Isabella had married Alexander Comyn, Earl of Buchan. He was the father (by a previous marriage) of John Comyn who claimed the throne. To complicate matters further, John Comyn had married Margaret Balliol, the daughter of Devorgilla and elder sister of John Balliol. Their son was John, commonly known as the Red Comyn, whom Robert Bruce, the future King of Scots, slew in Greyfriars Abbey, Dumfries, in 1306. Thus the Comyns were by turns allies and rivals of the Balliol faction.

For all practical purposes, however, the dispute resolved itself around Balliol and Bruce. By the law of primogeniture Balliol had the stronger claim, but the precedence of the grandson of an elder sister over the son of a younger sister was not clearly established. Whether Robert Bruce actually believed that he had the stronger claim is immaterial; he certainly acted as though this were the case, reinforced by the fact that he claimed to have actually been nominated as heir to Alexander II fifty years earlier when the succession, on a previous occasion, had not seemed secure. While the death of the Maid of Norway was still no more than a rumour, the Lord of Annandale and his henchmen assembled under arms and marched on Perth — a fact which Bishop Fraser was quick to point out to King Edward in his famous letter of 7 October.

Scotland in the winter of 1290 and the early months of 1291 was in danger of disintegrating into civil war. Again, the Bruces were at the bottom of the trouble. A large body of magnates rallied to their side. Towards the end of 1290 a document on behalf of the seven earls (only those of Fife and Mar were actually specified and the term 'seven earls' may have been intended to symbolise the leading magnates of Scotland as a whole), addressed a violent protest to the Guardians John Comyn and Bishop Fraser who had, by now, openly espoused the cause of John Balliol. 'In the name of the seven earls and their adherents I seek urgently the help of the king of England.' Precisely who 'I' was is not clear, for the document now preserved in the Public

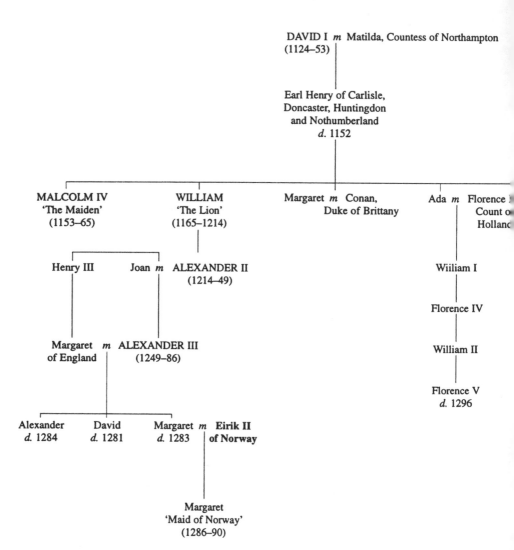

DAVID I _m_ Matilda, Countess of Northampton
(1124–53)

Earl Henry of Carlisle,
Doncaster, Huntingdon
and Nothumberland
_d._ 1152

MALCOLM IV   WILLIAM   Margaret _m_ Conan,   Ada _m_ Florence
'The Maiden'   'The Lion'   Duke of Brittany   Count o
(1153–65)   (1165–1214)   Holland

Henry III   Joan _m_ ALEXANDER II   Wiiliam I
(1214–49)

Florence IV

Margaret _m_ ALEXANDER III   William II
of England   (1249–86)

Florence V
_d._ 1296

Alexander   David   Margaret _m_ **Eirik II**
_d._ 1284   _d._ 1281   _d._ 1283   **of Norway**

Margaret
'Maid of Norway'
(1286–90)

Claimants to the throne in bold
Sovereigns in capitals

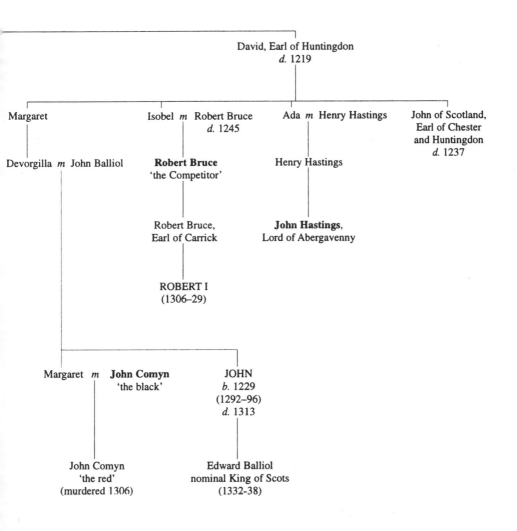

David, Earl of Huntingdon
d. 1219

Margaret

Isobel *m* Robert Bruce
d. 1245

Ada *m* Henry Hastings

John of Scotland,
Earl of Chester
and Huntingdon
d. 1237

Devorgilla *m* John Balliol

Robert Bruce
'the Competitor'

Henry Hastings

Robert Bruce,
Earl of Carrick

John Hastings,
Lord of Abergavenny

ROBERT I
(1306–29)

Margaret *m* **John Comyn**
'the black'

JOHN
b. 1229
(1292–96)
d. 1313

John Comyn
'the red'
(murdered 1306)

Edward Balliol
nominal King of Scots
(1332-38)

Records Office is only a copy, probably written by clerks employed by Edward I, from an original draft in which the name of the sender was denoted only by the Latin word *talis* ('so and so'). But from the general tone and the overall purpose of the petition, it seems likely that Robert Bruce was the instigator. The actual letter to the Guardians has not survived.

The chief objection of the seven earls (probably Angus, Atholl, Buchan, Fife, Mar, Menteith and Strathearn) was that their ancient right of instituting the king had been swept aside by the Guardians, but this did not imply that they would refuse to recognise any decision taken by King Edward. At first glance it may seem strange that Robert Bruce should go so far as to seek Edward's recognition of the traditional law of succession and the rights of the seven earls in this matter, but his background and training make this decision clearer.

Robert Bruce was the son of Robert de Brus and Isobel or Isabella, the second daughter of Earl David. The family appear to have lost their ancestral lands at Brix in Normandy but were extensive landowners in several English counties. A Bruce ancestor, while on a visit to the court of Alexander I, had secured the affections of the heiress to the lordship of Annandale, and by marriage brought this important Scottish barony into the family. Robert Bruce, son of Isobel and grandson of Earl David, was thus a degree nearer the common ancestor than Balliol. Besides being one of the great magnates of England and one of the principal vassals of Edward I, Robert Bruce the Competitor was an English lawyer, having been a puisne judge and Chief Justice of England in the reign of Henry III. The so-called petition of the seven earls, of course, dates from the autumn of 1290 when his position was much stronger than Balliol's, and he was anxious merely to get Edward's endorsement. Later, however, he was much less inclined to abide by Edward's decision, when the case was going against him.

John Balliol, born in 1229, was the younger son of the Lady Devorgilla, sole heiress of Alan of Galloway, and John Balliol of Barnard Castle in County Durham. The family was Norman, of course, originating in Bailleul with extensive lands round Neville which it still possessed. Fortunately, John's brothers died in their father's lifetime and he gradually fell heir to vast estates in France and England (notably in Durham and

Northumberland) as well as Galloway. Devorgilla's death in January 1290 brought her son to prominence in Scottish affairs and his close kinship to the powerful Comyn family has already been mentioned. His position in County Durham gave him an *entrée* to the influential Antony Bek, while his wife Isabella was the daughter of John de Warenne, Earl of Surrey, and he was thus also connected, by marriage, to the rapidly rising house of Percy, the greatest landowners in Northumberland. Balliol was now in his early sixties but still had fine, sensitive features and deep-set eyes, and was not without considerable intelligence. History has dealt rather unkindly with him, attributing to him a certain fecklessness and lack of character; but even a much stronger personality than he might have fared no better in the tricky political situation of the 1290s. He was probably much shrewder than people ever gave him credit for. He was also noted for his exquisite manners, but courtesy and chivalry were qualities which counted for little against such a ruthless character as King Edward.

At this point Edward's wife, Eleanor of Castile, died and any action he proposed taking was delayed by the period of mourning. In retrospect it can be seen that Edward was primarily concerned about maintaining law and order in Scotland rather than backing a claimant who would be pliant to his will, but fundamentally he was anxious to use the country's leaderless condition to advance his own position as feudal overlord of the northern kingdom. It has to be conceded that Balliol was legally the right choice for the throne, and in this aspect Edward acted as impartially as any arbitrator should; but in every other sense Edward acted unfairly and high-handedly. While the merits of the various claimants were being considered at a measured legal pace (a process which stretched over eighteen months), Edward used the interregnum to strengthen his own position.

It was only now that the true character of the man revealed itself. This high and mighty prince, the greatest of the Plantagenets, was descended from the Angevins who had a long reputation for evil-doing, pagan practices and witchcraft. They were said to have originated with a Breton bandit named Tortulf the Forester whose descendant, Fulk the Red, had attached himself to the dukes of France and received the county of Anjou as a reward. The name Plantagenet came from the spray of yellow broom (*Planta genista*) worn on the helmet of Geoffrey the Handsome, Count of Anjou, whose son became Henry II of England. Henry's sons, Richard the Lionheart and John, inherited the saturnine qualities of their Angevin forebears, both being noted for mercurial behaviour, violent tempers and a propensity to great cruelty. Edward inherited the drooping eyelid of his father, Henry III, and not a little of the brutality of his grandfather, but he was also of above average intelligence, articulate and possessed of a very sharp mind. Posterity in general remembers him for his legal reforms and the institution of Parliament, but he often twisted the law to suit his own ends and he was flawed by a malice and vindictiveness which made him a dangerous enemy. In hindsight, it seems that Eleanor of Castile exerted a moderating influence on her husband; but her death from fever on 25 November 1290 liberated him from any scruples he may previously have held. In fact, Edward had a long track-record of covert tyranny, although he did not always get away with his arbitrary and bullying tactics. In 1283, for example, he misappropriated the money collected for a new crusade but backed down when threatened with excommunication; eleven years later he resorted to the same tactics to extort over £80,000 from the hard-pressed clergy and on this occasion his effrontery paid off handsomely.

Edward apparently responded to Bishop Fraser's naïve letter and magnanimously agreed to give his advice to the Scots regarding the succession. At the same time, however, he informed his privy council that 'He had it in his mind to bring under his dominion the King and realm of Scotland, in the same manner that he had subdued the Kingdom of Wales.'[1] His innate genius, rapaciousness and insatiable greed were greatly helped by the fact that Scotland not only lacked a strong monarch of its own, but was singularly lacking in any disinterested national leader. On the contrary, the blindness of almost all the Scottish nobles to any interests but their own, the resulting division, distrust and lack of moral principle among the magnates of the kingdom, and the absence of any military experience after eight decades of Anglo-Scottish peace, all conspired to make Edward's task much easier.

Edward showed his hand on 16 April 1291 when he issued a summons to the barons of the northern counties of England, among whom were John Balliol, Robert Bruce, John Comyn and William de Ros, four at least of the expected claimants to the Scottish throne, to meet him at Norham-on-Tweed on 3 June. The choice of venue is significant for it was not only a convenient border crossing point but happened to have, close by, the formidable fortress of Antony Bek, Bishop of Durham. Even to this day, the ruins that tower above the wooded rising ground on the south bank of the Tweed, seven miles west of Berwick, are a spectacular reminder of Norman castle-construction at its grandest. Certainly in 1291 its massive walls and menacing fortifications must have impressed the Scottish emissaries with awe.

At the same time a mandate was issued to the sheriffs of York, Northumberland, Lancaster, Westmorland and Cumberland to assemble the feudal array of these counties at the same rendezvous. It appears that Edward had also, in some shape or other, invited certain of the nobility and clergy of Scotland to a meeting to be held at the same place on an earlier day. No document of this nature has survived but the terms of the invitation, its aims, and the parties to whom it was addressed may be inferred from what took place. Certainly there are still extant letters of safe conduct dated 4 May 1291 at Norham-on-Tweed, giving an assurance to the Guardians and other leading Scots that if they came to negotiate with Edward he would not put them at a disadvantage by virtue of their crossing the Tweed to the English side. When they did come to Norham, however, Edward promptly demanded that they acknowledge his suzerainty.

It has been postulated[2] that, had Edward possessed tact, moderation and a sense of justice, he would have achieved his aims in the end. He might gradually have tamed Scotland into a vassal kingdom without resorting to any actual exercise of force. He possessed immense diplomatic skills, in addition to his native cunning, and had he behaved in a reasonable manner it is quite probable that Scotland would have been peacefully absorbed within a matter of years. After all, the Scottish nobility were also, for the most part, holders of estates in England and their allegiance to Edward was a foregone conclusion. The common people might be a different matter, but through the feudal framework they owed unquestioning allegiance to their lords and masters, and could therefore be counted upon to fall into line. No doubt this reasoning governed Edward's subsequent behaviour; but it is singularly unfortunate that he should have treated Scotland with arrogance and high-handed disdain, and thus utterly misjudged the temper and character of the Scots.

While he was showing his hand to his privy council, Edward was also pursuing an apparently legal course of action. During the winter of 1290–91 he invited all the abbeys and monasteries of the kingdom to search through their chronicles for any entries dealing with Anglo-Scottish relations. Much of this material was pure myth concerning the origins of the Scots and the English. There was, for example, the tale of Dioclesian, King of Syria, who had thirty-three daughters by Queen Labana. These daughters killed all their husbands on the night of their mass marriage and for this dastardly deed the ladies were cast adrift in a rudderless vessel which bore them eventually to a distant island called Albion. Here the princesses mated with demons, the resulting offspring being a race of giants. Brutus, great-grandson of Aeneas of Troy, banished the giants, renamed the island Britain and left it in equal portions to his three sons, Locrinus, Albanectus and Cambrus from whom descended the people of England, Scotland and Wales respectively. Humber, King of Hungary, invaded Albyn and slew Albanectus, but was pursued and killed by Locrinus to whom Albyn (Scotland) reverted. From this incident derived the feudal superiority of the kings of England over the kingdom of Scotland. This ludicrous legend ignored the invasion and occupation of the island by Romans, Anglo-Saxons and Danes before the coming of the Conqueror; but, incredible as it seems, the greater part of this preposterous story was adopted and put forward in the claim of King Edward to be Lord Paramount of Scotland and was later solemnly set forth in the justification of his conduct addressed to Pope John XXII.

Armed with the results of these findings, Edward summoned an assembly of Scottish nobles and clergy who dutifully came on 10 May to Norham, in the ominous shadow of Bishop Bek's castle. If they were not overawed by the military might of the Prince-Bishop of Durham, the Scots must certainly have been overwhelmed by the spectacle of the puissant Edward, King of England, Lord of Ireland and Duke of Aquitaine, his mighty prelates and barons with their respective retinues, including several of the men who were claiming the Scottish throne for themselves. Ranked among the assessors and officials was a remarkable personage, in the shape of a notary public of the Holy Roman Empire no less, one Johannes Erturi de Cadamo, whose duty it was to record the proceedings, with all that formality and precision for which the Normans had become distinguished, showing how thoroughly Edward had prepared for what was to come.

Either within the castle, or after adjourning to a nearby church, in the presence of this great assembly of Scots and English, Edward the great impresario unfolded his plans. According to the chronicler Walter of Hemingburgh, a statement was drawn up by the Dominican provincial, William de Hotham, one of Edward's most trusted servants, and this was read to the Scots by Roger Brabazon, one of the King's justiciars. This asserted that, from the earliest times, the King of England had always held the overlordship of Scotland. Edward used this claim for the moment to justify his self-appointed position as adjudicator in the Great Cause, but inferred that, henceforward, he would have to be regarded as Lord Paramount of Scotland.

The Scottish magnates (or at least those of them who were not party to the scheme for their own ends) were alarmed, dismayed and confused by this turn of events. They protested their ignorance of any such claim to superiority and urged that, while the throne was vacant, the matter should not have been raised. Edward exploded at this unexpected show of resistance and cried out, 'By Holy Edward, whose crown I wear, I will vindicate my just rights, or perish in the attempt!' Hemingburgh adds that 'to make this speech good, the King had issued writs for the assembling of his army, so that, in case of the demand being resisted, he might conquer all resistance even to the death'.

Almost immediately Edward regretted his outburst and he quickly resumed the mask of the impartial lawyer. The Scots begged for time to consider the matter, so he graciously granted them twenty-four hours for consultation and deliberation. This was too obviously a mockery, so he relented and gave them nine days, later extended to three weeks, to bring forward whatever they could by way of a rebuttal. While the Scots were dithering, however, Edward took the precaution of summoning the feudal array, a large army which was within a day's march of the Tweed when the King again met the Scottish delegation on 2 June, this time at Holly-well-haugh (now Upsettlington) on the Scottish side of the Tweed opposite Norham.

No fewer than eight of the claimants (Robert Bruce, Florence of Holland, Sir John Hastings, Patrick or Cospatric Dunbar, the Earl of March, William de Ros, William de Vesci, Robert de Pinkeny and Nicholas de Soulis) took part in the inaugural meeting and all of them readily acknowledged Edward as their Lord Superior. The following day John Balliol took the same oath, and by proxy John Comyn of Badenoch also gave his assent. On subsequent days the three other claimants put in an appearance and took Edward's oath: Patrick Galythly, Roger de Mandeville and last, but not least, Eirik II of Norway. With the exception of the Earl of March, Galythly and King Eirik, all of the competitors were Norman or of Norman descent, and generally in possession of great estates in England. In fairness to the contenders, to have refused to take the prescribed oath would most certainly have resulted in the forfeiture of these estates. No fewer than nine meetings took place between Edward and the Scottish delegation between 2 and 11 June. Some were held on the village green at Upsettlington, others were held in Norham church and two were convened in the King's apartments in the Bishop's castle.

Edward himself seems to have taken no direct part in the proceedings. Instead, the Chancellor of England called on the magnates, prelates and community of the realm of Scotland to produce their answers to the claim of supremacy, and any evidence to prove the negative to Edward's claim. The prelates and nobles made no answer and it was assumed that the representatives of the common people likewise remained silent; but a copy of the roll was discovered in the nineteenth century which showed a brief passage, suppressed in the generally accepted version, to the effect that the community had made an answer, but that this was declared by Edward himself to contain *nihil efficax* (nothing effectual). As the Scots, to Edward's way of thinking, had produced nothing to the contrary, the King was now resolved, as Lord Paramount, to determine the question of the Scottish succession. Thereafter the competitors were asked whether they acknowledged Edward as Lord Paramount and were willing to ask and receive judgment from him accordingly. Bruce was the first to give his eager assent, closely followed by Balliol and Comyn and all the others. Ever the cautious lawyer, Edward had the details committed to writing and each claimant duly appended his seal to the document, copies of which were immediately sent to the various religious houses for preservation and publication.

Events now moved rapidly. On 11 June 1291 Edward ordered that every Scottish castle be surrendered to him. This was stated to be merely a temporary measure which would be revoked two months after the succession had been decided. As a further precaution Edward insisted that all Scottish officials be replaced by Englishmen. There was some measure of justification in this apparently high-handed action because Scotland was now teetering on the brink of all-out war between the Bruce and Balliol factions. As it happens, the majority of the candidates, including both Balliol and Bruce, issued statements acknowledging Edward's superiority and agreeing to submit to his arbitration. Furthermore, they acquiesced in Edward's demand that English forces take over the castles and other strongpoints in Scotland, even though none of the claimants had any power or authority to make such a concession. Interestingly, Edward also promised that in future, on the death of a Scottish king, he would demand nothing but homage and the rights incidental to it.

This important admission was probably wrung from Edward by the efforts of Bishop Wishart who, all along, strenuously resisted Edward's claim and reiterated the words spoken by Alexander III in 1278 when he stoutly refused to do homage for his kingdom, maintaining that he owed homage only unto God for it. On 14 June, the day after the negotiations ended, Wishart and Bishop Crambeth of Dunkeld made independent copies of Edward's concession and appended a document stating that the claimants' recognition of Edward's superiority had been made with the consent of the Guardians and the responsible men of the realm, thus indemnifying the claimants in case they had acted beyond their powers.

On 11 June the Guardians formally resigned their authority and were immediately reappointed 'by the most serene prince, the Lord Edward, by God's grace illustrious king of England, superior lord of Scotland'. At the same time, a new Guardian was appointed to secure Edward's interests, an English baron named Brian Fitz-Alan of Bedale.

Two days later, on the green of Upsettlington, the Guardians and leading nobility of Scotland gathered to swear fealty to Edward as superior and direct lord of the kingdom of Scotland. Sir Alexander Balliol, a kinsman of the claimant, was appointed Chamberlain of Scotland and numerous documents are preserved recording payments to this high official whom Edward himself described as 'Our chosen and faithful'. Among the magnates present on that momentous occasion were Robert Bruce of Annandale and his son Robert Bruce, Earl of Carrick. Seven other earls of Scotland did homage that day and in the ensuing six weeks barons, knights, freemen and religious leaders personally swore fealty to Edward, who set the seal on his success by making a grand ceremonial progress through the kingdom. Finally, to save everyone else the trouble of doing homage in person, Ayr, Dumfries, Inverness and Perth were designated as centres for those who had not already done so. The deadline for taking the oath was 27 July — comparatively short notice — and very severe penalties were to be imposed on those who refused or neglected to comply.

Responsibility for administering the oath at the first-named centre was Sir Ranald Craufurd in his capacity as sheriff; but conspicuous by its absence from the list of those complying with the order was Sir Malcolm Wallace of Ellerslie. When retribution was about to descend on his head (Ayr and Irvine being now garrisoned by English troops), Sir Malcolm and his eldest son fled north to the wild fastness of the Lennox. Sir Ranald took his daughter and her younger sons under his care for a time, before sending them to Kilspindie in the Carse of Gowrie where they were housed and looked after by another relative, possibly an uncle of Lady Wallace on her father's side, whom Blind Harry describes as 'an aged man'. This gentleman was the priest of the district and it was he who sent young William, now in his seventeenth or eighteenth year, to the church school in nearby Dundee.

This was in the nature of a seminary for young men intent on entering the priesthood. It was here that Wallace met John Blair who soon afterwards became a Benedictine monk.

Subsequently he left his monastery to attend his friend as chaplain and comrade in arms. Later on he would conduct diplomatic negotiations with Rome and the Hanse towns and, in retirement at Dunfermline Abbey, would eventually write the Latin biography of Wallace that served as the basis for Harry's epic poem. At this college William also met Duncan of Lorn and Sir Neil Campbell of Lochawe, youths who were to take part in his early exploits. It seems clear that William, as a younger son, was destined for a clerical career, following a tradition of both the Wallace and Craufurd families. The question has sometimes been asked why such a young giant, skilled in arms, should have settled on the priesthood, especially at a time when his father and elder brother were on the run and had sore need of his prowess. The answer is fairly obvious: the Church offered advancement to able young men and such a course would have seemed prudent in these unsettled times. Besides, the young student was living at Kilspindie and thus able to keep an eye on his mother and younger brother John. Oddly enough, Dundee was one of the few places at this time where there was the slightest opposition to the English takeover.

Although the submission of the Scots was far short of what Edward desired, it could not be said that they made much show of resisting his demands. The only sign of resistance was made by the Earl of Angus, Gilbert de Umfraville (an Englishman no less!), who refused to surrender the castles of Forfar and Dundee on the grounds that he had been appointed their custodian by the community of the realm of Scotland. This was merely a token show of resistance and the Guardians were not slow in finding a facesaving solution to this minor impasse.

Edward established a court of 104 auditors to decide who should have the crown, and the preliminary hearing was fixed for 3 August at Berwick. It has been suggested that Edward the lawyer took as his precedent the *judicium centumvirile*, the court of 105 which settled questions of property in the time of the Roman republic. The court was composed of twenty-four auditors seconded from Edward's council, and forty auditors each nominated by Balliol and Bruce. Thus the claim of the other candidates was summarily dismissed and the court concentrated from the outset on the merits of the pleas put forward by the two principal protagonists. On 3 August, however, all the competitors appeared at Berwick before Edward and the assembled auditors, formally to enter their petitions. These documents were sewn up in a sack secured with the seals of the earls of Buchan and Mar and the bishops of Glasgow and St Andrews, and the sack was then deposited in Berwick Castle. That done, Edward, who had pressing business elsewhere, adjourned the court until 2 June of the following year.

The court reassembled on 2 June 1292 but was then adjourned once more until 14 October in order to allow the eighty Bruce and Balliol auditors time to consider their replies to the question by what laws and customs the right of succession should be determined. The actual hearings lasted from 14 October till 17 November, when Edward gave judgment in favour of John Balliol. The eighty Scottish assessors were unable to agree about Scottish law and could not decide whether the rules of succession (which Edward had laid down for England in 1290) could or should apply to Scotland. In the end they referred the matter back to Edward's council which decided, at the beginning of November, that primogeniture rather than nearness of issue should be the criterion, and answered in favour of Balliol. The Scottish auditors were then asked to consider their verdict in the light of this decision and they, in turn, voted in favour of Balliol. Significantly, Bishop Wishart, James the Steward and a few others declared that although they had originally favoured Bruce they had now been converted to Balliol by these legal arguments. On 6 November Edward gave judgment in favour of Balliol against Bruce and then turned to consider the claims of the other contestants against Balliol.

Having lost his claim to the throne of Scotland and believing that a third of a loaf is better than none at all, Bruce now lent his support to the claim of John Hastings of Abergavenny. Hastings argued that Scotland was not really a kingdom at all, that its kings were never crowned or anointed, and that it was no more than a big barony held of the king of England. As such it was partible between the descendants of Earl David's three daughters — just as his earldoms of Chester and Northampton had been divided among Bruce and the fathers of Balliol and Hastings in 1237, following the death of John of Scotland. Edward held, however, that Scotland was an impartible kingdom, and dismissed the claim of Hastings.

On 17 November, within the great hall of the castle at Berwick-on-Tweed, Roger Brabazon delivered the judgment in Edward's name. By that time eight of the competitors had withdrawn, while two others, Comyn and Mandeville, failed to appear. Judgment was pronounced unequivocally in these terms:

> As it is admitted that the kingdom of Scotland is indivisible, and, as the king of England must judge of the rights of his subjects according to the laws and usages of the kingdoms over which he reigns; and as, by the laws and usages of England and Scotland in the succession to indivisible heritage, the more remote in degree of the first line of descent is preferable to the nearer in degree of the second line; therefore it is decreed that John Balliol shall have seisin of the kingdom of Scotland.[3]

Thus, by means of a great lawsuit, the Scottish crown and the fate of the Scottish nation were disposed. Two days later the constables of the twenty-three leading castles of the kingdom were ordered to surrender their charges to Balliol. The great seal of the Guardians was formally broken into four pieces and carefully stored away in the English Treasury at Westminster 'lest, if the seal remained intact, doubts should arise about the authenticity of documents, and as a sign of the king of England's full sovereign lordship in the Scottish realm'. On 20 November Balliol swore fealty to Edward at Norham, for the realm of Scotland held of him as superior lord. Ten days later, on St Andrew's Day, John Balliol was installed on the stone of Scone by John de St John, deputising for the infant Earl of Fife. At Newcastle on 26 December 1292, John Balliol did homage to his liege lord.

By the time Balliol ascended his throne, Scotland was effectively under English occupation. The surrender of the leading castles to King John must have been nominal rather than real, for their Anglo-Norman constables and custodians, together with their garrisons, remained in place. The nobility of Scotland might be quiescent and compliant with the new order; but the common people, coming in daily contact with the occupation soldiery, were another matter altogether. A fierce, proud people, angered at the manner in which their country was being treated as a chattel, and disgusted at the pusillanimity of their feudal superiors, could not let such an insult lie. Even before the Great Cause was settled there had been sporadic outbreaks in various parts of the country, beginning as brawls and riots between the overbearing soldiery and the irritated native populace and gradually escalating into ambushes and reprisals.

One such skirmish took place in 1291 on the flanks of Loudoun Hill at the head of the Irvine Valley. Blind Harry's account of this incident is confused, doubtless the oral transmission having become garbled in the course of several generations. He states that Sir Malcolm Wallace Senior was slain in this encounter by an English knight called Fenwick; but he goes on to say that his son, Sir Malcolm Junior, also perished in the mêlée. In a passage where he mentions that Lady Wallace's father was dead and her husband slain in battle, he continues:

> Her eldest son, who was large in stature, and whose name, in truth, was Sir Malcolm Wallace, had his hough sinews cut in that press; on his knees he then fought and slew many of the English, until being attacked by numbers on both sides, he was borne down by their spears; so died that good and renowned Knight.[4]

As Sir Malcolm Wallace Junior was still alive in 1299,[5] the story of the death of the hamstrung warrior must relate to his father. In any event it was a matter which left William with a smouldering resentment of the English, which gradually developed into an implacable hatred.

There has been some controversy over the date at which Wallace emerged as a guerrilla leader, one school of thought maintaining that his first acts of rebellion did not take place until 1296, after the fall of King John. This is supported by the theory that William was not born until 1278, but in view of the fact that he was commander of the Scottish army only months later, this theory is untenable. It seems obvious that such a skilled general must have served a long and hard apprenticeship in guerrilla warfare, and this is amply supported by the exploits narrated by Blind Harry, which some historians choose to ignore. Harry, to be sure, was often vague or confusing regarding chronology, but a careful study of his text helps to put the sequence of events in the proper context.

Thus, the period when the young Wallace first took up arms against the hated oppressors was unequivocally described. It was the time when 'they had haile the *Strengths* of Scotland; what they would do durst few against them stand'.[6] This was the term specifically used to describe the castles and strongholds surrendered to Edward while the claims to the throne were being adjudicated. This puts William's first acts of defiance fairly and squarely in the year 1291, probably soon after his father was killed at Loudoun Hill. Later on, Harry states that Wallace's campaigns against the English lasted 'six yeris and monthis sevyn',[7] which, dating back from the Battle of Falkirk, puts the first incident late in 1291.

The chronicler John of Fordun, who died in 1384 and was certainly living within a few years of Wallace's death, probably conversed with those who had known him well, and therefore his physical description of the hero, quoted in the previous chapter, may be taken as reasonably accurate. Lord Hailes, who was not disposed to credulity or romance, conceded that:

> This singular person had every popular excellence; strength of body; keen courage; a spirit active and ambitious. By his affability he conciliated the affections of his followers; by the force of native eloquence he moulded their passions to his will; by calm, intrepid, and persevering wisdom, he generally maintained authority over the rude and undisciplined multitudes who crowded to his standard.[8]

Blind Harry represented William, with dramatic truth at least, as brooding painfully over the death of his father, and as being stirred to uncontrollable resentment at the treatment of the Scots within his personal observation. The destruction of his family, the exile of his mother and the oppression of his countrymen had already nerved his heart and hand to take action. The moment when he would strike the first blow in retaliation for his family's sufferings was not far off.

The castle of Dundee had been handed over to the English baron, Brian Fitz-Alan of Bedale, along with other strongholds in Angus and Fife. Fitz-Alan, by now a Guardian of the realm and also one of the three Justices of Scotland, placed the castle in the hands of a constable named Selby, 'a fierce man of war who had done much injury to the Scots, a man despiteful and outrageous in his dealings'. He had a son about twenty years of age who, with three or four companions, used to go into the town every day: 'a proud, overbearing young rascal, wanton in mischief'. One day in December 1291 young Selby caught sight of William Wallace, brightly clad in green and towering head and shoulders over the others in the street. Selby accosted him saying, 'Thou Scot, abide; what devil clothed thee in so gay a garment? An Irish mantle were the right apparel for thy kind; a Scottish knife under thy belt to carry; rough shoes upon thy boorish feet.' So saying, he demanded the handsome dirk at William's belt. Wallace's response was swift and dramatic; grabbing the Englishman by the collar, he drew his blade and thrust it through his assailant's heart.

Selby's comrades pressed on William, but they were jostled by a crowd of onlookers and unable to draw their swords before Wallace killed or wounded some of them with his dirk. He then turned and fled to the town house of his uncle. At the close-mouth he ran into his uncle's housekeeper and swiftly told her what had happened. Promptly she bundled him inside, gave him a russet gown of her own to cover him up, placed a wimple and mutch on his head, and set the beardless boy to work with a distaff and spindle. Moments later a party of English soldiers came down the street, searching all the houses for the assassin. Wallace crouched in the corner spinning for dear life, but the ruse worked and the soldiers went off again, threatening to raze the town to the ground and burn the Scots in their dwellings unless they surrendered the killer. The housekeeper coolly con-cealed Wallace until nightfall, when he made his escape back to Kilspindie through the back courts and alleys and evading the English patrols.

By the time William returned to Kilspindie Lady Wallace was beside herself with despair, news of the incident having spread like wildfire. Shortly afterwards the governor of Dundee issued a proclamation summoning all Scots resident in Dundee and the surrounding district to appear at a court of enquiry. William decided that the time had come to leave the area. Disguised as a pilgrim but carrying a short sword under his gown, he and his mother left Kilspindie and set out for Dunipace. Whenever they were stopped and questioned by patrols they said they were on their way to worship at the shrine of St Margaret at Dunfermline. This pious reference to the English-born saint, who had begun the anglicisation of Scotland, obviously went down well with the troops checking passers-by. The pilgrims took the ferry across the Tay to Lindores and trudged through the Ochil Hills to Dunfermline where they lodged for the night. The following day they fell in with some English pilgrims, including the wife of the Constable of Linlithgow who took a shine to the well set-up young pilgrim. Attaching themselves to this lady's retinue, the Wallaces passed safely over the Forth, but declined an invitation to stay at Linlithgow, and went on to Dunipace.

This part of Stirlingshire was comparatively peaceful and William's uncle suggested that the fugitives would be quite safe there; but William insisted on pressing on, determined to return to Ayrshire and avenge the death of his father. Shortly afterwards mother and son returned to Ellerslie. Sir Ranald rode out from Ayr and brought them the bad news that William had been outlawed for the murder of young Selby. Sir Ranald's position as sheriff was in danger of being compromised; he hinted that while he could protect his sister, there was nothing he could do for her wayward son. He suggested that William remove himself from Ellerslie, where the English would sooner or later seek him out, and go to Riccarton to live with his uncle, Sir Richard Wallace. William went to Riccarton in February 1292 and stayed there until April. Harry states that Sir Richard had been blinded, disabled and enfeebled through loss of blood in some skirmish with the English, but gave the boy a good home.

On the twenty-third of that month, ironically the feast-day of St George, the patron saint of England, William went fishing at the Irvine Water nearby. On this occasion he was accompanied by a servant lad who carried his net and rod, but for once William had gone out unarmed — a mistake he never made again. Late in the afternoon, when William had caught several trout, the Lord Percy, then Captain of Ayr, rode past with a party of men. In this regard Blind Harry was surely mistaken, for Henry de Percy's appointment as Warden of Ayrshire and Galloway came some years later. Interestingly Percy, born about 1272–74, was of an age with both Wallace and Robert Bruce, the future King of Scots. The scion of a Norman-French family with extensive estates in Louvain, he was one of the able young men whom King Edward promoted to high office, over the heads of older men. It is unlikely, however, that Percy was in Scotland in 1292, and certainly not in the exalted position Harry claims. But the salient points regarding Wallace's encounter with troops of the Ayr garrison need not be disputed.

Later in the day, so goes the story, five of these Englishmen detached themselves from the retinue and rode down to the riverbank where they demanded Wallace's catch. William politely offered them half, but the leader of the group dismounted and seized the lot. When William remonstrated that the fish was intended for the supper of an elderly knight, the Englishman retorted that William had his permission to go on fishing. William answered civilly that the Englishman was in the wrong. The latter, now angered at being addressed so familiarly by an upstart Scot, drew his sword and lunged at him. William parried the blow with his fishing-pole and struck his adversary such a blow on the cheek that he was knocked off his feet, his sword sent flying. Deftly, Wallace picked up the sword and despatched the Englishman with a single blow to the neck. The other four soldiers had now dismounted and rushed to the aid of their fallen comrade. William's blood was up; he hacked one to the collarbone, another he struck on the arm with such force that both hand and sword fell to the ground. While the remaining pair fled, Wallace coolly ran through the man he had just maimed.

According to Harry, the two who escaped eventually caught up with their lord's party and urged him to return to avenge the deaths of their three comrades. When Percy was told that they had been felled by a single assailant he laughed loudly and implied that if they were killed by one man they were hardly worth avenging. Meanwhile, Wallace took the horses and gear of the slain, put away his rod and line for the day, and returned to his uncle's house. Sir Richard was crazy with despair, but William said that he would not remain any longer. He and his young page mounted two of the English horses and rode off to the east where the vast forests could give them refuge.

Harry's account was either derived from a local tradition, or in turn helped to perpetuate the story. Be that as it may, the legend of Wallace's encounter at Irvine Water was preserved locally by an ancient hawthorn known as the Bickering Bush.

Like Wallace's oak in Renfrewshire, this venerable tree survived into the early years of the nineteenth century, but by 1822 it was in decay and was then cut down and broken into small pieces by souvenir-hunters. The name survived in a local pub until it was demolished in the 1980s.

3

TOOM TABARD

Scotland was lost quhen he was bot a child,
And our-set throuch with our ennemys wilde.

Blind Harry, Buke Fyrst, lines 145–46

From the outset, the brief reign of King John was beset with problems. Although his main rival, Robert Bruce of Annandale, was eighty-two years of age, Balliol was disconcerted to learn that, on the day after judgment was given, the old man had drawn up a document delegating his claim to the throne to his son, the Earl of Carrick, and his heirs. This impressive document, now in the British Library, was sealed by Bruce and Gilbert de Clare, Earl of Gloucester. Two days later, on 9 November, the Earl of Carrick resigned his earldom to his son, the eighteen-year-old Robert. The Countess Marjorie had died earlier in the year and it was in the natural order of things for her eldest son to succeed to the title. In August 1293 the young earl was confirmed in the succession at the parliament convened at Stirling, James the Steward and the Earl of Mar acting as his sponsors. The elder Earl of Carrick, having divested himself of his responsibilities in Ayrshire, left Scotland to travel round Europe and thus studiously avoided having to do homage for his lands to a king whom he despised. In 1293 he was in Norway for the marriage of his daughter Isabel to Eirik II. This marriage resumed Norwegian interest in Scottish affairs. For the moment, however, it was a match with which Edward I was well satisfied, as the Bruces were at that time on good terms with the English court. Moreover, Bruce the Competitor, having resigned his claim, had faded out of the political picture. He retired to his castle of Lochmaben in the heart of his Annandale estates where he died on 1 April 1295 in his eighty-fifth year. In October that year the elder Earl of Carrick returned from his protracted European sojourn and was appointed governor of Carlisle Castle by King Edward. He held this position until October 1297, when he was dismissed because Edward was by then beginning to suspect the loyalty of his son.

But all that was still in the future. In 1293 young Robert Bruce stood in high favour with the man whom he regarded as his true liege lord and spent much of his time on his estates near Chelmsford or his impressive north London mansion, Bruce Castle. If the young Earl of Carrick posed any threat to the new King of Scotland by cultivating his contacts with the Scottish nobility, basking in the reflected glory of his sister's royal marriage and ingratiating himself with the King of England, King John was more concerned at his own relations with his powerful southern neighbour.

Judgment had no sooner been given in Balliol's favour than he was being solemnly exhorted by King Edward to be 'careful in doing justice to his new subjects, lest by giving cause of complaint he should render necessary the interference of his Lord Paramount'. John then again performed the ceremony of homage, putting his seal to a formal affidavit that he did so willingly and in good faith. On 30 November he was crowned at Scone, seated on the Stone of Destiny, yet even during this simple but intensely moving ceremony he was compelled to acknowledge his fealty to the English King, and on Christmas Eve that year he had to repeat his homage to Edward, this time in the character of a crowned king. The proud and ancient kingdom of the Picts and Scots had thus degenerated into little more than an Anglo-Norman province. In imposing his will on Scotland, however, Edward made one fundamental and eventually fatal mistake. In the words of the historian Burton, 'in his Norman sublimity, seeing only the persons worth seeing, the nobles, scarcely a step below himself in dignity and pretension, and of his own race, he had reckoned without that hitherto silent and inarticulate entity, the Scottish people.'

From the beginning it was abundantly clear that Edward intended that his superiority was to be real rather than nominal, and the pressure on Balliol was subtly increased. Before 1292 was out, Edward demonstrated at least one aspect of his paramountcy by deciding a case at Newcastle. This was an appeal by Roger Bartholomew, a prominent burgess of Berwick, against the judgment of the Guardians of Scotland in a complex triple lawsuit. Bartholomew claimed that he had been unjustly treated and therefore appealed to a higher authority. When King John protested at this clear violation of the Treaty of Birgham, which had agreed that all Scottish lawsuits would be determined in Scotland, Edward blandly declared that the Treaty had ended with Balliol's accession, and that he himself had the right to judge every Scottish case brought before him. Edward clarified the position, first through Roger Brabazon and then in a personal statement to King John, the prelates and magnates of Scotland and England assembled at Newcastle for the Christmas feast. A few days later, on 2 January 1293, Edward wrung from Balliol an agreement that the Treaty was null and void. Furthermore, John formally undertook to respect the validity of the acts done by Edward as lord while the kingdom was in his trust, in order to maintain the continuity of justice and government.

King John's position was weakened irrevocably by knuckling under in this way. In retrospect, however, it seems that John has been judged too harshly, for there was little, if anything, that he could have done. He was presented with a *fait accompli*, and support for any protest he might have made was conspicuously lacking among the Scottish nobility. Inevitably, the closer ties between Scotland and England, especially in the upper echelons of society, stretching back over two generations, created the right atmosphere for the events of 1293–96.

During that period Edward kept up social and legal contacts with influential figures in Scotland, and this insidiously undermined the independence and authority of King John. It was not surprising, therefore, that the mayor and burgesses of the Scottish town of Berwick could describe Edward, in a petition of 1294, as ruling the three realms of England, Scotland and Ireland by divine providence. Gradually a practice arose of appealing from the Scottish to the English courts. In 1293 alone Edward heard appeals from the court of King John, raised by John le Mazun or Mason of Bordeaux and Macduff of Fife, son of a previous earl, who claimed lands in Fife.

The latter case, in particular, highlighted the weakness of John's position. On the death of Malcolm, Earl of Fife, his heir was an infant. The earl's brother, Macduff, immediately claimed a portion of the estate. When his claim was dismissed by the Bishop of St Andrews, he appealed to King Edward during the Interregnum. Edward ordered that Macduff's claim be tried by the Guardians, who decided in his favour. This judgment was overturned by a council held by King John at Scone and Macduff was not only dispossessed but also thrown into prison for violating the law. On his release he promptly lodged an appeal with Edward, who ordered John to appear before him on 25 March 1293 to explain his conduct. When Balliol or his representatives failed to turn up, Edward and his legal advisers drew up a code of regulations, based on English common law, aimed at controlling and penalising John's disobedience — or 'feudal delinquency' as it was termed.

Edward might well have argued that he was only concerned with the maintenance of law and order in the northern realm, and he did not deliberately go out of his way to undermine John's position; but there were few people by the summer of 1293 who would have believed him. Matters came to a head during the Michaelmas session of parliament at Westminster when John appeared at last to answer in the case of Macduff. John refused to answer, or even to seek an adjournment (as that would have admitted recognition of the court). Instead, he backed down and begged, as Edward's man for the realm of Scotland, for a day to take counsel. He promised to give an answer in the next parliament. This issue was never resolved; the wars in Wales and Gascony intervened and by 1295 the situation had deteriorated beyond the point of retrieval.

In October 1293, however, Edward got a taste of his own medicine. As Duke of Aquitaine, he was a vassal of the King of France and Philip summoned him to answer for the crimes of some English seamen who had gone on the rampage in the port of La Rochelle. Although he avoided a personal appearance Edward was forced to send his representatives to Philip's court, to submit and make formal surrender of his French fiefs on 5 March 1294. Two days earlier, Philip gave orders for the suspension of all trade between France and England, Scotland and Ireland; but, interestingly, he waived this embargo in respect of the Scots when, on 10 May, he granted certain privileges to the Scottish merchants trading in Flanders, 'whom he does not hold as enemies, but rather as his friends'. This special treatment was reinforced by edicts on 14 July securing an indemnity for the goods of Scottish merchants at Amiens and giving general protection to the goods of Scots trading in Flanders.

Smarting under the humiliation inflicted by his feudal superior in France, Edward formed an alliance with his sons-in-law, the Duke of Brabant and the Count of Bar, and the rulers of Franche-Comté and the Low Countries and declared war on his liege lord in October 1294. Philip neutralised the Emperor Adolf, won over Florence of Holland (lately a contender for the Scottish throne) and made a treaty of friendship with Eirik II of Norway. The situation looked grim for Edward, who also had a rebellion in Wales to deal with, and he ordered King John to muster his forces and assemble at London no later than 1 September 1294. John received this summons at the end of June and within a few days took steps to defy his master. A parliament was hastily convened at Stirling a few weeks later and twelve advisers were appointed to assist the King — four representatives of the earls, the barons and the bishops respectively. Bishops Fraser of St Andrews and Crambeth of Dunkeld, together with two of the barons, formed an embassy despatched to the French court to arrange a marriage between Edward Balliol, John's son and heir, and Jeanne de Valois, Philip's niece. On 22 October King John came out in open defiance of his paramount lord; the treaties with Norway and Scotland were approved and made public in Paris and the impending marriage contract celebrated. Eirik II, in consideration of an annual payment of some fifty thousand pounds sterling, undertook to supply a battle fleet of a hundred ships for four months each year so long as hostilities between France and England continued. King John undertook, for his part, to invade England if Edward left the country or sent forces across the Channel to make war on France. In return, Philip promised support to Scotland.

By the summer of 1295 Edward was all too well aware of the

secret Franco-Scottish negotiations and early in October he prepared to secure his northern defences against possible attack.
On 5 October he appointed Antony Bek and Balliol's father-in-
law, Earl Warenne, custodians of the northern counties.
Warenne was also appointed governor of Bamborough Castle
and it was at this time that the elder Earl of Carrick received his
commission as constable of Carlisle Castle. Edward ordered
John to surrender the castles and burghs of Berwick, Jedburgh
and Roxburgh. Finally, on 16 October, he issued writs to all the
sheriffs in England for the seizure of the English estates, goods
and chattels of King John. Two months later he summoned more
than two hundred of his tenants to muster at Newcastle in
March 1296, fully armed and equipped. In February 1296 he
assembled a fleet of ships in East Anglia and proceeded up the
east coast, to rendezvous with his land forces at Newcastle. John
retaliated by issuing a national call to arms for 11 March and
summoning all free men to Caddonlee four miles north of
Selkirk.

The Bruces were conspicuous by their absence from the
muster. Since the accession of King John, the Bruce family, by and
large, had kept a very low profile. The marriage of Isabel Bruce to
Eirik II was sanctioned by King Edward and seemed at first to
cause embarrassment to the Scottish government; it was certainly a matter much debated by Balliol's council of twelve, who were
uncertain of the loyalty of the Bruce faction to the country. In 1294
the aged Competitor wangled the election of his own nominee,
Thomas Dalton of Kirkcudbright, as Bishop of Galloway.
Episcopal appointments were theoretically in the king's gift and
John had opposed this election. Furthermore, the diocese of
Galloway was conterminous with Balliol's own estates, yet the
neighbouring landowner of Annandale had had the effrontery to
challenge him in this way. The clergy of the diocese were split
down the middle between Balliol and Bruce and it was alleged
that the Bruces had bribed the prior and canons of Whithorn
whose privilege it was to elect the bishop. Dalton is a small village
some five miles south of Lochmaben and it is presumed that
Master Thomas had close family ties with Annandale. And now
the appointment of the new lord of Annandale as governor of
Carlisle indicated where the Bruce sympathies lay, in the event of
a confrontation between Edward and Balliol.

Several Scottish magnates, including the Bruces, ignored Balliol's summons and were promptly dispossessed. Annandale was assigned to the Earl of Buchan, and the earls of Angus and Dunbar were similarly ejected from their lands for siding with King Edward. The young Earl of Carrick and his brother Nigel were with their father in Carlisle in March 1296 when war actually broke out.

The first skirmish in the hostilities was a curious, half-cocked affair. Robert de Ros, Lord of Wark and an Englishman, was in love with a Scots girl whom he wished to marry. He deserted to the Scottish side and, late in March, led a party of Scots from Roxburgh to attack Wark Castle. The assault fizzled out and the Scots failed to take this strongpoint. Edward moved north and raised the siege of Wark, where he was met by the Bruces on 25 March and received homage from them for their lands in Scotland. The following day a Scottish army led by John Comyn, Earl of Buchan, crossed the Sark and entered Cumbria. By nightfall they had advanced as far as Carlisle, a town which was stoutly walled and resolutely defended by the earls of Carrick. The Scots had to content themselves with burning the cottages and hovels of the poorest classes dwelling outside the walls, before wheeling eastwards and indulging in an orgy of pillage and rapine, burning and looting the villages, monasteries and churches of Corbridge, Hexham and Lanercost. Laden with booty, Comyn's forces crossed the Cheviots and returned to Scotland well satisfied with their exploits.

About this time, however, the English army, consisting of three thousand foot soldiers and five thousand cavalry, advanced along the Northumbrian coast, crossed the Tweed and on 30 March invested the town of Berwick. Five weeks earlier some English merchants had been murdered in the seaport and the goods in their warehouses looted by the mob. Presumably Edward was quickly apprised of this atrocity and decided to make an example of the town. The attack on Scotland's largest city began inauspiciously. Four of the English ships taking part in combined operations ran aground in the mouth of the Tweed; the townspeople counter-attacked by the sea gate, burned the ships and killed or captured their crews. Apart from this initial success, however, the town was doomed. The richest commercial centre in Scotland was poorly defended by earthworks surmounted by a wooden stockade. Edward attacked in force from the landward side and his shock-troops swept over the palisade at the first assault. Later the Scots put out a story of English cunning, of cavalry flying false colours tricking the defenders into opening the gates, and it is not improbable that Edward (who had employed a similar stratagem at the Battle of Evesham in June 1265) resorted to such a trick; but the hard facts were more prosaic. The earthworks were pitifully inadequate — Edward is said to have led the cavalry in person, leaping over a dyke on his great warhorse Bayard. The English overran the ramparts, throwing the townsmen into confusion. Virtually the only resistance was put up by the small Flemish community (numbering about thirty merchants and craftsmen) who held the Red Hall. One of the Fleming archers, with an accuracy which had more than a little of luck, shot Edward's cousin, Richard of Cornwall, through the visor of his helmet and pierced his brain. The enraged King personally ordered the slaughter of the foolhardy foreigners, the Red Hall being set on fire and its defenders burned to death.

Quarter was given to the castle garrison, commanded by Sir William Douglas, known as le Hardi, who promptly swore fealty to his new liege lord and whom Edward retained as a hostage. In contrast, however, Edward did not spare the town itself. He had tried to parley with the burgesses of Berwick but they had taunted him with obscene doggerel and rude gestures. His revenge was thorough, even by the brutal standards of the time. Thousands of men, women and children were butchered in an orgy of rape and wanton destruction that lasted fully three days. Wyntoun said that Edward only came to his senses when he witnessed a woman giving birth to a baby as she was being hacked to pieces by a frenzied soldier. No less eminent an authority than Matthew of Westminster estimated the number of dead at sixty thousand, but this seems a gross exaggeration, given that the population of Berwick at the time was thought to be around twenty thousand. At the other extreme, the Scottish chronicler John of Fordun put the figure at seven thousand. Allowing for the fact that a body count was something to be proud of in medieval terms (and, conversely, Fordun would be anxious to minimise the 'success' of the English) it can be assumed that the true figure lay somewhere between these estimates; a more accurate assessment is that between seventeen and twenty thousand perished. The dead were so numerous that their corpses were dumped in huge pits or thrown into the sea. Large parts of the once-prosperous town were destroyed; from the rubble Edward personally supervised the fortification of Berwick which, henceforward, would be an English town. Although it was rapidly resettled from the south it would never regain its former position.

The destruction of Berwick, the worst atrocity ever to stain the pages of English history, was a deliberate act to terrorise and cow the Scots. The horror of this dark deed was heightened by the fact that it had been committed by a people supposedly friendly to the Scots for generations, after the briefest of assaults in which English casualties had been remarkably light. If he had anticipated an easy victory, however, Edward was soon proved wrong. The sack of Berwick belatedly united the Scots behind their monarch who, on 5 April, sent the Abbot of Arbroath to Edward with a letter formally renouncing his allegiance. 'What folly he commits!' exclaimed Edward grimly. 'If he will not come to us, we will go to him.' Later that month the Earl of Buchan and his army re-entered Northumberland. Marauding bands attacked Cockermouth, Redesdale and Tynedale and plundered the monastery at Hexham for the second time in as many weeks. Much of this destruction was aimless and seems to have been in the nature of reprisals for the Berwick atrocities.

A propaganda document, supposedly prepared for dissemination in France to show King Philip what savages he was allied to, stated of the Scots: 'They burned two hundred little scholars who were in the school at Corbridge learning their first letters and grammar, having blocked up the doors and set fire to the building.' The Lanercost Chronicle, however, gives a different location for this atrocity, saying, 'They collected a crowd of young schoolboys in Hexham school and, blocking the doors, set fire to the building and its inmates innocent in the sight of God.' Walter of Hemingburgh mentions the burning of Hexham and its priory but makes no mention of the murder of the schoolboys.

In fact, the Scottish punitive expeditions in Redesdale and

Tynedale served little purpose, and certainly did not deflect Edward from his grand designs for the subjugation of Scotland. Berwick was to be the pivot on which the administration of Scotland was to balance, and with characteristic energy Edward set to work as early as April to rebuild the town so recently sacked by his troops. He recruited a vast workforce in Northumberland and personally supervised at least the initial stages of the town's reconstruction. The ineffectual earthworks were replaced by a deep ditch and high, broad earthworks. Having secured the defences Edward then designated Berwick, in September 1296, as the administrative centre for the government of Scotland and appointed Hugh Cressingham, formerly chief itinerant justice for the northern counties of England, as Treasurer of Scotland with his headquarters in the town. In January 1297 a committee was established to advise on the planning of the new town, under Cressingham's direction.

Almost a month elapsed after the fall of Berwick before Edward resumed the offensive. No doubt he felt that time was on his side, and that the pacification of Scotland would be a relatively simple matter. The King of Scots had already been shown up as weak and ineffective — 'a lamb among wolves' is how one chronicler described him. The magnates of Scotland were divided, ranging from those like the Bruces who were actively engaged on Edward's behalf, to the Earl of Buchan, Constable of Scotland, who was attempting to co-ordinate Scottish resistance to Edward. In between lay the earls and barons who could not decide where their interests lay, or who would not serve under leaders with whom they disagreed.

On St George's Day, 23 April 1296, the main English army commanded by Balliol's father-in-law, Earl Warenne, set out along the coast road from Berwick north into the Lothians and four days later engaged the Scots under Buchan on the foothills of the Lammermoors, at Spottsmuir near Dunbar. The earls of Mar and Atholl, traditional supporters of the Bruce faction, decided at the last moment not to take part in the battle and the loss of their troops to the Scottish side was a grievous blow to Buchan. Like the Scots of 1651 before Cromwell's army, Buchan's army lost what little advantage they had by rushing headlong from the high ground to charge the English cavalry.

Edward's battle-hardened horsemen, veterans of campaigns in Flanders and Wales, skilfully regrouped and charged the Scots so effectively that the latter were totally routed. The ensuing struggle was unequal and Buchan's army was destroyed. With this signal defeat, resistance in Scotland crumbled rapidly. Among those taken prisoner at Dunbar were 130 important knights, the earls of Atholl, Ross and Menteith, the son of John Comyn of Badenoch and half a dozen other magnates, and they were speedily transported south, to be incarcerated in various English castles.

The Steward surrendered Roxburgh Castle after a brief siege on 8 May. Jedburgh capitulated a fortnight later, Edinburgh Castle was battered into submission by English siege-engines, and the Lothians were easily subdued. By the middle of June Edward was before Stirling, where an Irish contingent led by Richard de Burgh, Earl of Ulster, joined him, but when they rode up to the impressive castle they found it already deserted by its garrison. From there the English army proceeded in a leisurely fashion northwards through Perth, Montrose, Aberdeen and Banff as far as Elgin. Detachments were sent westwards into the Highlands but the main body moved south again at the end of July.

On 2 July John Balliol, from his temporary headquarters at Kincardine, formally confessed his error in making an alliance with France against his liege lord and surrendered his kingdom to Edward. The letter which he sent to Edward bore the Great Seal of Scotland, probably the last time he sealed documents with this device. Five days later, in the churchyard of Stracathro, Balliol publicly admitted his errors and confirmed his reconciliation with Edward. On 10 July he underwent two humiliating ceremonies: at Brechin, clad in the plain white gown of the penitent and carrying a simple white wand, he formally surrendered his enfeoffment to Antony Bek, and later the same day he repeated it to Edward himself at Montrose. His act of submission was total. Edward, with a fine sense of the dramatic, had the royal insignia ripped from Balliol's tabard or surcoat, and from this humiliating incident springs the nickname by which the luckless Balliol has ever since been known — Toom Tabard (empty coat). Later generations have confused this nickname, taking it to mean that he was a hollow king, a mere puppet manipulated by Edward, and this harsh though erroneous concept was repeated forcibly by Agnes Mure Mackenzie, maintaining that the quality of his reign made his subjects call him 'Empty Jacket'. In another age and in other circumstances John Balliol might have shown more positive and statesmanlike qualities. His principal misfortune was to take over a divided country which had been without a leader for six years, and to be faced with the ruthless opportunism of a powerful and greedy neighbour.

Early in August John Balliol and his son Edward were taken by sea to England under the escort of Thomas of Lancaster. Thereafter the erstwhile King of Scots was treated with surprising leniency. For a brief spell he was kept in the Tower of London but shortly afterwards he was allowed a measure of liberty — the modern equivalent would be house arrest — at Hertford not far from his former manor of Hitchin. He was given every comfort in accordance with a man of his position, including a huntsman and ten hounds. When the Scots rose in revolt in 1297 in the name of King John, he and his son were returned to the Tower. Two years later the Balliols, father and son, were handed over to the papal legate with whom they sojourned for a while, before departing from England on 18 July 1299 under the protection of the Bishop of Vicenza. At Dover King John endured the final indignity of a customs search. His baggage was found to contain a substantial quantity of gold and silver plate, as well as coined money. He was allowed to retain this property, but a gold coronet and the Great Seal of Scotland, which he had somehow managed to conceal, were promptly confiscated.

In 1302 John Balliol was released from the amiable custody of the Bishop of Vicenza and allowed to retire to his ancestral estate at Bailleul in Picardy where he died in 1314, the year of Bannockburn. His son Edward was to return to Scotland in 1333 and reigned for five years as a puppet backed by the forces of Edward III, but thereafter he faded from the scene and died, at an advanced age, in 1370.

The inherent weaknesses of Scotland, together with the character defects and vacillation of John Balliol, make this reign one of the most tragic in a history noted for tragedy. The submissions at Stracathro, Brechin and Montrose which brought this sorry reign to an end plunged Scotland into a decade in which the national identity was all but obliterated.

At Scone King Edward removed *Lia Fail*, the Stone of Destiny on which every Celtic king of Scotland had been crowned. Legend had it that the grey basalt stone had been the pillow on which Jacob slept when he dreamed of angels ascending a ladder to heaven. It was believed to have been brought from the Holy Land by Scota, the daughter of the Pharaoh of Egypt from whom the Scots took their name, and subsequently brought from Spain to Ireland by Gadalos or Gaelus, ancestor of the Gaels. In the sixth century Fergus of Dalriada brought the stone from Ireland to Scone where it reposed for eight hundred years. According to Blind Harry, King Edward had himself symbolically crowned on the stone at Scone before removing it to Westminster Abbey where it reposes, under the Coronation chair, to this day. Harry included a prophetic couplet:

> But where that stone is, Scots shall masters be,
> God haste the time Margretis heir to see.[1]

The prophecy would be fulfilled 130 years after this poem was written, when James VI, King of Scots, succeeded to the throne of England in 1603. An unsubstantiated myth, which persists to this day,[2] alleges that the monks of Scone, apprised of the approaching English army, hid the Stone and substituted a piece of rock hewn from a local quarry. By inference, the *real* Stone has been concealed ever since, no one knows where.

Be that as it may, Edward was well pleased with his conquest. He also confiscated the Scottish regalia, including the Black Rood of St Margaret, and transferred these precious and much revered symbols of Scottish sovereignty to London. Even more grievous a loss were the three chests crammed full of royal records and other archives of incalculable value which were shipped south from Leith, never to be seen again. Whether these documents were lost at sea or were deliberately destroyed is immaterial; Edward effectively obliterated the evidence of Scottish nationhood at a single stroke.

According to an anonymous account, Edward held his parliament at Berwick on 28 August 1296:

And there were all the bishops, earls, barons, abbots and priors; and there he received the homage of all, and their oaths that they would be good and loyal to him. To the well regulated people he forthwith gave up all their own goods and those of their tenants; the earls, barons and bishops he permitted to enjoy their lands, provided they came at All Saints to the parliament at St Edmunds. Then he appointed the Earl Warenne to be guardian of the land, and sir Hugh de Cressingham treasurer, sir Walter of Amersham chancellor. Then he tarried at Berwick three weeks and three days, arranging his affairs, and set out on his road to England on the Sunday after the feast of the Holy Cross.[3]

The main business of the Berwick parliament was the assembly of more than two thousand Scottish landowners, clergy, burgesses and representatives of communities to do homage to Edward, not as superior of Scotland but as King of England, Lord of Ireland and Duke of Guyenne. There has been some doubt expressed[4] as to the true size of this assembly, mainly on the grounds that such a multitude of important persons, together with their retainers, would have been impossible to handle, far less take each person through the prescribed ritual in turn. It is considered more likely that certain limited and well-defined classes of persons who held property in Scotland were required to provide written and sealed instruments of homage and fealty. The bulk of the names on the so-called Ragman Roll consisted of tenants-in-chief of the Crown and their heirs, substantial sub-tenants and their heirs, officers and leading burgesses of some eastern burghs, heads of religious houses and other clergy. The names were collected in order of sheriffdoms and for this reason certain people, with extensive holdings in several shires, appear on the Roll more than once.

Among the names were those of Robert Bruce, Lord of Annandale, and his son, the young Earl of Carrick, who had already sworn fealty to Edward the previous March. According to Fordun, the elder Bruce reminded Edward of a promise, made when Balliol first showed signs of rebellion, that the Scottish throne would be assigned to him. To this Edward replied testily, 'Have we nothing else to do but win you kingdoms?'[5] If the elder Bruce made any reply to this it has gone unrecorded. At any rate he returned to his duties at Carlisle without demur. From Edward's viewpoint it is understandable that, having just topped one figurehead in Scotland, he was not going to establish another. History has an impression of the elder Bruce as a somewhat colourless, spineless individual — not so very different from John Balliol, in fact — but Edward knew him personally and may have feared that Scotland would not be so easily handled under his rule. As for the young Earl of Carrick, those qualities of character — ambition, determination and resolution — which would later win him the throne would already have been well formed. In the autumn of 1296 the Earl of Carrick was turned twenty-two, a well set-up young man with a mind of his own.

On the other hand, absence of a name from the Ragman Roll may not be as significant as later generations have imagined. The Roll was pretty selective as regards the representation of the rising burghs of Scotland, and many knights and lesser gentry were not included. There may be no particular significance, therefore, in the fact that the name of Sir Malcolm Wallace younger of Ellerslie was absent. The name of his uncle, Sir Ranald Craufurd, was included and, indeed, he continued in office as hereditary Sheriff of Ayr, although real power in the county was wielded by the twenty-four-year-old Sir Henry de Percy, appointed by King Edward as Warden of Galloway and Ayr and Castellan of Ayr, Wigtown, Cruggleton and Buittle on 8 September 1296.

Edward himself left Scotland eleven days later. By that time the situation with France had deteriorated and there were matters much more important than Scotland to preoccupy him. His contempt for the Scots and their miserable country comes across most forcibly in the casual remark made to Earl Warenne at the time of his departure. As one old soldier to another, Edward is reported to have said, *'Bon besoigne fait qy de merde se delivrer'* (He who rids himself of shit does a good job).[6] For the moment, it appeared that Scotland had been pacified at a minimum loss to England. With the onset of winter most of the English host returned south and was demobilised, leaving garrisons of hand-picked men in all the castles of Scotland. Back in Westminster early in October, Edward doubtless congratulated himself on a good job well done. His self-satisfaction must have been short-lived.

North of the border, in the telling phrase of Fordun, the famous William Wallace, Hammer of the English, *caput levavit* — 'raised his head'.

4

FROM OUTLAW TO GUERRILLA

There was, at this time, a certain public robber or brigand,
Willelmus Walays by name, who had been many times outlawed. He, during his flight and wanderings, gathered around
him all outlaws like himself, who chose him as their leader,
and speedily increased to a multitude.

WALTER OF HEMINGBURGH, IN *WALLACE PAPERS*, P.33

At that time there was in Scotland a certain youth, Willelmus
le Waleis by name, an archer who obtained his living by
means of his bow and his quiver; of base descent, and mean
birth and training.

COTTONIAN MS, IN *WALLACE PAPERS*, P.8

B Y stating that the five Englishmen who tried to seize
William's catch of fish on the bank of the Irvine Water were
retainers of Henry de Percy, Blind Harry has led successive biog-
raphers and historians to assume that this incident must have
occurred late in 1296 or early in 1297. Thus the period of
Wallace's outlawry and brigandage, before emerging as a national leader, is invariably telescoped into a matter of months. If we
accept that William was in his early thirties at the time of his
death in 1305, and was eighteen when he slew young Selby, we
are faced with the problem of the empty years, before 'he raised
his head'. If the incident at Irvine Water took place in 1292, dur-

ing the Interregnum when the south of Scotland at least was occupied by English troops, then it must be assumed that William was an outlaw from that time onwards. Harry records that he was protected by his kinsman, Wallace of Auchencruive, and found refuge in Leglen Wood on the banks of the River Ayr, and that in later years this was one of his favourite hiding-places. Centuries later, this beautiful wooded dell was to be a haunt of the young Robert Burns, who would walk twelve miles from Lochlie on Sunday afternoons to pay his respects 'with as much devout enthusiasm as ever pilgrim did to Loretto; and as I explored every den and dell where I could suppose my heroic Countryman to have sheltered, I recollect (for even then I was a Rhymer) that my heart glowed with a wish to be able to make a Song on him, equal to his merits'. In 1929 the Burns Federation erected a cairn linking the patriot and the patriot-bard.

Remarkably little is recorded of the state of Scotland during the reign of King John. Of one thing we may be certain, however, and that is that the continuing independence of Scotland was largely illusory. It seems highly unlikely that Edward surrendered all the castles and 'Strengths' of the country to John Balliol and withdrew all his forces at the end of 1292. It is more probable that the more important fortresses remained in English hands for strategic purposes. How else could Edward have enforced his legal summons on his increasingly recalcitrant vassal? That there were Englishmen aplenty, throwing their weight about in a sullen, ever more resentful countryside, there can be no doubt. This uneasy situation, of a country where the normal processes of law and order were breaking down, and where the common people were gradually asserting themselves against an alien presence, explains the rather cryptic lines of Blind Harry regarding his hero:

> Although only eighteen years of age, he was seemly, robust and bold. He carried for weapons either a good sword or knife and with such he often had encounters with their English foes. When he found one without his fellow, such an one did no further harm to any Scot. To cut his throat or to stab him suddenly he did not miss. Nor could any one trace how he came by his death.[1]

This conveys the impression of Wallace going about the country, a cross between a serial killer and an avenging angel, striking down the hated Southron whenever the opportunity arose and leaving no clues as to the identity of the assailant. In Harry's matter-of-fact words, he was 'dispitfull and savage' against anyone of the Saxon race. Over the centuries historians have been embarrassed by these revelations in their national hero, seeking to mitigate them by imputing a degree of blood-thirstiness to the poet himself. Others, however, remind us that the 1290s was a brutal period in which the mortality rate was high at the best of times and life was cheap. Public hangings for a wide variety of offences were commonplace and even quite minor misdemeanours might be punished by a severe flogging or mutilation. Conversely, there was not the intricate machinery of law and order that emerged in much later centuries. Men often took the law into their own hands; vendettas and revenge killings were frequent and customary. Furthermore, the escalating oppression of the Scots was regarded as justification enough for killing the hated English and their collaborators. There are many references in the chronicles of the period to such acts of lawlessness by brigands and robbers in Scotland, but little or no reference to the atrocities and reprisals inflicted on the often innocent bystanders, for the simple reason that the chroniclers were Englishmen who had a vested interest in presenting a rather one-sided view of events. 'The iron of English oppression had already entered deep into the soul of Wallace.'[2]

As Blind Harry was weaving into the fabric of his poem many of the oral traditions concerning William Wallace, it seems probable that some at least of his adventures and exploits belong to the period before 1296, even though Harry places them in the context of a Scotland after the sack of Berwick and the downfall of Balliol. The sceptics, interpreting Harry literally, have tended to dismiss these feats of arms largely because they could not possibly have taken place in a matter of months. If, however, we can accept that they were probably spread over a period of three years (1293–96), they not only make more sense but explain how it was that, by the time Wallace emerged as a national leader, he had acquired the skills of generalship necessary to organise and lead a relatively large force, and take on what was arguably the finest, and certainly up to that time the most successful, army in Europe.

Historians who reject Blind Harry as pure fable, on the other hand, are faced with the problem of explaining the paradox of the landless younger son of a minor laird, a callow youth with neither wealth, land nor nobility, emerging as the undisputed leader of his country. One recent writer has raised the interesting speculation that William, unknown to his contemporaries far less posterity, had served his apprenticeship as a soldier. 'It follows from this that he had left Scotland to fight, for no opportunity was to be found in his homeland.'[3] Blithely overlooking the lack of any such foreign adventures, or even a hint of them, in the writings of Blind Harry, Wyntoun, Major or Fordun, it is further conjectured that William might have fought in Wales or France and that, *mirabile dictu*, he may even have fought for King Edward. Given the size and prowess of Wallace, and his undoubtedly charismatic qualities as a natural leader of men, it seems unlikely that such a young paladin could have gone for long in Edward's service without coming to his notice. The singular lack of any reference to the young Scottish giant in either the records or the chronicles of the period makes such conjecture rather pointless. A more important point is that, had William ever served under Edward, this would surely have been brought out at that farce of a trial in 1305, as inescapable proof of the treason with which he was then charged. And William's defiant denial of treason at that time surely rules out the possibility of service under Edward, even years earlier.

The likeliest solution to the enigma is that Wallace was a fugitive from the law. For some of the time he would have lain low in the great Selkirk Forest that spread over much of southern Scotland; but even in spite of his great height, which must have made him conspicuous, he might frequently have emerged in disguise from his lair to mingle with the crowds at fairs and visit the market towns. The youth who had been intended for the Church was apparently not averse to female company, if Harry is any guide in the matter, and this sometimes led him into narrow escapes from the forces of law and order.

The English chronicles, reviling the Scottish hero and indulging in character assassination, frequently refer to William as a brigand and a robber, and mention his 'repeated outlawries'. Apart from this and the embroideries of Blind Harry, the only shred of evidence regarding William Wallace before his emergence as a guerrilla leader is contained in a document of 8 August 1296 indicting one

> Matthew of York, accused by Cristiana of St John [Perth], of robbery, viz. on Thursday next before St Botulph's Day, he came to her house at Perth in the company of a thief, one William le Waleys, and there by force took her goods and chattels viz. beer, to the value of 3s, replies that he is a clerk and not bound to answer. The jury finds the charge proved, and he is adjudged to penitence.[4]

Of course, by that time Scotland was in the process of being pacified by Edward. If this thief William le Waleys is our hero, he may well have been one of those countless ex-soldiers, lately in the service of John Balliol or the Earl of Buchan, now made redundant by the turn of events. It is more likely, however, that William had been living the life of the wandering brigand, a latter-day Robin Hood, not so very dissimilar from the picture conveyed by Harry. In any case, a proud young man of warlike mien could not easily forgive or forget the way in which his father was done to death, and would be quick to resent the contemptuous behaviour of the English garrisons. In one incident, according to Harry, Wallace paid a visit to Ayr in disguise and could not resist taking on an English churl who had a formidable reputation as a weight-lifter. This buffoon, for a groat (fourpence), would let anyone who dared strike him across his back with the rough pole which he carried. When William heard of this he offered the man three groats, and struck him with such force that he broke the fool's back. The other soldiers tried to overpower Wallace but he brained one with the cudgel and broke the neck of another, then drew his sword, felled a third and slashed through the armpit armour of a fourth. Including the churl, Wallace killed five Englishmen in this brief but bloody encounter before leaping on his horse and making his escape to Leglen Wood.

William may have been lodging with his uncle Sir Ranald when there was yet another fracas in the streets of Ayr. On this occasion the sheriff's servant had gone to the market to buy some fish and was on his way home when he was intercepted by Percy's steward who demanded the fish. Wallace just happened to be passing by and interceded on behalf of the servant, telling Percy's man to leave the boy alone. The steward responded by lunging at William with his hunting staff. William ducked, grabbed the man by his collar and plunged his dagger into his heart. Again, men-at-arms converged quickly on the scene, with the usual deadly result; but gradually the sheer weight of numbers, and the fact that the English troopers were armed with spears, forced Wallace back to the sea-wall. Desperately he tried to fight his way out of the press but he was borne to the ground and overpowered. He was bound hand and foot and carried to the Warden's dungeon where he was closely confined in appalling conditions and deliberately weakened by slow starvation. Sir Ranald, at great personal risk, tried to ransom his young kinsman, but Percy was obdurate. The outlaw was left to rot in his dungeon, Celimus the gaoler being instructed to give him nothing but water and rotten herrings. Under these conditions it is hardly surprising that Wallace contracted a fever and hovered close to death. On the day appointed for his trial it was found that Celimus had gone too far; the cell door was opened to reveal that William was in a deep coma. Assuming that the prisoner was already dead, the English threw his corpse over a wall into a dungheap where he would be left to rot.

Fortunately news of this disgusting end came to an old retainer of the family, the woman who had been William's first nurse at Ellerslie. This woman, living in the Newton of Ayr, went to the English and sought permission to take away his corpse to give it a decent burial. With great reluctance they eventually agreed, so the woman and her friends bore away the body to her house where, as she was cleansing him, she noticed a faint flickering of his eyelids. She spoon-fed him — even her daughter, who had a twelve-week-old baby, suckled the young giant and brought him back from the brink. Because rumours were flying round the town, the women were compelled to arrange a wake for Wallace to keep up the pretence of his death.

Harry relates that, about this time, Sir Thomas Rymour of Ercildoune, then in his seventies, was visiting St Mary's monastery at Faile near Mauchline, when he heard the rumour of Wallace's death. He was so alarmed at this that he sent a servant into Ayr to seek the truth. On being told later that William had, in fact, survived his ordeal he declared:

For sooth, ere he decease,
Shall many thousands in the field make end.
From Scotland he shall forth the Southron send,
And Scotland thrice he shall bring to peace.
So good of hand again shall ne'er be kenned.[5]

Sir Thomas, known to posterity as Thomas the Rhymer, had foretold the death of Alexander III and was widely regarded in his own lifetime as a soothsayer and prophet. This latest prophecy would soon have spread beyond the monastic cloisters. In modern parlance, a prophecy by Thomas the Rhymer was probably the best bit of public relations Wallace could have got; even the English became alarmed when news of it, coupled with Wallace's miraculous escape, reached their ears. Incidentally, the effect on William himself would have been incalculable. In an age of superstition and a universal belief in the supernatural, such a prophecy by so renowned a personality must have given William a sense of his own destiny. His invincibility against the English, coupled with his resurrection, must have given him the feeling that he could achieve anything if he put his mind to it.

When he had recovered, William sent his old nurse, along with her daughter, baby and servant, to his mother at Ellerslie, fearing some reprisal once the truth leaked out. He himself could not return to Crosshouse as he did not wish to compromise his uncle. Instead, he set off on the road to Glasgow, 'without belt, boss, buckler or band', armed only with a rusty blade which he had found in a corner of the nurse's house. On the way he stepped aside to let pass an English esquire named Longcastle, accompanied by two stout yeomen. Longcastle, 'a soldier keen and terrible', was suspicious and insisted on taking the young wayfarer back to Ayr with him. Inevitably Longcastle paid for his suspicion, William's rusty blade slicing through the Englishman's neck. One of the yeomen he decapitated with a single stroke; the other tried to flee but William chased after him and made such a stroke between his ribs as to expose his liver and lungs. Thus providentially William acquired horses, armour and silver, 'for spending money he had none'.

At Riccarton he was reunited with his Uncle Richard who had mourned his death. This seems to have marked a turning point in William's career. Hitherto he had been a lone maverick, lashing out at individuals or, at best, getting into an affray with no more than a handful of the hated English. Now the prophecy of Thomas the Rhymer gave him a broader purpose. Could he, indeed, a landless younger son, succeed where the great magnates of Scotland had so signally failed?

He was now joined by Sir Richard's three sons Adam, Richard and Simon, as well as by Robert Boyd of Kilmarnock and other trusty companions. No longer the lone outlaw, but the leader of a band of desperate men, William became more ambitious. Adam, the eldest son of Sir Richard, was to become one of William's most distinguished lieutenants. Mention has already been made of William's nephews Edward Little and Tom Halliday who were his constant companions. Harry tells us that Halliday's eldest daughter married young Sir John Graham who was later to become Wallace's second-in-command, while a second daughter married Johnstone, whom Wallace subsequently appointed constable of Lochmaben Castle. Other relatives who joined his ranks about this time included young Patrick Auchinleck of Gilbank, William's 'eyme' or uncle by marriage. Kirkpatrick of Closeburn in Dumfriesshire (a relative of the Roger Kirkpatrick who would help Robert Bruce slay Sir John Comyn a few years later) was described as 'of kin' and 'to Wallace's mother near', suggesting a relationship on the Craufurd side. William Craufurd and one Kneland or Cleland are described by Harry as cousins. The network of nephews, cousins and far-out relatives was probably very extensive; far from being confined to Ayrshire it was spread right across Scotland from Dumfriesshire in the south to Moray in the north.[6] The importance of this kinship cannot be over-emphasised; it gave Wallace's band ties of blood as well as a common purpose, at a time when conspirators did not dare trust outsiders. More significantly for long-term success, this network cut across regional, linguistic and cultural barriers, giving Cymric, Picto-Scottish, Anglo-Saxon and Danish elements a solidarity in the face of their common foe.

That these and other young men were drawn to William Wallace there is no denying. By now his exploits against the hated English must have spread far and wide. His miraculous escape from death and his retrieval from the grave must have had the ring of a resurrection about it, and the biblical parallels would not have been lost on William's followers. His giant stature and extraordinary stamina inspired confidence in an age when men fought with weapons that relied on brawn rather than brain, far less technology. But he also possessed considerable personal magnetism and charm. He was an inspired leader and his men adored him. One of his earliest adherents was Kerly from Cruggleton, near the village of Sorbie in Wigtownshire. This Gallovidian Gael was his most faithful companion, accompanying him on many of his exploits and fighting by his side through thick and thin.

Blind Harry states that in July, 'when the sweet flowers and all edible vegetation grow abundantly in every glen and hollow', Wallace got the opportunity to avenge his father's death. No date is given, of course; but from a reference to Percy's men the year 1297 is implied. This would make a nonsense of chronology, so it has to be assumed that the ambush at Loudoun Hill took place the previous summer, before Sir Henry de Percy's appointment. Writing more than a century and half after the event, Harry can be forgiven for an anachronism regarding Percy's appointment. Some other English magnate would undoubtedly have preceded Percy but his name is not known. The death of Longcastle and his companions would have confirmed the rumour that the outlaw Wallace had cheated death. Harry has Percy debating how best this menace could be contained and draws the interesting conclusion that such a man must be won over to King Edward's interest by a reward of gold and estates. Given the facility with which the great magnates changed sides in the late thirteenth century, such a course of action is not as far-fetched as it might seem.

In the meantime, however, William's spies and informers brought him the news that Fenwick, the knight who had slain his father, was back in the south-west of Scotland, and had been entrusted with a delicate mission. He was in charge of a convoy bringing a large treasure of gold and silver, including the confiscated chattels of the Scottish churches, to Ayr. Harry has Fenwick travelling from Carlisle, which is unlikely in view of the fact that William laid a trap for Fenwick's men at Loudoun Hill — ironically, the very spot where Fenwick had killed Sir Malcolm Wallace five years earlier. It seems more probable that Fenwick and his men were travelling from that other English stronghold, Lanark. This would explain why their route lay through Avondale and thence to the Irvine Valley. Loudoun Hill, dominating the head of the valley, was the ideal place for an ambush, where the track passed through a steep defile. Master John Blair, the Benedictine monk from Dunfermline, was one of their number when Wallace's band took up their positions and was an eye-witness of the battle, for Harry cites him in describing the plan.

Harry also provides a detailed description of William's mode of dress and armour at this period:

> Ever since he left prison Wallace wore secure armour; from that time he always used good light harness in case of sudden strife; from it he would never sever. An habergeon he wore under his gown, a small steel helmet he had in his bonnet, and no more; his gloves, of plate cloth armour, well covered; and in his doublet, a close collar of steel. His face, which was always bare, he kept with his two hands, which worthy were and wicht.[7]

A habergeon was a neck-covering of chain-mail extending across the breast. The light armour worn by William could easily be concealed under tunic or jerkin, while the small steel basinet protecting his head could be covered by a cloth bonnet. Unlike the knights and pikemen of the period, however, William did not wear a closed helmet with a visor or eye-slits, hence the reference to protecting his face with his mailed hands.

According to Harry, Fenwick's men-at-arms numbered nine score, while Wallace had fifty men at his command and *right* on his side. More importantly, William had the element of surprise and had chosen his ground well, at a point where the English could not ride more than two abreast. The Scots partially blocked the pass with rocks and boulders and fought on foot, thrusting their spears and swords under the bellies of the English horses where their armour was thinnest or non-existent. Wallace, with a well-ground spear, ran it through the corselet bar of the leading horseman with such force that the shaft split asunder. Swiftly he drew his great two-handed sword and finished off the hapless knight with a deadly stroke. The English tried to ride down the Scots but the latter held firm, withstanding repeated charges. Fenwick himself, armed with a sharp lance, attempted to skewer Wallace, who neatly sidestepped and struck a blow which sliced through the Englishman's saddle-bow. Fenwick was unseated and toppled from his destrier, where he was finished off by Robert Boyd with a stabbing sword. Adam Wallace of Riccarton slew Beaumont, a renowned squire, his blade shearing right through the Southron's neck. In the general confusion riderless horses trampled many a warrior underfoot. Although greatly outnumbering their attackers, the English lost heart when their leaders were killed. About eighty of them managed to escape towards the south, leaving a hundred dead. Significantly, there is no mention of wounded in this tally, and it is assumed that no quarter was given. On the Scottish side three men were slain, two from Kyle and one from Cunninghame, who had left their homes to follow Robert Boyd. Quite casually, Harry recounts that the victors made the English servants lead the baggage horses to Clyde's Forest: 'when they were out of dread of being surprised they bound them fast and hanged them on the boughs of trees.' Then, as an afterthought, he adds hastily, 'Wallace spared none who were able for war, but he made his followers always forbear to injure women or priests.' Brigand he might be, but Wallace still had certain standards.

This ambush netted Wallace two hundred pack-horses, heavily laden with provisions and wine, as well as the armoured destriers of the knights and men-at-arms, armour, weapons and money. 'Both stuff and horses, in great abundance, he sent privately to friends round about, the remainder right happily they consumed on the spot.' News of the battle spread like wildfire, the English exaggerating the size of the force which had attacked them. The Scots, who knew better, marvelled that fifty lightly armed men could have achieved so much. It seemed as if Sir Thomas's prophecy was coming true. More importantly, however, William's success destroyed the myth that heavily armoured horsemen were invincible: confronted by a well-disciplined force, on ground which was chosen by the latter and used to best advantage, the much-feared English cavalry could be defeated.

For twenty days the Wallace band remained in Clyde's Forest. This densely wooded area south of Lesmahagow and extending to the Clyde is largely open moorland today, but

Wallace's Cave near Coalburn, a great sandstone fissure, is traditionally regarded as the outlaw's stronghold in this area. The fame of the giant outlaw spread far and wide and other fugitives, broken men and youths seeking adventure and revenge, flocked to him. Percy is said to have journeyed to Glasgow to take counsel with Sir Aymer de Valence, 'a powerful and false traitor, who dwelt in Bothwell'. This is poetic licence at its worst. Sir Aymer, Earl of Pembroke, and a nephew of Henry III, could not be described as a Scottish traitor by any stretch of the imagination. We have only Harry's word for it that he was in Scotland at this period — in fact he seems to have been in Flanders till late in 1297, and as far as can be ascertained from historical records did not come to Scotland until 1298. He was one of the Guardians of Scotland appointed by King Edward in 1306 and, in that context, was a formidable opponent of Robert Bruce, which may be why Harry confused him with the earlier struggle involving Wallace.

According to the poem, however, it was Sir Aymer who advised Percy to make a truce with this 'awful chieftain'. Sir Ranald Craufurd, threatened with dismissal and the forfeiture of his lands, was allegedly forced to act as intermediary in this deal. The sheriff sought out his nephew in Clyde's Forest and came upon his company as they were sitting down to dine on some of the spoils of the ambush. Sir Ranald laid out the terms offered by the English; Wallace, strongly urged by Adam Wallace and Robert Boyd, agreed. The truce was to last ten months. The band thereupon broke up, each man going his own way. William rode with Sir Ranald and his retinue back to Crosshouse. This truce was said to have taken effect in August. Wallace, however, was not one to sit back idly. Chafing at inaction, he longed to visit Ayr again. One day, when his uncle was away from home, William, in company with fifteen comrades in disguise, slipped into the town. On this occasion he witnessed a passage-at-arms, under the challenge of a famous English champion. After the challenger beat several opponents his eye lit upon the young giant and he called him out. Wallace accepted the challenge and without further ado slew the champion. Then, and only then, it dawned on the English soldiers that the victor was that redoubtable outlaw Wallace. A fierce skirmish ensued between the two parties but once again the outlaw made good his escape to Leglen Wood, leaving twenty-nine English soldiers dead in the market place. Notwithstanding the fact that Percy was alleged to have lost three of his own kinsmen in the affray, Harry claims that he merely sent a messenger to Sir Ranald charging him to take surety of Wallace that he should keep away from market, town or fair, 'so that he might be out of the way of the resorts of his soldiers'.

After a night in Leglen Wood, Wallace returned to Crosshouse where his uncle showed him Percy's letter. William agreed to behave himself and stayed at Crosshouse for sixteen days. The fourth book of Harry's epic begins in September 1296 with a great council at Glasgow, to which Sir Ranald and his retainers were summoned. William was with this entourage and rode ahead with his two trusty companions Gray and Kerly, overtaking Sir Ranald's sumpter horse ridden by a young servant. Ahead, on the road, however, they caught up with the tail-end of Percy's baggage train at Hesilden east of Cathcart, a few miles south of Glasgow. When Percy's men insolently commandeered Sir Ranald's fresher pack-horse for their master, William tried to remonstrate, but to no avail. He must have had a hard time controlling his anger, but he let the English soldiers take the animal and leave their own jaded beast to carry Sir Ranald's baggage. Presently William returned to the main party riding across the moor and reported what had taken place. Sir Ranald was philosophical about the matter and said it was better to lose a horse than the lives of good men over such a trifle.

As Harry reports it, the road to Cathcart was William's road to Damascus. His reply to his uncle was measured and dignified, but unequivocal:

> As surely as God shall save me, of this great wrong I shall have amends; and neither for truce, nor to please you, will I let it pass. With witness I herewith give up my allegiance, for, if in cowardice you choose to forfeit your rights, you, yourself, shall soon by them be done to death.[8]

Sir Ranald knew better than to argue with the young hothead, and let him go. He himself, however, thought it prudent to delay his journey and instead of pressing on to Glasgow that evening took lodgings at Mearns Cross. Meanwhile Wallace and his two comrades rode on and caught up with Percy's baggage-train at East Cathcart. They immediately recognised Sir Ranald's sumpter horse by its trappings, as well as the three horsemen and two foot soldiers who had behaved so insolently earlier in the day. The enemy, in turn, saw that the Scots meant business and turned with weapons drawn to meet this threat. Wallace dismounted, the better to fight on foot; drawing his huge sword he struck the leading horseman with such force 'that both hat and head he made to fly'. A second he slashed across the face, splitting his skull asunder, and left a third mortally wounded. Meanwhile Kerly and Gray had despatched the yeomen. They then took the best of Percy's pack-horses as well as the destriers, helped themselves to the pick of Percy's harness, equipment and arms, besides gold, silver and jewels, and went on their way.

By nightfall they had entered Glasgow, but, crossing the wooden bridge over the Clyde in the town centre, they kept on riding until they were well clear of the city, it being Wallace's intention to head for the Lennox, the wild, mountainous region around Loch Lomond. The three men made camp that night, but the following day rode on to a hostelry kept by true Scots who gave them shelter.

Meanwhile the council met and formally outlawed William Wallace. To this council may belong the undated document which granted to Edward de Keith, in the name of King Edward, 'all goods and chattels of whatever kind he may gain from Messire William le Waleys the King's enemy'.[9] When Sir Ranald and his retinue arrived at ten o'clock, he and several of his party were arrested by the English and brought before the court to answer for the highway robbery and murder. Sir Ranald, however, produced a cast-iron alibi and denied all knowledge of Wallace's murderous actions. The charges were dropped against the sheriff, but his nephew and his companions were publicly posted as outlaws. Now all men's hands were turned against them. Sir Ranald was forced to swear a mighty oath that he would not communicate with his nephew. Wallace's band was widely dispersed and this seemed to represent the nadir in his fortunes, but in the Lennox he made contact with Sir Malcolm, Earl of Lennox, who offered him sanctuary and even promised to make him master of his household. Contrary to Harry's statement that Earl Malcolm 'had not made bond', he had in fact sworn fealty to King Edward not once but twice (on 14 March and 28 August 1296), but he was one of the few Celtic magnates of Scotland left and, secure in his island fortress of Inchmurrin in Loch Lomond, he could take his allegiance to the English sovereign lightly.

Wallace, however, declined the offer. He was not content to lie low in the wilds of Dunbartonshire; instead, he soon recruited another band, eventually having 'sixty likely men at wages'. Some of these were apparently Irishmen, driven out of their own island by one of Edward's lieutenants named MacFadyen, and numbering among them one Stephen of Ireland who was to become, like Kerly, one of William's most trusted supporters. Another adherent at this time was a strange character called Fawdon, 'melancholy of complexion, heavy of stature, dour in countenance, sorrowful, sad, ever dreadful and without pleasance'. All in all, this seems to have been a pretty rough bunch of murderers and cut-throats; William ordered Gray and Kerly to stick close to him at all times, until he trusted the others better.

Wallace's exploits in the ensuing months make him sound like a latter-day Robin Hood: killing and robbing the English and giving the spoils to the Scots 'with judgment and in a handsome manner', disdaining property himself although he had an abundance of gold to spend.

With his sixty desperadoes, Wallace headed north. Their first exploit was the capture of the pele-tower at Gargunnock, a little west of Stirling. He sent two scouts at midnight to spy out the land; they returned to report that the garrison security was lax, the sentry asleep, the drawbridge down and workmen going in and out without question. Wallace and his men managed to gain entrance to the castle but found the door secured with a stout bar. William wrenched the bar with his bare hands, ripping out some of the masonry with it, then smashed down the door with his boot. The noise awoke the sentry who lashed out with a pikestaff which William wrested from his hands and then brained him with. By now the constable, Thirlwall, and his troops had been roused but they were speedily despatched to the last man. The women and children of the garrison were spared, though confined in the dungeon. The corpses of the garrison were concealed in the ditch and the drawbridge was raised. Wallace and his gang remained in the pele for four days, undetected, before they gathered up their spoils, liberated the women and children, torched the little castle, and made their getaway.

Travelling under cover of darkness and mostly on foot, they made their way with Stephen as their guide to the River Forth, crossing at Kincardine. On the thickly wooded bank of the Teith William shot a large deer which gave them ample fresh meat. Crossing the deep waters of the Teith, they entered Strathearn and holed up during the daytime in a thicket, sallying forth at dusk to kill each and every Englishman they ran across: 'Some they took by sleight and some they slew by force.' At Blackford in Perthshire, for example, they encountered five riding to Doune, whom they slew and stripped before throwing the corpses into the river. Thereafter they crossed the Earn and headed for Methven Wood where they found 'a land of great abundance' and rested for some time.

William was not a man to remain inactive for long. He was curious to visit St Johnstone (Perth) so, leaving Stephen in command during his absence, he set forth with seven men. At the gate to the town he was accosted by the mayor or provost, to whom he gave his name as Will Malcolmson from Ettrick Forest. The mayor explained that his men were on the lookout for the outlaw Wallace. William replied that he had heard tell of this man but could give no news of him. The governor of Perth at this time was Sir Gerard Heron and his lieutenant was Sir John Butler, son of Sir James Butler of Kinclaven. Regretting that he had neither the men nor the arms to seize this town, William reconnoitred it thoroughly, learning of the strength and disposition of the enemy.

On discovering that Sir James Butler was returning to Kinclaven, Wallace retraced his steps to Methven Wood and gathered his band. The following day they advanced on Kinclaven, on the right bank of the Tay, a little above the confluence with the Isla. There the outlaws hid in a wooded hollow near the castle. Early in the afternoon William's scouts brought news that three outriders had gone past, but Wallace waited until the main body of ninety horsemen, with Sir James in their midst, had come up. The numbers were more evenly matched on this occasion, but the English cavalry thought that they were far superior to the lightly armed Scots, who were mostly on foot. With lances levelled they charged forward but, mindful of the lesson learned at Loudoun Hill, the Scots stood their ground and slashed at the legs and bellies of the horses, disabling them and throwing their riders to the ground where they could be more easily put to the sword. Wallace himself clove Sir James 'deeply into bone and brain right through all his armour'. After the death of their commander the remnant turned tail and fled, leaving sixty dead on the field. The panic-stricken survivors clattered into the castle with the doughty Wallace hard on their heels; single-handedly he secured the drawbridge until his men could catch up. Then they entered the fortalice and slew every man, sparing only the women, Lady Butler, the children and two priests, all of whom they confined closely while they systematically plundered the castle and dismantled its fortifications. Setting the women and priests free, the Scots burned down the castle and withdrew into Shortwood Shaw. In this action Wallace lost five of his own men.

Lady Butler and her party hastened to Perth to give the alarm. Immediately Sir Gerard Heron mustered a thousand heavily armed cavalry to pursue the marauders. Five squadrons were ordered to surround the wood while the sixth, led by Sir John Butler, made a direct assault. Wallace had taken up a strong position, a cleugh fortified on three sides by a hastily improvised stockade of tree-trunks, with an open space in front. Here he was determined to make a stand. Butler had a hundred and forty Lancashire longbowmen with eighty spearmen in close support. Wallace had only twenty archers, and few of them were skilled with the longbow, being more used to handling spears and swords. William himself was equipped with a strongbow which, like Ulysses in Greek mythology, none but he had the strength to draw. He had only fifteen arrows but he made each one count and despatched the enemy with deadly accuracy. The English archers, however, had an unlimited supply of arrows and rained down a deadly hail on the Scots, who were saved only by the thickness of the surrounding woods. William himself had a very narrow escape when an English marksman shot him 'under the chin, through a collar of steel, on the left side, and hurt his neck some deal'. This, incidentally, explains the near-contemporary French description of Wallace which states that he had a wen or scar on the left side of his neck. Fortunately, on this occasion, William spotted his assailant and, darting out from his lair, struck the archer with his great sword, cutting his head off.

At a crucial point in this skirmish, the attackers were re-inforced by a company of three hundred men-at-arms led by William Lorn (Sir William de Lorraine) from Gowrie, intent on avenging the death of his uncle, Sir James Butler. This was a des-perate moment for Wallace. He swiftly harangued his men: 'Here is no choice but either do or die. We have the right with us.' The Scots, now reduced to fifty men, were confronted with a well-armed force numbering ten times as many. The battle raged fiercely and, in spite of his arduous efforts with his 'burly brand', Wallace was forced to withdraw his men and seek refuge in the thickest part of the wood, where the ascent was steep and craggy. Here they made a desperate defence against their vio-lent foes. In the mêlée Wallace came face to face with Butler whose father he had so recently killed, but the English knight was saved by the bough of a tree which William sliced through, bringing it down on his head. Lorraine, coming to the aid of his cousin, was cut down by Wallace who managed to get back into his little stronghold unscathed. The news of Lorraine's death spurred on Sir Gerard Heron who ordered his squadrons into the wood, to close in for the kill; but the Scots managed to slip out on the north side, leaving seven of their comrades for dead. In the confusion Wallace's band was well away before the Englishmen realised it.

That night the Scots retreated into Cargill Wood to tend their wounds. Mercifully the English did not pursue them, being more intent on recovering the booty which Wallace had taken from Kinclaven, but all they found was Sir James Butler's horse. They then withdrew back to Perth, more despondent than elat-ed. The following night, however, the Scots returned cautiously to Shortwood Shaw and recovered their cache of booty where they had concealed it under the rocks. By dawn they had reached Methven Wood again and established themselves in a 'strength' in Elcho Park where they remained for some time, undetected by their foes.

It was at this juncture that William's human frailty almost let them down. Chafing at inaction as usual, and keen to return to

Perth where he had a 'leman' (mistress), he disguised himself as a monk and went into the town to keep a tryst with a girl whom he had presumably met on his first visit. On this occasion, however, he was recognised on account of his great height which no monkish garb could conceal. The English kept him under surveillance and after he had departed they interrogated the frightened girl who divulged the date and time of their next assignation.

On that day, however, the girl blurted out to William what had happened and was in a wretched state, wondering what would happen. With great presence of mind, Wallace resorted to a subterfuge which had helped him before. He donned the largest of her gowns and crammed her cap on his head. Then, secreting his sword under the gown and wrapped in her voluminous hooded cloak, he proceeded by the nearest way to the south gate. To the guards he said in a falsetto voice, 'To that chamber, quickly, Wallace is locked in!' They were deceived and let him pass, but two watchmen outside the gate noted this 'stalwart quean' walking with large, rapid strides, and went after her. On the South Inch, William turned to face his pursuers whom he left dead in a matter of seconds. Meanwhile, the troopers stormed the house where Wallace was supposed to be confined. In the great commotion, the girl somehow managed to escape. Shortly afterwards the discovery of the corpses on the South Inch led to a hue and cry. Sir Gerard Heron despatched six hundred well-armed men in hot pursuit; but by that time Wallace and his men were back within Elcho Park.

Heron was equipped with a bloodhound of the best Gilsland breed and this animal tracked Wallace back to the park. Heron and half his men surrounded the park — in reality a thick woodland — while Butler, as before, led the attack with three hundred against forty-three. In the first furious encounter the Scots killed forty but lost fifteen. Finding this ground indefensible, they hacked and slashed their way through Butler's throng and reached the River Tay, hoping to cross to safety, but the water was deep and half of them could not swim. The Scots had no alternative but to fight on, with their backs to the water. In this desperate skirmish they killed sixty of the enemy but lost nine. Now reduced to a mere handful, Wallace's gang seized their opportunity as Butler's troops were reforming, and dashed pell-mell between them and Heron's men, heading for Gask Wood.

It was early November and nightfall saved the Scots from annihilation. The way was uphill and rough, the Scots were footsore and battle-weary, and when they were still east of Dupplin Moor and a considerable distance from their goal, Fawdon broke down and refused to go on. Having entreated and cajoled him to no avail, Wallace angrily drew his blade and lopped off the mutineer's head. Blind Harry justified this drastic act, saying that Fawdon was suspected of treachery. Besides, the corpse would serve a useful purpose in holding up or distracting the bloodhound. Wallace is described as arguing with grim logic: if Fawdon were false, he would join the enemy; if he were true, the enemy would assuredly slay him when he fell into their hands. At least in this way Fawdon's death would help his comrades.

The fate of the tardy Fawdon is hard to rationalise, especially as Stephen and Kerly now hung back while the others pressed on. These two, Wallace's most trusty men, concealed themselves behind bushes near Fawdon's body, to see what would happen when the pursuers caught up. Sure enough, the English stopped in their tracks and gathered round the headless corpse, speculating on what had happened. As they were doing so, Stephen and Kerly crept out and mingled with the crowd. Kerly gradually edged forward and when Heron was bending to examine the body, he suddenly struck him dead. Again, in the confusion, Stephen and Kerly made good their escape towards the Earn. Butler sent a party back to Perth with Heron's body while the rest of his force pressed on to Dalreoch, about half a mile north of Dunning.

Meanwhile Wallace and his depleted band, now down to thirteen men, had gained the safety of Gask Hall (later immortalised in a song of Lady Nairne). Here they rested for the night. Wallace fretted about the fate of Stephen and Kerly and was conscience-stricken about the death of Fawdon. In this context Blind Harry develops a strangely atmospheric passage culminating in the dramatic appearance of Fawdon's ghost. This apparition was heralded by mysterious horn-blowing and William sent out his remaining men to discover the source. In this strange manner he was totally isolated and seems to have lost contact with his men. Harry has him wandering along the banks of the Earn, all alone and moaning with self-pity. In this uncharacteristic guise he was intercepted by Sir John Butler who had ridden out, ahead of his men, to check the fords. Butler, sceptical of the explanation given by this strange young man, drew his sword and prepared to dismount, but William was too quick for him. Drawing his own blade, Wallace struck the knight a mighty blow across the thigh. William seized his horse and with a second stroke cut his adversary's throat. An esquire who tried to ride him down with his lance, lost his life and his weapon. William rode away with a troop of cavalry in close pursuit. In the course of a running fight William slew a score of them, but at Blackford his horse broke down and he had to continue through the moorland on foot.

Eventually he came to the River Forth not far from Stirling. He dared not cross the river by the narrow bridge which was closely guarded. Instead, he bundled his sword and armour and swam the icy current at Cambuskenneth. He struggled to the south bank and hastened to the Torwood where he got shelter in a widow's hut. Later, two of her sons guarded him while he slept in a nearby thicket; a third son ran off to Dunipace to inform the priest, Wallace's uncle, of his presence.

Tired and bleeding, apparently deserted by even his staunchest comrades, Wallace was now at the depths of despair:

> What I have had in war before this day —
> Prison and pain — to this night was but play . . .
> I moan far more the losing of my men
> Than for myself, had I ten times such pain.[10]

Harry has the old priest counselling his nephew to make peace with King Edward who would surely grant him a lordship with great lands. William retorted that he preferred 'to see the Southron die, than land or gold that they can give to me', adding 'from war I will not cease till time that I bring Scotland into peace, or die before'. This encounter with his uncle stiffened his resolve, and the arrival of Stephen and Kerly soon afterwards raised his spirits again. This time he was also accompanied by two of the widow's sons, the parson of Dunipace providing them with good horses and fresh equipment. So Wallace and his tiny cohort crossed Dundaff Moor. The northern campaign, if one could call it that, had ended in the virtual annihilation of the Wallace band, but tales of their exploits were circulating far and wide and fanning the flames of resistance.

At Dundaff, a wild, rugged tract in Stirlingshire, Wallace made contact with Sir John Graham. According to Harry, this lord of Dundaff was an old man who paid tribute to the English to remain at peace. Harry seems to have confused him with Sir David de Graham, who was the landowner in this area;[11] this knight was among those captured at Dunbar and subsequently held in St Briavel's Castle in England for a time. Sir David, however, had a son named John, and it was this brave young knight who was later to play such a prominent part in Wallace's campaigns. Wallace remained three nights at Dundaff and decided to move on, on the morning of the fourth day. Young Sir John was keen to go with him, but William turned down his offer, saying that the time was not right. The loss of so many men in the recent campaign weighed heavily on his conscience. He planned to go south into Clydesdale and rally his friends there. If and when he could raise a force again he would send word to Graham.

Wallace and his closest friends rode south, skirting Glasgow and resting at Bothwell Moor where they were sheltered by one of his Craufurd kinsmen. From there they travelled to Gilbank, a small estate in Lesmahagow parish held by Patrick Auchinleck, another kinsman of Wallace on his mother's side. There Wallace and his four faithful attendants spent the Christmas of 1296. Indirectly William heard that news of his exploits in the north was well known, but was comforted by the thought that the English, believing him to have perished in Strathearn, were no longer looking for him. Although he passed the time at Gilbank as unobtrusively as possible, Wallace was not inactive. Discreet messages were sent forth by means of Kerly who traversed Douglasdale to Muirkirk and thence to Ayr where he informed Sir Ranald that his nephew was alive and well. Kerly also contacted Robert Boyd at Kilmarnock and Adam Wallace in Riccarton. It is also likely that Lady Wallace, William's mother, died about this time.

From time to time, William would slip into the nearby town of Lanark 'for sport'. What sport was intended Harry is quick to specify. 'When he journeyed to town from Gilbank and found any men of that false nation, they never did more grievance to

Scotland' was his elliptical way of saying that Wallace murdered Englishmen on sight. Some he stabbed with his dirk; others he slew by slitting their throats in some dark alleyway. One can imagine the terror this caused in Lanark, a town which was strongly invested by English troops at the time. A killer was on the loose, but no one knew who was perpetrating these deeds.

To the modern mind, these violent acts seem inexcusable; but in the context of the late thirteenth century they were understandable. To William the only good Englishman was a dead one, and he proceeded to practise what he always preached. We do not know for certain how the English authorities reacted but we can imagine that these mysterious slayings did not go unpunished. The chronicles are silent regarding reprisals, but Harry gives a hint. At Lanark there dwelled Sir William Heselrig, the English Sheriff of Clydesdale, 'cruel, outrageous and despiteful in his actions; many therefore stood in great dread of him'. Heselrig stepped up the number and frequency of patrols in and around the town. No longer did Wallace slip his sharp blade across Southron gizzards; seeing that these patrols exceeded him in numbers he would step aside and courteously salute.

It was during this period that William is alleged to have met, and fallen in love with, Marion Braidfute. She was the eighteen-year-old daughter and heiress of Hugh Braidfute of Lamington who appears to have died shortly beforehand. Rather than return to Lamington, Marion preferred to reside in the Braidfute town house in Lanark, paying her taxes and accepting the king's peace and protection. Harry adds, however, that her elder brother had been put to death by Heselrig, but she bore this tribulation with becoming resignation.

> She suffered all and bore herself right lowly; so amiable she was, so benign and wise, courteous and sweet, full of noblesse, of well-ordered speech. Comely of countenance, and worthy of being commended for her virtues. Humbly, she bore herself and purchased a good name of every wight, keeping herself free of blame. True and righteous persons all lent her great favour.[12]

Wallace is said to have clapped eyes on this attractive girl one day in the Church of St Kentigern near Lanark. 'The smart of love pierced him at last so keenly' although he remembered how his last affair, with the girl at Perth, had cost his men dearly. He discussed the dilemma with Kerly who advised him, if he really loved her so much, to take her in marriage. William felt that love and war did not mix, and that until he had achieved his goal of liberating Scotland he could not afford to marry and settle down. For some time, however, he continued to see her whenever he came to town, although he had to be very discreet about it, as her dwelling was in the very centre of the town, at the lower end of the high street. Marion obviously gave him every encouragement, for she even arranged for him to come to the house by an alleyway leading to a gate in the wall of the back garden. The affair was complicated by the fact that Heselrig himself had designs on the girl, or rather her valuable estate, and planned to wed her to his son. Of the courtship of William and Marion, Harry says very little. In another context (William and his leman in Perth) he glosses over such matters by saying 'I cannot speak of the intercourse they had — very ignorant am I of Venus' pleasures'. According to the poem, William and Marion pledged themselves to each other, it being understood that William would come back and claim her as his bride once he had freed his country. Elsewhere in the poem, however, Harry claimed that Marion and Wallace got married and that she bore him a daughter who eventually married a squire named Shaw, bearing him 'right goodly men'. Interestingly, the printed edition of 1594 inserted some lines not in the manuscript of *The Wallace*, asserting that this daughter of Wallace married a squire of Balliol's blood and that their heirs succeeded to Lamington. This points to a second marriage with Sir William Baillie of Hoprig. Sir William, second of Hoprig, a son-in-law of Sir William Seton, obtained a charter of the barony of 'Lambiston' as late as 1368 which seems to accord with the legend.[13] The obvious flaw in this story is the difficulty of reconciling dates. If William did not come to Clydesdale until December 1296, are we expected to believe that he met, courted, married and impregnated Marion soon enough for her to give birth no later than May 1297 when she was murdered? It is more probable that they had met and formed some sort of liaison at a much earlier date, probably in July 1296 when Wallace and his band were lurking in Clyde's Forest. This would explain the birth of the daughter about April 1297. Strange as it may seem, the notion of Wallace having fathered a child, in or out of wedlock, has caused embarrassment to some nineteenth-century historians. Chief among them was the Revd Dr Charles Rogers who robustly dismissed the story: 'The entire narrative is baseless; the patriot died unmarried. Nor does he seem to have had any illegitimate offspring.'[14]

Soon after Christmas Wallace left Gilbank and, accompanied by his quartet, rode to Corheid in Annandale where they were joined by Tom Halliday and Edward Little who rejoiced to find that rumours of his death had been unfounded. Another staunch adherent who now returned to the band was Master John Blair. According to Harry, this redoubtable cleric had spent some time in Paris after leaving Dunfermline. He had been at Loudoun Hill the previous summer but had not accompanied Wallace on the northern campaign. Henceforward he would remain close to his leader, chronicling his adventures.

With fifteen companions, Wallace now rode towards Lochmaben. Leaving most of his men in Knock Wood, he set out with Halliday, Little and Kerly to celebrate mass in the parish church. While they were at worship, young Clifford, nephew of Sir Henry de Percy, with some of his friends espied the Scotsmen's horses hitched to a rail outside the hostelry, and spitefully cut off their tails. On returning from church and finding their horses in pain, Wallace asked the wife of the innkeeper who had done such a thing. She pointed to Clifford and his companions whom William accosted, saying that he wished to reward their services. With a single stroke he slew the practical joker and spilled the brains of one of his companions onto the road. Halliday, Little and Kerly made short work of the other three. Mounting their injured horses, Wallace and his men fled with a large number of English cavalry baying at their heels. Their mounts being weak from loss of blood, Wallace and his companions made a stand at one point and slew some fifteen of the leading horsemen. The others then held back and the Scots managed to reach the safety of Knock Wood where they rejoined their comrades. In an ensuing skirmish William cut down the redoubtable Sir Hugh de Morland and mounted his fine charger; on this occasion a score of Englishmen were killed or mortally wounded. Sir John de Graystock, the English commander, was furious and kept up the pursuit; but Wallace and Halliday fought such a skilful rearguard action that the Scots escaped unharmed.

By now they were well to the north-west of Lochmaben, on the open moorland on the slopes of Queensberry. Here, by chance, they met up with Sir John Graham with thirty men, and Kirkpatrick of Torthorwald, who had been holding out in Eskdale Wood with his band of twenty men. Immensely cheered by these timely reinforcements, Wallace wheeled about and charged towards the English cavalry, putting them to flight. Noting that a bunch of horsemen, about a hundred in number, had maintained their ranks, Wallace brusquely ordered Sir John to attack them. The Stirlingshire contingent obeyed the command and took the Englishmen by surprise with the ferocity of their charge, Graystock being slain by Sir John himself. Afterwards William apologised to Sir John for the curtness of his order given in the heat of the moment. Remarkably, in this running battle, the Scots did not lose a single man.

Flushed with success, the Scots, now almost seventy in number, held a brief council and decided on a change of tactics. Previously they had engaged in hit-and-run raids as well as isolated opportunist attacks on the enemy. Now the time had come to attempt something more spectacular — nothing less than an assault on Lochmaben Castle.

This fortress was the chief stronghold of the Bruce family and was located near the centre of the village. It should not be confused with the present Lochmaben Castle situated some way to the south-east and constructed at a somewhat later date. The original castle was a much less pretentious edifice, probably little more than a pele tower such as those at Gargunnock and Kinclaven. But it was sited on an eminence and from its battlements the garrison commanded a fine view of the surrounding countryside and controlled the movement of traffic through Annandale. More importantly, this was the seat of the Bruce family. The aged Competitor had died here barely a year previously and it was the chief stronghold of the elder Earl of Carrick although at this time he was resident in Carlisle where he was governor.

Shortly after the victory on the flanks of Queensberry, therefore, Halliday and John Watson, both men of Annandale, rode boldly up to the gate of the castle as dusk was falling. The unsuspecting gatekeeper recognised Watson as a local man and opened the gate without question, whereupon he was slain by Halliday. The gate was thrown open wide and Wallace and a small group of hand-picked men entered. Inside they found only a couple of men-servants whom they promptly despatched, and some women whom they confined as usual. By now the stragglers from the running battle were returning in twos and threes. As they were admitted to the castle by Watson, Wallace and his companions, waiting in the shadows inside, unhorsed and killed them. In this manner the castle was secured by the Scots. Hitherto Wallace had been content to plunder such fortresses and then despoil them; now he planned permanent occupation. Johnstone, the husband of Halliday's second daughter, and probably the same Johnstone of Eskdale mentioned by Harry later in his poem, was appointed captain. Lochmaben was thus the first castle that William attempted to hold. Wallace and Graham, with forty men, then rode north into Lanarkshire, captured and dismantled the stronghold of the Lindsays at Crawford, and returned forthwith to Dundaff until the winter had abated.

In a matter of months Wallace had fought campaigns in the west, north and south-west, defeated much larger forces at Loudoun Hill, Shortwood and Queensberry, plundered the castles at Gargunnock, Kinclaven and Crawford, and gained control of Lochmaben. Even if we make allowances for Harry's exaggeration of numbers killed and deeds performed, these short, sharp and bloody campaigns undoubtedly placed Wallace before his countrymen as the foremost champion of Scottish liberty, and witnessed his transformation from an outlaw into a guerrilla of great courage and resourcefulness.

5

FROM GUERRILLA TO COMMANDER

In the month of May . . . the perfidious race of the Scots began
to rebel.

HEMINGBURGH

They caused a certain bloody man, William Wallace, who had
formerly been a chief of brigands in Scotland, to revolt against
the King, and assemble the people in his support.

LANERCOST

IN the spring of 1297 Wallace left Dundaff. Accompanied by
only nine men, he made his way south to Gilbank, and some
time in April he went heavily disguised to Lanark to visit
Marion. Blind Harry implies that they got married at this time,
'beginning by a bond, with sure witnesses', adding 'my author
[i.e. John Blair] says she was his lawful wife'. That this event
probably took place shortly before the birth of Marion's baby
seems implicit in the ensuing lines: 'I cannot say precisely how
long they enjoyed this happy state, but in course of time a child
was born to these two lovers, a goodly child, a maiden bright
and beautiful . . .'[1]

Nowadays St Kentigern's Church is a majestic ruin in the
eastern suburbs of Lanark. In the thirteenth century the burgh
was confined to the crown of the hill and this ancient church lay
outside the town walls. Wallace was accustomed to go there on

Sundays to celebrate mass. Marion's house was at the other end of the town, at the foot of the high street close to the western extremity of the town walls, of which little vestige now remains. The site of this house, near St Nicholas Church and its life-size statue of Wallace, is marked to this day by a plaque.

After a time, William began to move about the town more openly, apparently confident that the English would not molest him. By now he and his companions had been joined by Sir John Graham and a band of fifteen well-armed men. Where this gang, numbering twenty-six in all, was accommodated we can only imagine, but they were probably too formidable a force for the occupying powers to tackle head on. Sir William Heselrig, Sheriff of Clydesdale, was not the man to tolerate such a show of defiance for long, though. With Robert Thorn, captain of the garrison, he devised a plan to capture the infamous outlaw.

The opportunity arose one fine Sunday morning in May when Wallace and some of his men were coming out of St Kentigern's Church after worship. On this occasion William was not clad in concealed armour as usual, but sporting a new suit of green cloth, a long-established custom at the advent of summer. As he and his companions traversed the busy high street, William was accosted by the strongest soldier in Heselrig's command. The soldier addressed him sarcastically, in a mixture of English and French: '*Dieu garde*, good day, *bon Seigneur* and good morn!' Wallace responded in a medley of Scots and Gaelic: '*Gud deyn, dauch lard, bach lowch banyoch a de*' (good evening, lazy lord, if you please, God bless you). By now some other Englishmen had sidled up and joined in the taunting. William, sensing danger, refused to be baited; but one of the soldiers mockingly snatched at his long sword, crying, 'What should a Scot do with so fair a knife — as the priest said who last fucked your wife.' This was accompanied by further taunts, implying that one of the priests of St Nicholas was the true father of Marion's child.

William must have felt his anger rising as these coarse jibes continued, but by now the English crowd had swollen to about two hundred, and somewhere at the back of this throng were Heselrig and Thorn themselves. The odds were overwhelming but William, sensing that the English meant to take him, struck suddenly and with customary deadly force. The fight was fast and furious, Harry's only descriptive note focusing on a particularly gory moment. Wallace struck off the sword-hand of an Englishman; the blood from the stump gushed forth so strongly that it struck William in the face and temporarily blinded him. In the narrow street, however, the English could do little by sheer force of numbers and the Scots, veterans of many such encounters, skilfully fought a rearguard action and withdrew through the town gate in good order. They took immediate refuge in Marion's house, then escaped through the garden and back gate into the open countryside, where they concealed themselves in a little stronghold amid the sandstone Cartland Crags, a spectacular chasm about a mile north-west of Lanark forming the bed of the Mouse Water.

Fifty dead and wounded Englishmen littered the Lanark streets. The rest, led by Heselrig and Thorn, regrouped and marched up to the door of Marion's house, demanding the surrender of the gang of ruffians. From the upper window Marion played for time to give her husband a chance to escape, and argued with the sheriff; but when the English realised that the Scots had got away Heselrig in his anger had the door smashed in. Marion was seized and put to death on the spot. Harry adds laconically, 'I cannot tell you how,' but Wyntoun's account is slightly different and rather fuller. According to this chronicler, Heselrig came to Lanark after the disturbance, ordered Marion's arrest and then caused her to be put to death. Improbably, he adds that Wallace, in disguise, was actually a witness to her execution. The exact circumstances will never be known.

What is incontrovertible is that Wallace was maddened beyond control at this atrocity. His father had been slain, his mother had been persecuted (and is believed to have died about this time) and now his wife had been cruelly put to death. Honour demanded that he take the life of Heselrig; but Wallace was determined that the death of the sheriff should be such a frightful spectacle that it would strike terror into the hearts of the hated enemy. Patrick Auchinleck, hearing of Marion's death, journeyed to Cartland Wood with ten men. That night Wallace and his band prepared to go to Lanark. Little suspecting that the outlaws would return to the town, the English security was lax. The soldiers guarding the various gates in the town walls gave no thought to the men who came through singly at different times; but once within the town the little band formed up. While

Graham's party headed for the house occupied by Robert Thorn, Wallace and his men went straight to the sheriff's residence, a tall building. Smashing in the brass-bound door with his foot, Wallace rushed upstairs and found the sheriff in his bedroom where he felled him with a single downward stroke of his great sword, cleaving his skull right down to the collar bone. For good measure, young Auchinleck 'made siccar' with three stab wounds to the fallen sheriff's inert form.

By now the alarm had been given and others of the household rushed upstairs. Young Heselrig, coming to his father's aid, was struck a mortal blow by Wallace who toppled him over the staircase. The raid took the English by complete surprise. Thorn's house was set alight and he and his household were burned to death. The Scots went on the rampage that terrible night and slew many Englishmen — Harry puts the number of dead at 240. Only the womenfolk and priests were spared, but they were forcibly ejected and sent on their way without goods or provisions. Thus runs the account given by Blind Harry and, without so much detail, by Andrew of Wyntoun.

What makes this episode so significant, setting it apart from William's earlier exploits, is that, for the first time, we have an incident that is independently corroborated. At his trial in 1305, amid a general list of killings, arson, destruction of property and sacrilege, the first specific charge brought against Wallace was that he had murdered the Sheriff of Clydesdale, whose name, oddly enough, was rendered in the indictment as Hesebrig (clearly a clerical error). That this crime was singled out for special mention was symbolic, for, in English eyes, it was regarded as the signal for the widespread resistance which triggered off the first War of Independence.

Uprisings, revolts and disturbances there had been in plenty over the previous months — Wallace's own contribution had been not inconsiderable — but the murder of Heselrig and the massacre of the garrison at Lanark was on a larger scale than anything that had gone before; more importantly, it encouraged Scots everywhere to believe that the hated English were not invincible after all.

Immediately after this incident Wallace and his band of followers moved westwards to their old familiar territory in Ayrshire. From all over the south-west of Scotland men flocked to his side. Old comrades, such as Adam Wallace and Robert Boyd, were joined by new allies, such as Sir John Tinto, and a thousand men on horseback were raised from Kyle and Cunninghame alone. By midsummer the whole south-west was aflame with revolt; Wallace was now at the head of three thousand well-armed men, together with a large number of others who lacked 'horse and gear'. News of the uprising spread like wildfire, but inevitably the English authorities were alarmed and sent word to London. That the Scots were in revolt was common knowledge in England that summer, for among the fighters who flocked to Wallace's encampment was Gilbert de Grimsby whom the Scots nicknamed Jop. He was a man of great stature, born at Riccarton and therefore someone who would have known William since childhood. He had enlisted in the English army and served under Edward in Flanders and Picardy. A fine figure of a man, he was selected by Edward himself to be a pursuivant or herald and to him had fallen the honour of bearing the sacred banner of St John of Beverley at the head of the English army which paraded through Scotland after the Battle of Dunbar in 1296. His distinguished services in that campaign were rewarded by King Edward who, on 13 October that year, issued a directive to Earl Warenne stating that 'Gilbert de Grimmesby' should be found an appointment worth twenty marks per annum.[2] On hearing of Wallace's rebellion he had deserted and made his way secretly north to join the rebel ranks. He brought invaluable intelligence concerning the English army and its disposition, and William rewarded him by making him his standard-bearer.

Although discontent with English rule gave the rising its spontaneous character, it would not have succeeded as far as it did without the support of certain influential men. Chief among these were James the Steward and the Bishop of Glasgow, the two surviving Guardians of 1286. Robert Wishart belonged to the family of Wishart or Wiseheart from Pittarrow in Angus and was either a nephew or cousin of William Wishart, Bishop of St Andrews and Chancellor of Scotland in the reign of Alexander III. William Wishart was bishop-elect of Glasgow in 1270, but before he was installed he was transferred to the bishopric of St Andrews, and Robert, then Archdeacon of St Andrews, was preferred to the see of Glasgow in his place. No record of his early career survives, and the earliest documentary record of him concerns his consecration at Aberdeen in 1272. He rapidly achieved a leading position among the prelates who directed the affairs of state in Alexander's reign, and his appointment as one of the six Guardians on 16 March 1286 was an obvious choice. As has already been mentioned, he was responsible for the administration of Scotland south of the Forth (along with James the Steward and John Comyn of Badenoch). Subsequently, he was one of the Scottish commissioners who negotiated with Edward at Salisbury, and his signature appears on the letter sent to Eirik II informing him of the marriage proposed between the Maid of Norway and Prince Edward.[3] At this juncture Wishart, with Bishop Fraser of St Andrews, seems to have supported Edward and later he acquiesced in the elevation of John Balliol to the throne.

Wishart's gradual disenchantment with King Edward probably arose from the attempts by the latter to anglicise the Scottish Church. Wishart was the most ardent champion of the rights and liberties of the Church in Scotland and strenuously opposed the ejectment of Scottish clergy and the appointment of English priests in their stead. In treating the Scottish Church in such a high-handed manner, Edward clearly misjudged the prelates of that country. Unlike the magnates, most of whom were committed to Edward's cause on account of their extensive English estates, the prelates, by and large, were men of a more independent turn of mind. They were more likely to have risen from the ranks of the Scottish community and were therefore not so susceptible to Anglo-Norman influence. It may be stretching a point to suggest that opposition to English rule was co-ordinated and orchestrated by the hierarchy, but those of its priests who had not been replaced by English appointees were certainly at the heart of the passive resistance in 1296–97. Master John Blair of Dunfermline, Thomas Gray of Libberton and the uncles of Wallace at Dunipace and Kilspindie were by no means isolated examples.

In the early months of 1297 Wishart was already engaged in intrigue against the alien government which had been foisted on the Scots. Suspicions of Wishart's disloyalty were conveyed to King Edward who wrote specifically to Pope Boniface VIII asking to have Wishart deprived of his see. To this the Pope would not agree, although he sent a letter to the Bishop of

Glasgow commanding him to desist from his opposition to Edward and denouncing him as 'the prime mover and instigator of all the tumult and dissension which has arisen between his dearest son in Christ, Edward, King of England, and the Scots'. This admonition had no effect on Wishart who, by midsummer 1297, had come out in open support of Wallace. This signal act of defiance was to cost him dear later on. Imprisoned after the sorry débâcle at Irvine in July 1297, Wishart was singled out for close confinement, though he was later released. For his continued intriguing with such rebels as Wallace, however, the bishop was one of those expressly excluded from the generous terms offered to the defeated Scots at Strathord in February 1304. Wishart not only granted absolution to Robert Bruce for the murder of Comyn on the altar steps of Greyfriars in March 1306 but officiated at Robert's coronation at Scone later that month. When he was captured by Aymer de Valence after the Battle of Methven the following July (where he had fought with the best of them, clad in armour) he was sent in chains to Nottingham and thence to Porchester Castle where he was kept for eight years in strict confinement, eventually losing his sight as a result. Not till after the Battle of Bannockburn did he regain his liberty, being one of the five prisoners then exchanged for Humphrey de Bohun, Earl of Hereford. He returned to his diocese where he died in November 1316. His impressive tomb, bearing a recumbent effigy of the bishop-statesman, can be seen in Glasgow Cathedral to this day.[4]

The possibility that Wallace and Wishart met in the early summer of 1297 cannot be ruled out, although it remains no more than supposition that they did.[5] Whether such a meeting took place or not is immaterial, for Wishart would have been kept well informed of the revolt. Indeed, he would have been aware of the exploits of the young outlaw over the preceding months. Wishart had many kinsmen well placed in the Church, and the medieval Church was admirably suited to subversive activities, providing the organisation and the communication whereby the revolt was co-ordinated and maintained. It is probable that Wishart was responsible for giving the rebellion a cloak of respectability by claiming that it was a just war in the name of King John, the anointed sovereign of Scotland. While he was trying to persuade the ever-cautious Steward to lend his support to this cause, Wishart learned that Wallace had gained a valuable ally and this, in turn, persuaded the Steward to back the uprising. Sir William Douglas, 'le Hardi', late governor of Berwick Castle, had been released from confinement late in 1296 and lost no time in aligning himself with the rebels.

Blind Harry represents Douglas as attacking and capturing the castle at Sanquhar before being himself besieged there by the Captain of Durisdeer. A message is sent to Wallace who promptly heads south and raises the siege, defeating the English at Dalswinton and killing some five hundred of them in the process. Douglas is then appointed constable of all the castles between Drumlanrig and Ayr. Whatever the truth of all this, it is significant that, on 12 June 1297, King Edward declared forfeit all Douglas's lands and property in Essex and Northumberland as a consequence of his actions.

When Edward heard of this important defection, he ordered the Earl of Carrick to muster the men of Annandale and launch an attack on the Douglas stronghold. According to Hemingburgh, the Bishop of Carlisle suspected the loyalty of the younger Bruce and made him swear, on the bible and the sword of St Thomas à Becket, a special oath of allegiance to Edward before setting out on the expedition, but this may be no more than a fiction of hindsight.

From the absence of any mention of Lochmaben, it must be assumed that the occupation of that Bruce stronghold by Wallace's men was short-lived. At any rate Robert Bruce, the future King of Scots, marched his forces over the hills from Dumfriesshire and down the valley of the Clyde to Douglasdale whose castle was being held by Sir William's English wife, Eleanor Ferrers. She was his second wife, a widow whom Douglas had forcibly abducted while she was visiting Scotland; she was not only won over by his charm but became an ardent supporter of the Scottish cause. Incidentally, his first wife was the sister of James the Steward. Sir William himself had gone to Ayr to join the main body of the rebels. The young Earl of Carrick made no more than a token attack on Douglas Castle, but then abruptly, and for no apparent reason, changed sides. Hemingburgh explains this *volte face* naïvely by saying that Bruce joined the Scots because he was a Scotsman. Young Robert addressed his father's tenants of Annandale before the walls of

Douglas Castle: 'No man holds his own flesh and blood in hatred and I am no exception. I must join my own people and the nation in which I was born.' He said that his oath at Carlisle had been given under duress and he appealed to the Annandale men to join him, but with the exception of a few they apparently declined. The Annandale levies slipped back over the hills to Dumfriesshire while the young earl and his supporters, with the men of Douglasdale and Lady Douglas and her family, journeyed westwards into Ayrshire. In Carrick he had no trouble in recruiting his own tenants.

The action of the Earl of Carrick at Douglas was his crossing of the Rubicon, but it was a baffling one. He had a strong position in Scotland and was almost a protégé of Edward. Why give up all that for some vague concept of Scottishness which barely existed? Wishart and the Steward were life-long supporters of the Bruce faction, but Sir William Douglas was a staunch Balliol man — and the uprising was nominally on Balliol's behalf. Why go against family interest in support of the traditional rival of his house? It has been suggested that as early as 1297 the Earl of Carrick had aspirations to the throne, but this is extremely unlikely and there is nothing, in the events during the revolt from 1297 to 1304, to support this.

Far more important than the Earl of Carrick's change of heart was the emergence, in the north of Scotland, of another outstanding rebel leader. Among the Scottish knights taken prisoner after the Battle of Dunbar were Sir Andrew de Moray of Petty, his brother Sir William (known as 'le Riche' from his vast wealth), and the son of the former, also Andrew de Moray. The two knights were imprisoned in the Tower of London while the younger Andrew was held at Chester Castle for a time. He was released, or escaped from custody, some time later and made his way back north, arriving in Moray in the spring of 1297. Sir William de Moray had already been set free, having agreed to join Edward's army for the campaign in Flanders, but Sir Andrew had chosen to remain in prison rather than fight for the English. With his father languishing in an English prison and his uncle effectively a hostage in English hands, the action of young Andrew in raising revolt was rash to put it mildly. No reason for taking up arms has ever been suggested; it is sufficient to say that by April 1297 Andrew de Moray had raised the whole of

Moray against the English who maintained a strong presence in the area, with large garrisons in the castles of Inverness, Urquhart, Nairn, Forres, Elgin and Lochindorb.

The Morays were a powerful family of Celtic stock, possessing extensive estates at Dingwall, Petty, Alturlie, Avoch, Boharm, Botriphnie and Croy in the region that bore their name, as well as the powerful lordship of Bothwell in Lanarkshire. As previously noted, Blind Harry says that Sir Aymer de Valence held Bothwell at this time; and if not Sir Aymer, then certainly some other powerful English baron must have been in occupation of such a strategically important stronghold. The priest of Bothwell was, in fact, David de Moray or Moravia, youngest brother of Andrew and William, and following their incarceration he assumed the position of head of the family and administrator of its estates. His promotion in the hierarchy was thereafter nothing short of meteoric, evidence of the strong support of Bishop Wishart. He was appointed a canon of Elgin in 1298 and Bishop of Moray and Caithness a year later, though his lasting achievement was the foundation of the Scots College at Paris in 1325. David de Moravia seems to have lent much more than spiritual support to his nephew's insurrection, being not only the conduit to Wishart and the Steward but giving Andrew immense logistical back-up. Moray was one of the few districts in Scotland in which the normal feudal system did not operate; its inhabitants owed their allegiance direct to the sovereign without the intermediary of a feudal superior. Thus the revolt, when it erupted, was unequivocally in the name of King John.

It is a measure of how slowly news travelled in the thirteenth century that King Edward was not apprised of this northern revolt till June; even then he seems to have been unaware of its leader till much later, for as late as 28 August 1297 Andrew de Moray was granted letters of safe-conduct to journey south to London, there to visit his father in the Tower.[6] Needless to say, young Andrew had much weightier matters on his mind by that time and the visit never took place.

In the spring of 1297 Andrew de Moray raised his standard at Ormonde Castle in the Black Isle and harried the English garrisons in the north-east. This was a rising of the common men, led by minor gentry. Moray's chief lieutenant, in fact, was Alexander Pilche, a prominent burgess in Inverness of German or Flemish origin, and it has been suggested that he was the real force behind the uprising.[7] Be that as it may, Andrew de Moray was, by birth and upbringing, the rightful leader of the revolt in the north. His forces, though small, were well mounted and knew their terrain. They were organised into flying columns which harassed and attacked the English at will, striking with ferocious rapidity and vanishing just as swiftly, leaving terrible carnage and destruction behind them. Little is known for certain about Moray's activities, although there is extant a very graphic account in a letter addressed to King Edward from his 'diligent and faithful friends' which stated that Moray led 'a very large body of rogues' and besought the King to come north and rid them of this menace.[8] Moray's first essay on a grander scale was the siege of Urquhart Castle on the western side of Loch Ness, but he lacked the ballistic engines necessary to reduce it by force. Other castles, however, fell into his hands, including the strongholds of Banff, Elgin and Inverness itself.

Significantly, opposition to Moray came from the northern nobility led by the formidable Effie, Countess of Ross, and closely supported by Henry le Cheyne, Bishop of Aberdeen, whose brother Sir Reginald was governor of Moray. Interestingly, the Earl of Ross was, at this time, still held in the Tower of London where he had been confined since the Battle of Dunbar. His son was to have accompanied Andrew de Moray to London that August when they had been given permission to visit their fathers, and it is not known whether the young Ross made the journey or not. Edward's immediate response to Moray's activities was to release from his continental service John of Badenoch and the Earl of Buchan, both members of the powerful Comyn family, who were then despatched to Scotland to stiffen the feudal faction and restore law and order in the north.[9]

It was perhaps unfortunate for Edward that not only was he himself out of the country at the time, but the Earl of Surrey, Warden of the Kingdom and Land of Scotland, had also taken himself off to the south for the good of his health as the winter of 1296 set in, and then delayed his return north by making great play of his activities in Northumberland and County Durham.[10] When apprised by Edward of the insurrection of Wallace in south-west Scotland, Warenne wrote to his royal master complacently, 'And know, Sire, that the delay which we have made will cause you no harm whatever, if God pleases.'[11] Hemingburgh would later write that the earl's attitude was ever afterwards 'the fountain and origin of all our troubles'. On 14 June 1297 Edward gave Warenne an explicit order to return to his post forthwith, but it was not until the end of July that he reached Berwick. Even then he lost much valuable time by despatching his grandson Henry de Percy to negotiate with the Scots. In the meantime Scotland was nominally in the hands of Hugh Cressingham whose seat of administration was at Berwick. Far from governing Scotland with the firm hand which his master required, Cressingham was proving to be thoroughly inept at carrying out Edward's orders regarding the refortification of Berwick. The stone walls which the King had commanded had yet to be built. There was more than a suspicion that the Treasurer was diverting into his own coffers the funds which had been earmarked for this project.

English rule was more rigorously maintained at Glasgow, however, where Antony Bek, Bishop of Durham, backed by crack troops of St Cuthbert's Host, was in residence. Edward had decreed that the bishopric of Glasgow should henceforward be subordinate to Durham, a matter that only made Wishart more rebellious. Scone, where the Scottish kings had been crowned for centuries and which was therefore a symbol of national unity, was the seat of William de Ormesby whom Edward had appointed Justiciar of Scotland. From this ancient and sacred site in the very heart of the country, English justice was dispensed in a brutal manner. Ormesby's chief remit was to seek out and bring to Edward's allegiance the men of lesser importance whom the King desired should swear fealty to him, over and above the magnates who had already done so. Those who were reluctant to take the oath were coerced by bands of soldiers, fined, sequestered or outlawed. Even those who made the journey to Scone and took the oath were taxed a silver penny each by the clerks of the court, who became very wealthy as a result.[12]

Some time in June Wallace, arguably at the behest of Bishop Wishart, planned and executed a daring raid that aimed at striking terror into the very heart of the English regime. Riding north with a hand-picked body of cavalry, he met up with Sir William Douglas at Perth and together they advanced on Scone a few miles to the north-east. Ormesby's troops melted away as the Scottish army drew near and the Justiciar himself barely escaped with his life, fleeing southwards and not stopping until he was safe back within his estates in Northumberland. He abandoned a great quantity of goods and chattels. Tradition maintains that Wallace and Douglas slew many Englishmen in this brief campaign and laid siege to several castles, but details are lacking.

By late June, southern Scotland was in a ferment. Everywhere English troops had withdrawn into their castles and were in a state of virtual, if not always actual, siege. It was now apparent how illusory had been the subjugation of Scotland. The English in effect were confined to the towns and larger burghs, but only those which could be supplied by sea were tenable, for the Scots had cut their overland lines of communication, and bands of armed rebels roamed the countryside at will. The focus of discontent consisted of four men, clearly named in the English chronicles as the Bishop of Glasgow, James the Steward, Andrew de Moray and William Wallace. The Lanercost Chronicle stated trenchantly that the bishop,

> ever foremost in treason, conspired with the Steward of the Kingdom, named James, for a new piece of insolence, yea, for a new chapter of ruin. Not daring openly to break their pledge to the King, they caused a certain bloody man, William Wallace, who had formerly been a chief of brigands in Scotland, to revolt against the King, and assemble the people in his support.

Blind Harry's account of the early summer of 1297 is very confused. He avers that King Edward came north with an army of sixty thousand men which was scattered like chaff by the invincible Wallace in a pitched battle near Biggar, an astronomical number of the slain being close relatives of the King. Notwithstanding the strong local tradition which persists to this day, this is pure myth, although it may be that Harry got mixed up with the later Battle of Roslin. There are also conflicting accounts regarding Edward's awareness of what was actually happening in Scotland at this time. Edward, it is known, was busy making preparations for his latest expedition to Flanders although he was not wholly negligent of the northern troubles. Early in May he was having his siege-engines overhauled at

Carlisle and on 24 May he addressed a circular to his leading lieges in Scotland. During May and June he received the oaths of fealty of a number of Scottish magnates to serve him 'in Scotland against the King of France'.

If the Battle of Biggar is total myth, the strange episode known as the Barns of Ayr may also be partly apocryphal, for it does not sit well with the known facts, nor with the chronology of the period, although it figures in *The Brus*, John Barbour's epic poem which, written about half a century after the event, is generally trustworthy regarding historical events. According to Blind Harry, an eyre-court was summoned, by a judge whom he names Arnulf of Southampton, at Ayr for 18 June. To his credit, Henry de Percy would have nothing of this plot and deliberately went to Glasgow in order to absent himself from the proceedings. The leading Scots of Ayrshire were summoned in the name of King Edward to appear at a lofty building known as the Barns (used as barracks) on the town's outskirts. The entrance was strongly guarded and the Scots were admitted one by one. No sooner were they inside the door than a noose was slung over their heads and they were hauled off their feet and strung up from an enormous beam running the full length of the building. In this treacherous manner some 360 barons, knights and gentlemen were summarily executed without trial. First to hang was Sir Ranald Craufurd, Sheriff of Ayr, followed by Sir Bryce Blair and his uncle Sir Neil Montgomery and many others including Kennedys from Cassilis, Campbells of Loudoun, Barclays, Boyds and Stewarts and the flower of Ayrshire nobility. Afterwards the bodies were stripped and thrown into the yard.

Barbour mentions this atrocity in passing, in lines lamenting the death of Crystal Seton: 'It was great sorrow assuredly that so worthy a person as he should in such manner be hanged. Thus ended his worthiness.' The ensuing passage mentions Sir Ranald Craufurd and Sir Bryce Blair 'hangyt in till a berne in Ayr'. The *Complaynt of Scotland*, a work of the sixteenth century and therefore long after the event, spoke of the incident as a matter of great public notoriety whose barbarity was common knowledge.

Wallace himself had gone to Kingace that day and thus evaded the trap. When he entered Ayr in the afternoon he was intercepted by a young woman of the Craufurd family who gave him the frightful news. William sent her off to rally Robert Boyd, Adam Wallace and such other friends and kinsmen as had survived the slaughter. He himself was set upon by a cavalry patrol and only escaped to Leglen Wood after he and his closest comrades had slain ten of the enemy. A day or two later, however, his band being reinforced, Wallace returned to the town. He instructed a girl to mark with chalk the doors of the houses wherein lived the English, and then gave orders that these doors were to be securely fast, so that the residents were trapped. With Boyd and fifty men keeping a close watch on Ayr Castle, William took the rest of his men to the Barns where the English judge and a large company were sleeping off a late-night carousal. Kindling and brushwood being placed all round the huge wooden building, Wallace gave orders to torch the place. With great relish Harry describes in the most lurid detail how the inmates perished. A hundred and forty English troops quartered at the priory were subsequently slain by Prior Drumlay and his monks in a subsidiary incident ever afterwards known as the Prior of Ayr's Blessing. The garrison of the castle, seeing the dreadful conflagration at the Barns, sallied forth but were ambushed by Boyd's men and slaughtered. Harry estimated the English death toll at five thousand.

This legend, though manifestly exaggerated, may well have a grain of truth in it, despite some glaring discrepancies. In the first place, Sir Ranald Craufurd was certainly alive after 18 June 1297. It has been suggested, though not very plausibly, that Arnulf the Justice was, in fact, the Justiciar Ormesby whom Wallace had attacked at Scone. It may be that this incident was loosely based on the fact that, more than a year later (26 August 1298), King Edward entered Ayr with his troops and found that the castle had been razed to the ground by the Scots, but the Barns themselves seem to have been the figment of someone's imagination. Lord Hailes, in his *Annals*, suggested that perhaps the story had arisen out of the pillaging of the English quarters at Irvine in July 1297. Somewhere in this distorted and garbled tale there may be the dim recollection of some atrocity and grim reprisal, for the incident figures in the writings of John Major as well as in the poems of Barbour and Blind Harry.

According to local legend, Wallace is said to have watched the conflagration from the top of a hill about two miles south of

Craigie. In 1855, on the 550th anniversary of Wallace's death, a castellated tower was erected on the summit of Barnweil Hill as a tribute to the great patriot. The story goes that the hill got its name from a comment of Wallace as the Barns went up in flames: 'Don't they burn weel.' The name, however, is of much greater antiquity than 1297.

In June or July 1297 there was an uprising in Fife fomented by Macduff, the claimant to the earldom. This may have been an act of sheer opportunism, for it did not gain wide popular support and was speedily suppressed by the pro-English Earl of Strathearn. On 1 August Warenne reported back to Edward that Macduff and his two sons had been captured and 'they shall receive their deserts when they arrive'. Around the same time, Sir Alexander of Argyll was reported to have seized the Steward's castle of Glasrog (Glassary) and to have attacked Alexander of the Isles, a loyal supporter of King Edward. This ties in with Harry's account of an expedition by Wallace to Argyll to rescue Neil Campbell of Lochawe, his old schoolmate from Dundee, from the clutches of MacFadyen whom Edward had made Lord of Argyll and Lorn. Wallace was alleged to have defeated MacFadyen and installed Duncan of Lorn and Sir Neil Campbell in his place.

There was also the strange sideshow in which Douglas burned Turnberry Castle, a Bruce stronghold, and in retaliation the young Earl of Carrick ravaged Douglasdale, seizing the wife and children of Sir William and carrying them off to Annandale. This may tie up with the fact that the Bishop of Carlisle summoned the elder Bruce after the Wallace-Douglas raid on Scone, and forced him to swear his allegiance again. Perhaps the raid on Douglasdale was intended to demonstrate the loyalty of the Bruces to King Edward.

Robert Bruce, the future King of Scots, has often been accused of deviousness and untrustworthiness, and this curious episode would, on the face of it, seem to prove the point; but there is also the possibility that he made a show of allegiance to Edward at this time to conceal the fact that he was actually conspiring with Bishop Wishart, James the Steward and the latter's brother, Sir John of Bonkill. Some time that summer young Bruce attempted to muster his father's men in Annandale but they were singularly lukewarm regarding this enterprise. He had more luck with his own tenants in Carrick and they went on an orgy of burning and slaying, summarily evicting the English from southern Ayrshire. The English chroniclers, touching on this affair, were particularly outraged by Bruce's brutal treatment of the English clergy. It has been suggested that this independent action by Bruce was evidence of his ambitions of gaining the throne, and there is always the possibility that he embarked on this course of action as a counterweight to the success and rising popularity of William Wallace. It has been argued that Bruce would naturally despise Wallace as a man of relatively low birth — and a man who was now openly espousing the cause of the rival Balliol; but there is nothing to support this contention and, indeed, all the evidence, scanty though it is, seems to point in the opposite direction, as will be seen in due course.

By midsummer 1297 Scotland appears to have been in a state of almost total anarchy. Most historians take the line that the revolt was caused by the arrogant and overbearing behaviour of the occupying forces. But even if the English had been the model of diplomacy and discretion and had handled the Scots with kid gloves, a general uprising was probably inevitable. The Scots may have quarrelled and fought amongst themselves, but they were certainly never going to knuckle under to any alien power however benevolent that might be. Ironically, the English occupation probably gave the Scots, for the first time, a real sense of nationhood. Hitherto Scotland had been inhabited by men of different races and languages, with different traditions and outlook. Now they were drawn together by the sense of dwelling within the same country, beginning to feel in their hearts that they were the same people when, regardless of race, they had a community of ideas, of interests, of memories and of hopes. This is what eventually made them a nation, but it was to be a nation tempered in the fire of the long drawn-out Wars of Independence.

Edward, however, could tolerate the deteriorating situation no longer. Early in June, while Warenne continued to vacillate, Edward appointed Sir Henry de Percy and Sir Robert de Clifford 'to arrest, imprison and justify all disturbers of the peace in Scotland and their resetters'. Having eventually, and with the utmost difficulty, raised an army of three hundred horse and forty thousand foot in England north of the Trent, Percy and

Clifford crossed the border early in July and advanced through Annandale. Marching north through Nithsdale, they came through Sanquhar and Cumnock and advanced into Kyle where they came upon the Scottish army encamped at Irvine. To honour this rabble with the title of an army is an exaggeration; it was a motley assemblage of earls, barons and knights with their tenants and vassals, together with the burgesses of the towns and probably many others who owed allegiance to no lord but were attracted to the coming showdown by the prospect of adventure and booty. From the outset the magnates could not agree on leadership and the chain of command, far less a common strategy for dealing with the imminent English expedition. In fact, the bickering between the various magnates who had condescended to take part in this campaign so disgusted Sir Richard Lundie or Lundin, a professional soldier who had never previously sworn fealty to Edward, that he now changed sides and took his own contingent of men-at-arms over to Percy, declaring vehemently that he would 'no longer serve with men who were at discord and variance'.[13]

This defection might have been expected to bring the Scottish lords to their senses but, in the memorable words of Lord Hailes, 'All the leaders were independent, all untractable. They would neither fight, retire, nor treat by common consent.' On 7 July the Scottish army surrendered ignominiously, apparently without firing an arrow, and its commanders submitted to Percy and Clifford. Significantly, the Earl of Carrick was forced to agree to hand over his infant daughter Marjorie as a hostage and two days later Wishart, the Steward and Sir Alexander de Lindesay became sureties for the young earl's good faith. Despite this, it appears that the wily Bruce managed to hang on to the little girl. Douglas and Wishart were less fortunate. First Douglas and then the bishop surrendered their liberty, allegedly stung by insulting slurs on their honour. On 16 July Osbert de Spaldington, governor of Berwick, informed King Edward that Sir William Douglas had failed to provide hostages or guarantors and was now 'in your castle of Berwick, in my keeping, and is still very savage and very abusive, but I will keep him in such wise that, please God, he shall by no means get out'. Earl Warenne himself wrote to Edward on 1 August on the same subject, saying that Douglas was 'in good irons and in good keeping'. Spaldington kept his unruly prisoner in irons, pending his shipment south where, on 12 October, he was incarcerated in the Tower of London. By 20 January 1299 Sir William was reported as being 'with God', a euphemism that probably concealed the brutal imprisonment which brought this doughty knight to an early death. Bishop Wishart was subjected to no less brutality, being confined in chains in Roxburgh Castle. Sir William's harsh treatment, however, was to be avenged many times over by his son. Then a boy of thirteen, he grew to manhood and, as Sir James Douglas, was renowned as one of the greatest fighters in the later Wars of Independence.

The ignoble collapse of the magnates at Irvine contrasts vividly with the dauntless resolution of William Wallace, who continued to operate in the field with a mixed army of Scots and Gallovidians (as Hemingburgh was careful to describe it). This partisan force conducted a brilliant campaign in the classic guerrilla pattern, harrying Percy's baggage train, cutting lines of communications and killing stragglers. The death toll from this action alone was conservatively put at over five hundred. Edward may have cowed the Scottish magnates, many of whom were conscripted into the expedition to Flanders, but Wallace and Moray were unbowed. The English chronicler Knighton succinctly described the situation:

> The whole followers of the nobility attached themselves to Wallace; and although the persons of their lords were with the King in England, their hearts were with Wallace, who found his army reinforced by so immense a multitude of Scots that the community of the land obeyed him as their leader and prince.[14]

According to Hemingburgh, the surrender at Irvine filled Wallace with disappointment which grew to fierce wrath against his pusillanimous colleagues, and found expression in his attack on Bishop Wishart's palace in Glasgow which was plundered and sacked. On the face of it, this seems highly unlikely, for Wishart had been Wallace's staunchest supporter and, unlike most of the magnates, had surrendered himself honourably into English captivity. Indeed, King Edward later suspected that Wishart had deliberately sacrificed himself, and submitted to internment in Roxburgh Castle in order to plot its betrayal to the

Scots. That an attack on Glasgow took place about this time appears to be confirmed by a story by Blind Harry. With three hundred horsemen Wallace rode across Glasgow bridge before the English authorities were aware of their presence. While Adam Wallace and Patrick Auchinleck led 140 men to attack along the North East Row from the rear, Wallace and Boyd led the main onslaught up the High Street. Apart from the minstrel, this engagement in Glasgow is documented from other sources. On this occasion there occurred the following conversation, often repeated as a specimen of Wallace's wit. William asked Auchinleck which squadron he wished to command. 'Uncle, whether will ye upbear the bishop's tail, or pass before and take his benison?' Auchinleck quipped in return, 'As you yourself are still, to my knowledge, unbishoped [i.e. unconfirmed], you shall take the blessing; and, as for us, we shall do our best to bear up the bishop's tail' — an allusion to carrying the train or ceremonial robes of high ecclesiastics on occasions of state.[15] Harry has Wallace engaging the forces of Percy and Bishop Bek, slaying the former and defeating the latter, with four hundred casualties on the English side. Percy, of course, was not killed at Glasgow and was probably nowhere near that city at the time, but Bek had made it his administrative headquarters and it was Bek, rather than Wishart, that Wallace was striking against. The battle was fast and furious, commencing at nine o'clock in the morning and over by midday, Wallace and his victorious troops being well south of Glasgow again by one o'clock.

Whatever the truth of the matter, Wallace was now the only Scottish general in the field south of the Forth. He regrouped his forces at Dundaff where he spent five days. To this place came Duncan of Lorn, with an elderly guide named Gilmichael, bringing the bad news that the earls of Atholl, Menteith and Buchan, now making common cause with the English, were harassing the Scots in Argyll, led by Sir Neil Campbell of Lochawe. Duncan had been ousted by his kinsman, John of Lorn, who had come into the King's peace and been ennobled by him. John was now allied to MacFadyen whose Irish troops joined in the fray. To take the pressure off Campbell and Duncan, Wallace now led an expedition into Argyll and defeated MacFadyen at the Pass of Brander, at the head of Loch Awe. Harry speaks of the earls and MacFadyen combining to produce a force of fifteen thousand that pillaged through Argyll, slaying men, women and children and laying whole districts waste. Although this is clearly exaggerated, there must have been some substance to it. The showdown came at Craig Bhuidhe (the yellow rock) which Campbell was determined to defend as long as possible, and with three hundred men he held up the enemy advance until Wallace's band arrived. Curiously, Harry singles out Sir Richard Lundie as one of the able knights who fought on Wallace's side in this battle, but this must be discounted for Lundie remained firmly in the English camp throughout this period, as will become apparent later. Similarly, the story that Malcolm, Earl of Lennox, also brought a contingent of troops to this engagement seems unlikely, for that earl was at this time, if not wholly on the English side then certainly sitting on the fence. Here again, Harry is the sole source for evidence of this battle, but despite such discrepancies regarding Lundie and Lennox, the details of numbers involved on the Scottish side, as well as the accurate description of the locale, could only have come from the results of some real event.

Throughout the summer of 1297 Wallace conducted a campaign in the Highlands. In the meantime Percy and Clifford had journeyed across country from Irvine, and were in Roxburgh on 15 July. Here they met up with Cressingham with three hundred armoured horses and ten thousand foot soldiers. Eight days later, the Treasurer wrote to King Edward at length. From this we gather that Percy and Clifford considered that they had achieved their objective, but Cressingham urged the King that 'even though peace had been made on this side of the Scots water [i.e. the Firth of Forth], yet it would be well to make a *chevauchée* on the enemies on the other side' — a clear reference to Wallace and his allies who were continuing to combat the English and their collaborators in Dunbartonshire, Stirlingshire and Perthshire. Cressingham then went on to specify his enemy and what should be done about him: 'An attack should be made upon William Wallace, who lay then with a large company — and does so still — in the Forest of Selkirk, like one that holds himself against your peace.' This vast wilderness, often referred to simply as the Forest, in fact extended far beyond the Borders as its name implied, reaching the southern bank of the Forth. It seems likely that Wallace and his band were then encamped on the northern side of the Forest, not far from Stirling.

On 24 July Cressingham wrote again to the King. Edward, who had been encountering considerable difficulties in equipping his Flanders expedition, not least from a fractious baronage who insisted on the reconfirmation of Magna Carta before they would support him, had written to Cressingham ordering him to raise money from the rents and taxes of Scotland to finance Warenne and Percy in their military operations. In reply, the Treasurer now informed his royal master, 'Not a penny could be raised, until my lord the Earl of Warenne shall enter into your land and compel the people by force and sentence of law.' He then went on to explain the situation more fully:

> Sire, let it not displease you, by far the greater part of your counties of the realm of Scotland are still unprovided with keepers, as well by death, siege, or imprisonment; and some have given up their bailiwicks, and others neither will nor dare return; and in some counties the Scots have established and placed bailiffs and ministers, so that no county is in proper order, except Berwick and Roxburgh, and this only lately.[16]

Cressingham's letter speaks volumes for the passive resistance of the Scots, painting as it does a stark picture of the reality of the English occupation. The selfish and cowardly magnates might have grovelled before Percy and Clifford, but the country as a whole was not at peace. No doubt realising that he had blurted out more than he had intended, however, the Treasurer concluded on a note of false optimism. 'All this will be speedily amended, by the grace of God, by the arrival of the said lord the Earl, Sir Henry de Percy, and Sir Robert de Clifford, and the others of your Council.' Quite how the situation was to be improved by the arrival of these men Cressingham did not specify.

The trouble in the north was by no means confined to Wallace and his forces. Further north Andrew de Moray's insurrection was gathering momentum. Under instructions from their English overlords, the Bishop of Aberdeen and Gartnait, son of the Earl of Mar, had attempted to combat this menace. Early in June King Edward had ordered the Earl of Buchan, and later the Earl of Mar, to give them assistance. On 25 July Mar, Comyn and Gartnait reported that, eight days earlier, their forces had encountered 'Andrew de Moray with a great body of rogues' at a place called Launoy on the River Spey which most writers could not identify, although Barron (1913) argued convincingly in favour of the district known as the Enzie (which would be rendered in Norman French as L'Ennoi or phonetically as L'Aunoy).

In the thirteenth and fourteenth centuries this large, wild tract was covered by dense woodland and was one of the principal royal forests in the north of Scotland. Just inside its western boundary was a great marshland extending eastwards from the Spey and known as the Bog of Gight, immediately to the north of which Castle Gordon was afterwards built. The road from Aberdeen to Inverness ran through the Enzie, skirting this bog to reach the ford at Bellie, and it was therefore a logical place at which to mount an ambush of the advancing English forces. This was confirmed by Comyn's letter: 'The aforesaid rogues betook themselves into a very great stronghold of bog and wood, where no horseman could be of service.' Sir Andrew de Rathe (Rait) was despatched by Comyn and Gartnait to Cressingham at Berwick, with an up-to-date situation report. Characteristically, Cressingham played down Rathe's information when he wrote again to Edward, on 5 August, saying that 'it is false in many points, and obscure, as will be well known hereafter, I fear'. Cressingham's attempt to make light of the troubles in the north was confounded the very same day, when the Constable of Urquhart reported how Moray had besieged his castle; and shortly afterwards Sir Reginald le Cheyne, the King's Warden in Moray, complained to the King that Andrew de Moray and his 'malefactors' had spoiled and laid waste his goods and lands. Sir Reginald himself fell into the hands of the insurgents shortly afterwards, probably when Inverness Castle capitulated to Moray.

For Wallace's progress during the summer of 1297 we have, once more, to fall back on Blind Harry to a large extent, and the problem that perplexes us is that while much of what the minstrel says has the ring of truth there are some glaring discrepancies. The encounter with MacFadyen at the Pass of Brander seems to have been inconclusive. Harry states that Wallace decided to lay siege to Stirling Castle, but this anecdote must be taken with a very large pinch of salt, as Harry gets the name of the constable wrong, and says that when the castle fell Wallace entrusted it to the Earl of Lennox which, in view of the fact that the earl was on the other side at the time, is an impossibility. At any rate, the story goes that Wallace and Sir John Graham rode through the town at the head of a hundred men on horseback, daring the constable to come out and fight. Harry names this official as Rokeby, although the records show that the constable was Sir Richard de Waldegrave, who had been appointed to this post on 8 September 1296. The story of the assault and capture of Stirling Castle at this time seems to be entirely apocryphal.

Stirling was, in fact, to remain in English hands until mid-September. Meanwhile MacFadyen was still at large and his men, mainly Irish, were rampaging through Argyll. Sending Gilmichael ahead to spy out the land, Wallace and Duncan of Lorn advanced through Strathfillan. This was an arduous march which took its toll of the foot soldiers, and even the horses began to fail. According to Harry, Wallace had set out with over two thousand men, but the problems of providing food for such a large number induced him to leave the bulk of his men in Strathfillan while he went ahead with a hand-picked body of a hundred cavalry. Behind him there followed Sir John Graham with a similar number, and then Adam Wallace of Riccarton with a reserve force of five hundred men. In Glendochart, Gilmichael and Sir Neil Campbell came to report. Beyond Loch Dochart, Gilmichael ran into one of MacFadyen's scouts and slew him. The Scots dismounted and crossed the moss and crags on foot to join up with Campbell's local forces. Although outnumbered by MacFadyen's Irishmen, the Scots had the element of surprise when they attacked at dawn the following day. The ensuing battle lasted more than two hours and at one stage even the experienced campaigner Jop (Gilbert de Grimsby) was uncertain how it would go. Those Irishmen who were not killed in battle were drowned when they tried to escape across the loch. The Scots in MacFadyen's army threw down their weapons and begged for mercy. Wallace gave instructions that the Scottish prisoners should be spared, but to the Irish he gave no quarter.

MacFadyen himself escaped, and took refuge with a bodyguard of fifteen in a cave under Craigmore. He was pursued by Duncan of Lorn and a large force who slew the enemy and brought back MacFadyen's head, 'which Lord Campbell placed high in Craigmore upon a stone, for the honour of Ireland'. At Ardchattan, a mountainous fastness in Lorn on the shores of Loch Etive north-east of Oban, Wallace held a council at which he formally handed over Lorn to Duncan, bidding him 'hold it for Scotland with the Right, and thou shalt well enjoy this inheritance', and he even promised that, should his treacherous nephew John of Lorn (who was then in London) return to Argyll, he, too, would get his lands back. 'I would lose no one whom righteousness may save.'[17]

Harry, apparently drawing heavily on the Latin account by John Blair, enumerated some of the leading knights who attended this assembly. In particular he described Sir John Ramsay of 'Ouchterhouse' (Ochtertyre) and his son Sir Alexander who, he says, subsequently captured Roxburgh. Interestingly, Harry interpolates a brief passage (after saying that Alexander held that stronghold until traitors plotted and caused his death): 'I have been blamed, to tell the truth, regarding this statement, and therefore will but lightly pass this tale; but it was an event openly spoken of, and for such I trow they ought not to deem me worthy of blame.'

Another prominent figure at this council was 'the Bishop of Dunkeld' whom Harry describes without actually naming. It has been presumed that he was referring to Matthew Crambeth who, in 1289, had been co-opted as a Guardian of Scotland after the deaths of Alexander Comyn and the Earl of Fife. Harry, by describing him as 'of high lineage, of St Clair blood', however, clearly meant William Sinclair, Crambeth's successor, who did not become bishop until 1304, if not later. On the other hand, Sinclair is believed to have been Co-Adjutor of Dunkeld during the time when Bishop Crambeth had been abroad, in France and Rome, on diplomatic missions for King John. He had been living quietly in Bute, under the protection of the Steward, since being evicted from the diocese in 1294. Possibly with a view to restoring Sinclair to his cathedral, Wallace now ordered a cross-country march which brought his little army eventually to the gates of Perth, although Harry hints that the ensuing siege was intended by way of revenge for the way Wallace had been mishandled in that town the previous year.

Sir John Ramsay pointed out that the walls of Perth were low because they were surrounded by a very deep moat; if this obstacle could be passed, the town would be easily captured. The Scots tarried at Dunkeld for four days making elaborate preparations for the assault. Some fifty lines (970 –1020) of Harry's epic were devoted in such detail to the preliminaries and the assault itself as to give an air of truth to his narrative. This appears to have been the first time that Wallace employed siege-engines of any sort, which were constructed in the forest, employing the best wrights of the surrounding district, and then floating the contraptions down the Tay to the outer defences. The English put up a stout defence with their artillery (arbalests and mangonels capable of hurling large rocks). Graham and Ramsay led the attack on the turret bridge while Wallace conducted the main assault at the centre of the town. Harry says that two thousand Englishmen perished in the carnage, but even allowing for pardonable exaggeration the slaughter must have been horrendous. A young knight named Ruthven, who had brought thirty men to the conflict, distinguished himself so well that day that he was afterwards appointed captain and Sheriff of Perth, with the hereditary lieutenancy of Strathearn.

Having first made a lightning attack on Cupar, whose English abbot fled at his approach, Wallace swept over the north-east with characteristic vigour. At Glamis he was joined by the Bishop of Dunkeld and that evening they reached Brechin. Gathering men as he went, Wallace marched through the Mearns and advanced on Dunnottar Castle, an enormous fortress with impressive natural defences, standing on a promontory. Some four thousand Englishmen and their supporters had fled there as the Scots approached. The bishop begged Wallace to spare their lives and let them depart; but the Scots suspected that some day they might return, and their wholesale slaughter was ordered. Many of them sought refuge in the church which formed part of the castle complex; with grim economy the Scots merely set this building alight, roasting alive the unfortunate inmates. Those who ran out of the building were promptly put to the sword. It was a reprise of the Barns of Ayr. Others jumped off the cliffs to their death rather than let themselves be taken by the dreaded Scots. Incredibly, when the massacre had been completed, many of the Scots went down on their knees and asked the bishop for absolution. Wallace laughed sardonically: 'I forgive you all. Are ye men of war, and repent for so small a matter? They rued not how they did to us in the town of Ayr, where they hanged our true barons.'

Hastening on up the coast to Aberdeen, Wallace attacked the shipping in the harbour and destroyed it. The impression is given of the English trying to flee, a hundred vessels being heavily laden with goods and a great company of soldiers. At the ebb-tide the Scots rushed down on this armada, slaughtered the troops, plundered their goods and burned their boats. 'None got away but priests, wives and children,' adds Harry as a matter of course. This Scottish host swept all before it, heading north to Crimond in Buchan and then westwards to link up with Andrew de Moray on the Spey. No record of the first meeting of the two great guerrilla leaders exists, but it appears that there was an immediate rapport and from then onwards, until Moray's death, the two generals acted in concert.

Wallace was back in Aberdeen by 1 August, making elaborate arrangements for the administration of the north. This appears to tie up with a report made by Earl Warenne on that very day to Edward, saying that Sir Henry de Lazom or Latham had seized the castle of Aberdeen 'and there makes a great lord of himself'. Warenne went on to say that he had not heard of Lazom's fate, but promised that 'if caught, he shall be honoured according to his deserts'. Interestingly, Sir Henry was an Englishman who went over to the Scots; this renegade subsequently had his estates in Lancashire confiscated in retaliation, he being described in the sequestration as 'a rebel adherent of the Scots'.[18]

From Aberdeen Wallace rode south, to supervise the siege of Dundee. Unlike Perth and Aberdeen, which had fallen with relative ease, Dundee was stoutly defended, as was Stirling. Despite obvious errors and discrepancies in his narrative, it seems that Blind Harry is essentially correct; Scotland north of the Forth was largely in Scottish hands by August 1297 with the exception of these two great strongholds.

It was in a bid to relieve these fortresses and crush the rebel Scots that Earl Warenne finally made his move. On 14 August he was replaced as Warden of Scotland by Sir Brian Fitz-Alan, the energetic castellan of Angus. This move was made at Warenne's own request, he being ill at the time and anxious to return to his

Surrey estates. However, he was ordered to remain at his post for the time being, and in obedience to Edward's wishes he pressed on from the Borders with the intention of reinforcing Stirling and raising the siege of Dundee. Edward, confident that the veteran Earl of Surrey would carry out his orders, departed for Flanders a fortnight later aboard his flagship, the *Cog Edward*. Dundee had not yet capitulated when Wallace got word that an English army under Warenne and Cressingham was moving northwards in the direction of Stirling. Leaving Alexander Scrymgeour to continue the siege of Dundee, Wallace and Moray, now acting in concert, marched their men from the east and north to converge on this strategic position.

6

STIRLING BRIDGE

*Omnes autem hanc legem sive pro lege concorditer approbantes
ipsum in capitaneum elegerunt.*

With everyone harmoniously approving this law, or substitute
for law, they chose him as their captain.

SCOTICHRONICON, XI, CAP. 28.

STIRLING, at the very heart of the kingdom, was of immense
strategic importance. The lofty crag which towered over the
surrounding plain was capped by one of the most impregnable
castles in the British Isles. Through this plain meandered the
mighty River Forth, tidal as far inland as Stirling and rapidly
widening below the town to form that Scots Sea which so effectively kept the wild Highlandmen from overrunning the
Lowlands. Stirling was, in the Middle Ages and for many centuries thereafter, very much the gateway to the Highlands, and
the key to that gateway was the narrow wooden bridge which
spanned the swirling Forth a little above the town. This solitary
bridge was vital in any confrontation between the Scots and the
might of England. With the exception of the beleaguered
fortress of Dundee, all of Scotland north of the Forth was in
Scottish hands. The large army which Earl Warenne and
Treasurer Cressingham now led through the centre of the
country aimed at relieving Stirling Castle and seizing the
bridge, whence they could pour into the Highlands and pacify

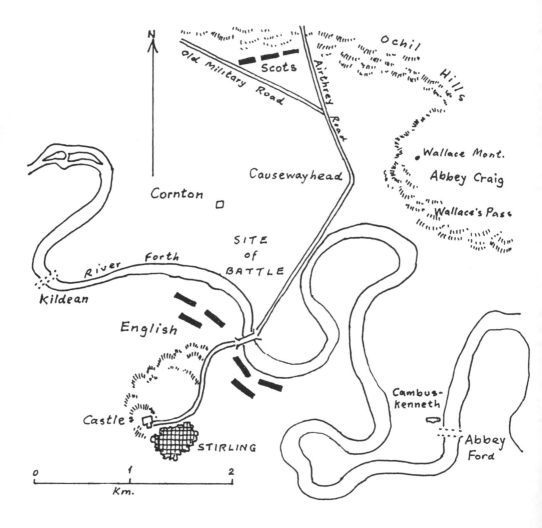

N

Ochil Hills

Scots

Old Military Road

Airthrey Road

Causewayhead

• Wallace Mont.

Abbey Craig

Cornton

Wallace's Pass

River Forth

SITE of BATTLE

Kildean

English

Cambus-kenneth

Castle

Abbey Ford

STIRLING

0   1   2
Km.

STIRLING BRIDGE 1297

the territory then controlled by Moray and Wallace.

Both sides, in effect, were gambling everything on a single throw of the dice, but the stakes were high. If the English succeeded, then Moray and Wallace would be forced back on the defensive, reduced to mere partisan leaders. If they succeeded, however, they would be in a very strong position not only to drive out the English but to take the power over Scotland into their own hands. Never before had the community of the realm of Scotland stood up to the might of an English army. At Dunbar and Irvine the Scottish levies had been commanded by their feudal superiors; in one they had been soundly defeated, in the other ignominiously forced to capitulate. It says much for the common people, the lesser gentry, the burgesses and the peasantry who rallied to the Wallace banner on this occasion, that they were prepared to risk everything now. It also speaks volumes for the leadership and courage of the two young generals, both hardly out of their teens, who took the field against one of the most seasoned warriors of the period and the most experienced army in all Europe.

The forces under the command of Warenne and Cressingham now amounted to about a thousand horse and fifty thousand infantry, drawn from all the counties of England north of the Trent but also including sizable contingents from Ireland and Wales. A second army of eight thousand foot and three hundred horse was heading north from Carlisle under Percy. This formidable force included veterans of wars in the Holy Land and France, of campaigns in Wales and previous conflicts in Scotland. It was well equipped and armed; more importantly, it was an army which had never known defeat and the rank and file had enormous confidence in the generalship of their leaders. On the other side, the Scots had shown poor fieldcraft at Dunbar and a general lack of discipline, while the disunity of their leaders, so evident at Irvine only two months previously, was common knowledge in the English ranks. Warenne would have known how few of the Scottish magnates were ranged against him. His intelligence sources would have kept him well informed of how pitifully few Scots noblemen were supporting the upstart brigand Wallace. Young Andrew de Moray, Sir John Graham, Sir John Ramsay and the like were of little or no account. The great nobles had been tamed: they were either serving with King Edward in Flanders, languishing in the Tower and other English prisons, or hamstrung by hostages and sureties for their good behaviour, ever fearful of losing their lands and property in England if they did not toe the line. Those at liberty to make up their own minds were extremely unlikely to give support to — far less serve under — a landless younger son who did not hold even the lowest rank of nobility.

What the Scottish army had, though, was an unquenchable spirit. Its ranks were motivated mainly by patriotism. They were men who had endured the insolence and arrogance, the high-handedness and brutality of English rule in one form or another for seven years, and now they had reached the point at which they were prepared to give their lives rather than endure English tyranny a day longer. This was a volunteer army, and what it lacked in experience it made up for in motivation. The English army, on the other hand, was essentially a feudal host, its ranks drawn largely from men who were pressed into service as part of their obligations to their feudal superiors. Many of the foot soldiers had been conscripted under the system whereby the yeomen and peasantry were liable for call-up through the levies on each county. The army also included a sizable contingent of Welsh archers whose skill with the longbow would, in a few decades, give England the advantage over the French at Crecy and Agincourt. But in 1297 the Welshmen had only recently come under English rule; many of them would have fought against Edward in the campaigns of the 1280s, and their loyalty was questionable at the best of times.

The medieval concept of warfare placed heavy reliance on two factors, mail-clad cavalry and the feudal chain of command through the great earls and barons, the knights and lesser gentry, the esquires, yeomen and men-at-arms. The Scots, lightly armed and poorly trained, were a new phenomenon, a force composed of common people fighting on their own account, for a purely national idea and object.

One can scarcely imagine a grander setting for a great national showdown. On the south side of the Forth stood the ancient burgh of Stirling, clustered about the majestic and lofty rock crowned by its castle. On the far side of the plain were the beautiful Ochil Hills, sweeping up from the east and then dipping away towards the north, leaving the great outcrop known as the Abbey Craig as an outpost. The height of the castle rock and the Abbey Craig was accentuated by the flatlands in between, virtually at sea level, through which lazily wound the river in enormous loops. From the castle esplanade, or from the top of the Wallace Monument, that magnificent Victorian folly erected on the summit of the Craig, the views in all directions are breathtaking, but between them the battlefield would have been spread out at the spectator's feet.

There has been perennial controversy regarding the precise location of the battle, for the wooden bridge which was the bone of contention has long since vanished without trace. One school of thought maintained that this bridge was at Kildean, much higher up the river than the existing bridges, but this does not accord with the description of the terrain given by the contemporary English chroniclers, who had no reason to lie about it. In more recent years the consensus of opinion is that the bridge spanned the river only a few yards upstream from the fifteenth-century stone bridge which still stands. At this point the Forth is about thirty metres wide. The current is relatively slow-moving, but the river is deep. There were only two fords, at widely separated points above and below the town and usable only at low tide, so that the narrow wooden bridge was effectively the only means of crossing the river. From the end of the bridge on the north side there was a paved causeway heading in a north-easterly direction terminating in the hamlet of Causewayhead (which exists to this day). The causeway lay across a broad haugh, a low-lying area of marsh, subject to inundation at high spring tides. If the bridge was so narrow that only two horsemen could ride abreast, the causeway was not much wider. Four horses at most could move side by side. To the left and right of the causeway the ground would have been much too soft and swampy for cavalry to operate.

In the approved medieval manner, the English commander gave the Scots the opportunity to surrender before the armies engaged in battle. This tactic had worked well enough at Irvine, when the Scottish magnates had caved in before Percy and Clifford without exchanging a single blow. On 10 September Warenne sent an envoy to the Scots, demanding their submission. This herald would later report back that the Scottish army was 'on the other side of the hill, above the monastery of

Cambuskenneth, with that robber William Wallace'.[1] The writer of this manuscript also commented ominously that 'there was not in the kingdom a spot where the English could have been so effectually shut up in the hands of the Scots, or a multitude in the power of a few'. Hemingburgh uses precisely the same language.[2] Neither of these things could be said of the open ground at Kildean (where, in fact, lay the upper of the two fords). The hill above the monastery of Cambuskenneth was, indeed, the Abbey Craig which derived its name from that ecclesiastical establishment. Until the 1930s it was commonly supposed that the Scottish army was drawn up on the Craig itself (hence the location of the Monument erected in the nineteenth century) but James Fergusson then demonstrated cogently that this was impossible.[3] The heavily wooded nature of the Craig today conceals the fact that its face is virtually sheer and there is no way that the Scots could have charged down it in battle order. Hemingburgh's actual words are *mox descenderunt de monte* ('presently they came down from the mountain') which accords with the notion of a descent from ground considerably higher than the swampy haugh. This puts the Scottish army on the slopes and braes some way to the north of Causewayhead, and thus accords with the suggested location of the bridge. With consummate skill Wallace and Moray had drawn up their army on the lower flanks of the Ochils, north-west of the Abbey Craig, facing almost due south to the causeway and the river, above the modern suburb of Cornton.

Ironically, Hemingburgh prefaces his description of the battle with the statement that the Scots magnates had surrendered at Irvine because, though outnumbering the English in foot soldiers, they were woefully deficient in heavy cavalry. To Walter of Hemingburgh, what took place at Stirling was a contest of skill and strategy. At first it looked as if the events at Irvine might be repeated. Two or three days before the battle some of the Scottish magnates, including James the Steward and the Earl of Lennox, rode into the English camp and promised to parley with the Scots to prevent unnecessary bloodshed. They returned on 10 September, their mission unfulfilled, but as an act of good faith, they promised to contribute sixty men-at-arms to the English cause. That evening, however, there was a slight skirmish between the Lennox party and some English soldiers who had been out foraging. It may be that the earl was incensed at seeing the Englishmen laden down with their booty, for he himself mortally wounded one of the soldiers in the neck with a spear.

> When this became known in our army, the men instantly ran to arms, and bringing the wounded, covered with blood, to the Earl Warren, demanded vengeance, at the same time calling out that faith was broken. To them the earl replied, 'Have patience for this night, and if tomorrow their promise be not fulfilled, you shall take vengeance, the deeper on account of what has just happened.'

Taking a charitable view of the magnates' action, it is probable that Lennox and the Steward were merely spying out the land for their compatriots and had no intention of taking part on the English side.

That evening Warenne gave orders that all should be prepared to cross the bridge early the following morning. At dawn, some five thousand foot soldiers, including the Welsh contingent, did cross the bridge but the earl, still recovering from his recent illness and obviously exhausted by his exertions, was fast asleep. This was a moment of indecision. In default of positive orders to advance the troops turned round and recrossed the bridge, an operation which must have done little to soothe the temper of the excitable Welshmen. When Warenne did get around to rising from his couch and donning his armour, he proceeded to hold a parade at which, in the custom of the period, the rank of knighthood was conferred on a number of youthful aspirants, many of whom would perish before the day was out.

During the accolade ceremony Lennox and the Steward reappeared, together with a handful of retainers well short of the squadron of cavalry that had been promised. The bland excuse proffered was that they had been unable to persuade the others to defect from the Scottish army. Even now, Earl Warenne dithered about attacking. From his vantage-point, gazing across the river to the foothills where the spears of the Scottish host glinted in the summer sunshine, it appeared that Wallace's men were in an unassailable position, threatening the left flank of any force which crossed the river and advanced along the causeway. The lofty escarpment of the Ochils, rising steeply from the plain at sea level, must have seemed more formidable than it really was. An experienced warrior like the Earl of Surrey would have noted the swampy ground, unsuitable for armoured destriers, the distance to be covered, the fact that his army would be fighting uphill, and the fact that the Scots, with the hills at their back, had a ready means of melting away whereas the English force, once across that infernally narrow bridge, had no means of escape. If only he could entice the Scots down on to the plain to the north of the town where his cavalry could make mincemeat of them, just as they had done at Dunbar. But here the positions were reversed . . . Warenne's unease as he appraised the situation is perfectly understandable.

But the English army was eager for battle; there would be muttering in the ranks and exasperated pleas from young bloods anxious to win their spurs; even the horses, sensing the tension in the air, would be restive. Still Warenne hesitated uneasily and, playing for time, he now despatched two Dominican friars across the bridge and up the causeway to offer the Scots terms for surrender. This parley was inconclusive, and the friars returned to Warenne with the news that Wallace appeared to have about 180 horsemen and a vast army of foot soldiers which they wildly estimated at forty thousand. Wallace's answer to Warenne was unequivocal and uncompromising:

> Tell your people that we have not come here to gain peace, but
> are prepared for battle, to avenge and deliver our country. Let
> them come up when they like, and they will find us ready to
> meet them even to their beards.[4]

Wallace's defiant answer took the English commanders by surprise. Far from seeking a way out, as the Scottish magnates had done two months earlier, this upstart brigand was, in effect, inviting the English to attack him. This, and the obviously strong defensive position adopted by the Scots, unnerved the English and spread dissension among the general staff. Some hotheads urged an immediate attack to call the robber's bluff, but saner counsels prevailed and, in time-honoured fashion, Warenne called a council of war to debate the issue. By now some part at least of Percy's army had joined the main body, for one of the more conspicuous officers taking part in the deliberations was none other than Sir Richard Lundie who had changed sides at Irvine. This gives the lie to Blind Harry's assertion, followed by some historians, that Lundie had fought alongside Wallace in his lightning northern campaign that summer. Sir Richard was a seasoned campaigner who also knew the terrain round Stirling intimately. With pardonable exaggeration Hailes says of him that he was 'to all appearance, the only man of true judgment in the whole English army'. Sir Richard now addressed Warenne's staff:

> My lords, if we go on to the bridge we are dead men; for we cannot cross it except two by two, and the enemy are on our flank, and can come down on us as they will, all in one front. But there is a ford not far from here, where we can cross sixty at a time. Let me now therefore have five hundred knights and a small body of infantry, and we will get round the enemy on the rear and crush them; and meanwhile you, my lord Earl, and the others who are with you, will cross the bridge in perfect safety.[5]

This was sound advice but, incredibly, Lundie was overruled. Some field commanders probably did not repose too much trust in the turncoat knight anyway, mindful of the behaviour of Lennox and the Steward, but the general feeling was that it would be unwise to split the army. There were some who vociferously argued Lundie's case, but the council degenerated into chaos at this point, everyone squabbling with his neighbour. At this juncture Cressingham spoke up. The Treasurer was totally lacking in charisma, and appears to have been despised and loathed by the English almost as much as he was hated by the Scots. Physically repulsive and grossly overweight, he had now exchanged his clerical vestments for armour and chain-mail. The sight of this pompous, fat clergyman accoutred for war was incongruous and was probably regarded with derision by the professional soldiers. Now he shouted down the babble and addressed Warenne. 'There is no point in dragging out this business any longer, and wasting our King's revenues for nothing. Let us advance and carry out our duty as we are bound to do.'

Warenne was annoyed by this interjection, and stung by the Treasurer's reminder of the costs which had been incurred so far. At length, worn out by all the bickering and argument, the Earl of Surrey gave the command to cross the bridge. Just as Lundie had pointed out, this wooden structure was so narrow that no more than two horsemen could ride abreast, and even then only with the greatest care and difficulty which would have slowed up the proceedings even further. By now it must have been mid-morning at the very least, and the negotiation of the bridge took several hours. By eleven o'clock, therefore, only a part of the English army had crossed the river.

In the vanguard was Sir Marmaduke de Thweng, one of the few knights to distinguish himself on that historic day. Marmaduke, later first Baron Thweng (died 1322), was the son of Sir Marmaduke de Thweng of Kilton Castle in Cleveland and Lucy, sister of Peter Bruce. The Thwengs were thus vassals of the Earl of Carrick in his capacity as Lord of Cleveland, as well as closely related to him. Marmaduke's elder brother Robert (dead by 1283) was, in fact, godson of Bruce the Competitor.[6] Thweng rode ahead of the main body with a small band of knights to secure the northern end of the causeway and cover the English advance. Among the notable figures who did succeed in crossing the bridge were Cressingham himself, the standard-bearers carrying the banners of St George and the Earl of Surrey, Sir Robert de Somerville and his eldest son, and the Constable of Stirling Castle, Sir Richard de Waldegrave.

The heavily armoured knights and their great warhorses, the royal banners, the guidons, pennants and oriflammes of the leading knights and barons, all the pageantry and panoply of medieval warfare, must have made a stirring sight. The tension in the Scottish ranks less than half a mile away must have been fearful. It says a lot for the discipline which Wallace and Moray had instilled that the Scots held firm and resisted the urge to rush madly down the slope, as they had done at Dunbar, to engage the enemy. No doubt this tension mounted as more and more English troops slowly made their way across the bridge and fanned out on to the marshy haugh. It also says much for the nerve of the Scottish generals as, from the summit of the Abbey Craig, they observed the crawling files of the enemy far

below and weighed up the chances of their spearmen and piti-
ful handful of cavalry. The main factor in Wallace's favour was
that he could choose exactly against what odds he would fight.
It must have been a nerve-wracking business, trying to gauge
the right moment. If he launched the counter-attack too soon,
his troops would stand a better chance of defeating the smaller
English force which had managed to cross the river, but this
would leave the main army intact, to strike again and ravage the
southern districts in revenge. If he waited until Surrey's entire
army had crossed, his lightly armed troops would be outnumbered and overwhelmed. According to Hemingburgh, the Scots
waited until 'as many of the enemy had come over as they
believed they could overcome', a point which seems to have
been reached around eleven o'clock.

From his vantage-point Wallace gave the signal to attack by
a single blast from a horn, it having been agreed previously that
he, and only he, should blow a horn when the moment was
right. The Scots had been waiting for the signal with great
expectancy. As soon as the sound rang out and reverberated
round the crags, the Scots, like some gigantic coiled spring,
surged forward *en masse*, brandishing spears and swords and
giving vent to blood-curdling yells as they charged. The spearmen on the right wing sped through Cornton Vale, hell-bent on
securing the bridgehead. The speed and ferocity of this
onslaught took the English by surprise and, indeed, it was
apparently several minutes before the main party was even
aware that it had taken place. The Scots hacked and stabbed
their way to the bridge and neatly closed the trap. There was a
stampede on the bridge itself, the closely packed troops unable
to move forward and pressed hard by those coming behind.
Many of them jumped or fell into the river and were drowned
in the deep water, weighed down by their armour and equipment.

Meanwhile the main Scottish forces had descended the
slopes, gathering momentum as they ran, spears levelled,
straight into the English mass. The heavy cavalry, floundering in
the marshy ground, proved ineffectual while the shock and
impact of the Scottish charge sent the disorganised and unpre-
pared English infantry reeling. Almost instantaneously came the
realisation that the Scottish spearmen had seized the bridge-

head, and this triggered off blind panic in the English ranks. By all accounts, the only man who kept his head on the English side was Thweng, whose squadron encountered the Scottish cavalry riding down the causeway. Thweng gave the command to charge and easily dispersed the more lightly armed Scots. His heavy cavalry would have given chase but Sir Marmaduke now quickly took in the general situation. To his dismay he noted that Edward's and Surrey's giant standards had disappeared in the confused mêlée half a mile to the south. More disturbing was the large mass of Scots now milling about the bridgehead and blocking retreat. One of Thweng's knights suggested that, despite their heavy armour, they should try to swim across the river — one of its great penannular loops was only a few yards away and the water did not seem too deep; but Sir Marmaduke declared that he would not drown for any man, and called his knights to follow him closely, confident in his ability to clear a path through the Scots. Then, spurring his charger, he rode straight through the Scottish infantry, cutting a swathe with his great broad sword. His squire came close behind him, the body of Sir Marmaduke's nephew (who had been mortally wounded) slung across his saddle, and, accompanied by a handful of other knights, they managed to reach the bridge and miraculously recrossed it.

About a hundred knights on horseback, some three hundred Welsh archers and almost the whole of the five thousand foot soldiers who had crossed the bridge perished that day. The Scots attacked in force from the north and drove the English into the loop of the river east of the causeway and the bridge. The bowmen had no room to manoeuvre and were speedily cut down, leaving the foot soldiers at the mercy of the infinitely greater numbers of Scots. The carnage was well-nigh indescribable. With their fierce cry of 'On them! On them! On them!' the Scots pressed forward relentlessly until the last English soldier had been trampled into the mud or driven into the treacherous water. The slaughter was virtually total. No more than a handful of foot soldiers managed to divest themselves of their armour and swim the river to safety. Incredibly, one knight allegedly performed the impossible feat of crossing the river, horse, armour and all. Sir Marmaduke was the only notable figure to make his escape, and his gallantry was subsequently rewarded when he was appointed lieutenant to Sir William Fitz-Warine whom his kinsman Surrey installed as Constable of Stirling Castle in place of the unfortunate Waldegrave.

The Scottish losses were negligible except in one important respect: Sir Andrew de Moray received a severe wound from which he died several weeks later. The leading casualty on the English side was the Treasurer, who either toppled off his horse or was yanked off it, and was trampled to death under its hooves. The battle must have been lost by midday but the grim mopping-up operation would have gone on much longer, as the Scots took no prisoners as usual. All the while, Earl Warenne was a helpless observer of the massacre. His archers had been in the van and had been among the first to be cut down, otherwise he might have been able to direct deadly fire across the river. As it was, the force on the south bank could only look on aghast, as their comrades were butchered less than fifty metres away. As soon as Thweng and his knights had recrossed the river Warenne ordered that the bridge be cut down and set on fire to prevent the Scots crossing in hot pursuit. Some accounts state that it was the Scots who destroyed the bridge — indeed, Harry says that John the Wright, concealed under the bridge, on hearing the blast from Wallace's horn, had pulled out the roller with such skill that the structure collapsed. But that would have been against the Scottish interest, and Hemingburgh is quite explicit on this point. Pausing only to tell the new Constable of Stirling Castle that he would return with a relieving force within ten weeks, Surrey gave orders for a speedy evacuation. Disregarding his age (he was sixty-six, which was old by the standards of the time and really too old for the commander of a great army) and his infirmities, Warenne mounted his horse and led his army southwards with due despatch, not pausing until he was safely on the far side of Berwick.

Where Sir Richard Lundie was during the battle is unclear, but he was presumably with the main force south of the river and had the grim satisfaction of seeing his gloomy predictions justified. Blind Harry, making the error that Lundie was on the Scottish side, has him fighting valiantly alongside Graham, Boyd and Ramsay but this is quite erroneous. When the Scots charged down from the slopes, however, the Steward and the Earl of Lennox, who had been somewhere at the rear of the

151

main English force on the south bank, slipped away through the town with their handful of men and rejoined the main band of their retainers concealed in the Torwood south of Stirling. Opinion remains divided regarding the motives and intentions of these wily magnates; but once the outcome of the battle was certain they came out firmly on the Scottish side. From the Torwood they sallied out to harass the retreating English army, killing the stragglers and attacking the baggage-trains.

We do not know what the state of the tide was on that fateful day, but as soon as it had ebbed sufficiently the Scottish cavalry crossed by the ford near Cambuskenneth and began that relentless harassment of the English army which was to continue unabated all the way to the banks of the Tweed. Harry states that Wallace and Graham made a great slaughter of the retreating English at Hathyntoun (Haddington). They continued to harry the English as far as Belton near Dunbar but, wearied with the slaughter, they broke off the chase. The Lanercost Chronicle observed that Warenne only 'escaped with difficulty and with a small following, so hotly did the enemy pursue them'. The demoralised English forces, mostly on foot, would have taken several days to reach Berwick, and in the ensuing period the Scots seized their pack-animals and repeatedly attacked them from the rear. The Earl of Surrey, in spite of his illness, rode at such a pace that his horse, according to Hemingburgh, 'never tasted corn again'. Ironically, from Westminster on 12 September the Prince of Wales, regent during his father's absence in Flanders, sent a directive to Warenne ordering him to remain in Scotland at all costs until the revolt in that realm had been put down. By the time this missive caught up with Surrey he was in York, intent on putting as many miles of English soil between himself and the ferocious Scots as he could.

Blind Harry claims that Wallace himself slew Hugh Cressingham, 'with a great sharp spear, the head of which pierced right through the plates of the corslet and through his body, stabbing him beyond rescue', but this must be regarded as poetic licence. Interestingly, the minstrel has nothing further to say on the subject, but this defect is remedied by the English chroniclers. Cressingham's squire, who was lucky enough to escape the carnage, maintained afterwards that the Treasurer was so obese that he had the greatest difficulty in remaining in the saddle, and when he tried to turn and flee he toppled off his horse and could not mount again. To a Scot wielding a Lochaber axe he cried out, 'For mercy, give me quarter,' but as the Scot was unacquainted with Norman French he whacked him anyway. After the battle, as the Scots stripped the dead of their arms and armour, they came upon the corpulent body of the late Treasurer. Not content with stripping the corpse of armour and every shred of clothing, the Scots skinned their arch-enemy and otherwise mutilated him, his genitals being cut off and stuffed down his throat. The chronicler of Lanercost Priory (which the Scots had earlier ravaged) was particularly outspoken on this brutal matter. According to this writer, the Scots dried and cured the Treasurer's hide and 'of his skin William Wallace caused a broad strip to be taken from the head to the heel, to make therewith a baldrick for his sword'. The *Scalacronica*, on the other hand, merely notes that 'it was said that the Scots caused him to be flayed, and in token of hatred made thongs of his skin' (a statement which led some of the more fanciful Scottish writers of the eighteenth century to aver that the Scots had made it into saddle-girths). Walter of Hemingburgh, however, recorded more reasonably that 'the Scots flayed him, and divided his skin among themselves in moderate-sized pieces, certainly not as relics, but for hatred of him'.

7

THE INVASION OF
ENGLAND

Then was the destruction of the English of such a kind and
magnitude as the northern regions have never experienced
the like.

SCOTICHRONICON, XI, CAP. 30.

THE Scots victory at Stirling Bridge was important psycholog-
ically for it finally gave the lie to the myth of English invincibility in general and the power of heavy cavalry in particular.
What the common foot-soldiers of Scotland achieved that day,
the Flemish at Courtrai and the Swiss at Morgarten would
repeat with a vengeance. But Stirling Bridge was by no stretch of
the imagination a decisive victory in the same sense as
Bannockburn, fought seventeen years later a mile or two down-
stream. Wallace's defeat of Earl Warenne did not put an end to
English designs on Scotland — far from it. The humiliation of
the English was something that King Edward now addressed
himself towards avenging. For the time being, however,
Wallace's star was in the ascendant. If his role in securing the
Scottish victory has been debated (notably by Evan Barron, a
tireless champion of Andrew de Moray), there is no doubt that
the guerrilla leader who had so dramatically been catapulted
into the role of Scottish dictator was very much the man of the
hour. Now William's considerable intellect, administrative
genius, diplomacy, charisma, personal magnetism, call it what

you will, were pressed into service to consolidate his position and weld his battered country into a nation once more. Stirling Bridge expunged the scandal of Irvine and handsomely atoned for the defeat at Dunbar.

It also dealt a severe blow to the concept of feudalism, and goes far to explain the jealousy and fear of Wallace felt by the magnates as a whole. The Anglo-Norman upper classes were a self-serving bunch at the best of times, as their disgraceful behaviour at Irvine had shown. Now they were to hamper and eventually undo Wallace's tireless efforts to govern Scotland. It is significant that, shortly after the battle, missives were sent from England to the individual Scottish magnates, praising them for their fidelity to King Edward and urging them to join forces with Brian Fitz-Alan for the purposes of putting down the rebellion. The nobles thus addressed included John Comyn of Badenoch; the Earl of Buchan; Patrick, Earl of Dunbar; Umfraville, Earl of Angus; Alexander, Earl of Menteith; Malise, Earl of Strathearn; James the Steward; Malcolm, Earl of Lennox; William, Earl of Sutherland; Nicholas de la Haye; Ingelram de Umfraville; Richard Frazer and Alexander de Lindesay of Crawford.[1] The younger Earl of Carrick was conspicuous by his absence from this list, implying that his loyalty was suspect, to say the least.

For the moment, however, Scots of all classes rallied to Wallace. After pausing briefly at Haddington again after harrying the retreating English, William went straight back to the scene of his recent victory. The garrison at Stirling Castle apparently had no faith in Surrey's promise, for it surrendered to the Scots after a very brief siege. On this occasion Wallace seems to have spared the lives of the defenders. Fitz-Warine, who had previously lost Urquhart Castle to Moray, was now marched away to captivity in Dumbarton Castle, along with Sir Marmaduke de Thweng. These knights were repatriated two years later in exchange for some Scottish prisoners.

Wallace now concentrated on reducing Dundee, which was continuing to hold out. This was the less glamorous aspect of warfare, and it is significant that Wallace should give priority to clearing out the pockets of English resistance before succumbing to the temptation of carrying the war into the enemy's own country. According to the *Scotichronicon*, the defenders of

Dundee Castle did not put up much of a fight once news of the disaster at Stirling reached them. This proved to be a rich prize, in arms and cash, and William rewarded Alexander Scrymgeour by appointing him governor of Dundee, with orders to dismantle the fortifications which had cowed the town. According to the *Relationes* of Arnald Blair, a chronicle which is not very highly regarded as to historical accuracy, Wallace's men captured Cupar Castle and put its garrison of two hundred men to the sword.

This left only four castles in English hands. Edinburgh Castle continued to hold out under the redoubtable Sir Walter de Huntercombe, while Robert de Hastings held Roxburgh and Osbert de Spaldington hastily fortified Berwick. Dunbar also remained in the hands of the Earl of March, a rabid Anglophile. A Scottish force under Henry de Haliburton, continuing the good work of harrying the retreating English army, came eventually to Berwick where they found the town abandoned by its garrison, 'because they had neither leader nor defender' as Hemingburgh laconically records. The Lanercost Chronicle confirms this, saying that 'the Scots entered Berwick and put to death the few English that they found there; for the town was then without walls and might be taken as easily by English or Scots coming in force. The castle of the town, however, was not surrendered on this occasion.' Be that as it may, Haliburton occupied the town and remained there with his forces until Wallace's invasion of England.

Meanwhile, another strong force was sent to besiege Roxburgh. By the first week in October, less than a month after the victory at Stirling Bridge, Wallace had cleared the English out of Scotland and recovered almost all of the castles and other strongholds. By the efforts of one man, with precious little help from the nobility and a great deal of hindrance, the power of King Edward had been ripped asunder and Scotland was, for the first time in almost a decade, free of alien domination.

Hitherto Wallace had been regarded merely as a successful guerrilla and latterly as a skilful general. Now his political as well as physical stature became apparent. The *de facto* power lay in his hands, nominally shared with Andrew de Moray although he was hovering between life and death and would not survive much longer. Scotland was in the hands of a young man of twenty-three or thereabouts, a person of good family and impeccable antecedents perhaps, but a younger son without land or vassals — and in the late thirteenth century such a lack of status mattered. By the force of his personality alone, however, William Wallace emerged as the leader of Scotland. Overnight, the guerrilla chieftain became supreme ruler of the Scots. This position was dramatically underscored by a remarkable Latin document which was discovered in the archives of the Hanseatic city of Lübeck in 1829 and which is quoted here in full:

> Andreas de Moravia and Willelmus Wallensis, leaders (*Duces*) of the army of the kingdom of Scotland, and the community of the same kingdom, to the prudent and discreet men and well-beloved friends, the mayors and commons of Lübeck and Hamburg, greeting and increase always of sincere friendship.
>
> It has been told to us by trustworthy merchants of the said kingdom of Scotland, that you of your own goodwill are giving your counsel, aid, and favour in all matters and transactions touching us and the said merchants, although our merits had not deserved this; and so all the more are we bound to you, to give you our thanks and a worthy recompense, whereto we willingly engage ourselves to you; and request you that you will be pleased to make it known among your merchants that they can have safe access to all the ports of the kingdom of Scotland with their merchandise; for the kingdom of Scotland, God be thanked, has been recovered by war from the power of the English. Farewell.
>
> Given at Haddington in Scotland on the eleventh day of October in the year of grace one thousand two hundred and ninety-seven.
>
> We further request you to have the goodness to forward the business of our merchants John Burnet and John Frere, according as you would wish us to forward the business of your merchants. Farewell. Given as before.[2]

In other words, Wallace was letting Scotland's trading partners know that it was a case of 'business as usual'. It will be recalled that the most strenuous resistance to the English at the sack of Berwick the previous year had been put up by the company of thirty Flemish merchants who fought to the bitter end in the Red Hall. A reciprocal arrangement with Flanders found expression in the Scottendyk, the Scots mercantile colony in Bruges. The golden age of Alexander III had witnessed a remarkable growth in Scottish trade with the Low Countries, Scandinavia and the Hanseatic League, but this must have been wrecked by the upheavals of the past eighteen months. Now that Scotland was rid of the English, Wallace's first priority was to resume diplomatic and commercial relations with foreign countries. Doubtless other letters were sent abroad about the same time, couched in the same proud and dignified terms, to let the world know that 'the kingdom of Scotland is recovered by war from the power of the English'.

Evan Barron, in *The Scottish War of Independence* (1934), continually sought to promote Andrew de Moray above and beyond William Wallace. As the proprietor and editor of the *Inverness Courier*, Barron may be forgiven for his uncompromisingly partisan stance on behalf of the northern leader. In showing that there was another great patriot as well as Wallace, he often provides a valuable corrective to the uncritical adulation accorded the latter by many nineteenth-century historians. But occasionally Barron oversteps the mark. Whether Moray or Wallace was the main architect of victory is a matter for conjecture, but in support of his view that Moray was the real victor of Stirling, Barron cites the Lübeck document which places Moray's name first. Other writers have ascribed the order of names merely to Wallace's innate modesty; no one appears to have pointed out that, both in Christian name and surname, Andrew de Moray would have taken precedence in alphabetical order anyway. Both men were of equal social standing, the sons of knights, but Moray's father was a substantial landowner whereas Sir Malcolm Wallace of Auchenbothie and Ellerslie was but laird of two insignificant estates. William's connections with the Wallaces of Riccarton and the Craufurds of Crosshouse and Craufurdland were of little account compared with the Moray family which had vast estates in Clydesdale and even England as well as the county from which they derived their name. Andrew de Moray was probably older than Wallace, although the fact that he was married does not make this necessarily the case. His young wife was pregnant at the time of his death, but a few months later she gave birth to a son, named Andrew de Moray after his father, and this young knight would become one of the staunchest supporters, as well as the brother-in-law, of King Robert Bruce.

Significantly, the letter to Lübeck was written from Haddington on 11 October. This town, one of the leading burghs of Scotland and a favourite royal residence, was an important administrative centre for the Lothians. We have seen how Blind Harry claims that Wallace stayed there before and after his pursuit of the English to Belton, but the minstrel may have confused that with a somewhat later date, when Wallace paused briefly before mounting his invasion of England which began exactly one week later, on 18 October. The date of Moray's death is not known, but it has been surmised that he succumbed to his wounds in November, as letters were still being issued in joint names up to that time. Certainly he could not personally have had a hand in the composition of these letters sent out in his name.

From the list of magnates addressed in the name of King Edward, it will be seen that Wallace had a great deal to contend with if he were to win the great nobles over to his cause. Some of the magnates must have been giving covert support — the ambivalent position of the Steward and Earl Malcolm has already been noted — but among the other earls were some of Edward's staunchest supporters and, by the same token, Wallace's most implacable enemies. In particular, Patrick, Earl of March, was a thorn in the flesh that could not be left unattended. Earl Patrick who, in the words of the chronicles, 'held the key of the eastern marches at his girdle', continued to hold the castle of Dunbar for Edward even after the English army had fled south, and it was therefore essential that he be won over. Accordingly, Wallace summoned Earl Patrick to a council at Perth early in October to swear his loyalty to the Scottish realm. The recalcitrant earl, however, had no intention of submitting to this young whelp and sent an insulting reply, with a jocular reference to William's origins. He would not submit to this 'King of Kyle', alluding to the legendary King Cole or Coill as well as Wallace's Ayrshire birthplace.

Now Earl Patrick, or Cospatric as he is sometimes known, was a prime target. As the Scottish army headed south round the coast the earl summoned up reinforcements, contingents being sent to him by Bishop Bek and allegedly also by the young Earl of Carrick. It is curious that Earl Robert was not included in the missives sent from Westminster, and his role, before and after Stirling, has been a matter of controversy ever since. At any rate, Wallace's forces reduced the castles and strongholds of Earl Patrick in the Merse and the Lothians, known as his Seven War Steeds. Patrick himself fled south with Bek's men and sought refuge at the English court.

Once this formidable adversary had been eliminated, the Scots were free to advance on Berwick. The town had, since its sack the previous year, been resettled by English families, and Wallace's army now took their revenge by indulging in an orgy of destruction. Later the citizens of Berwick would petition Westminster concerning the losses they sustained in this attack after which 'the earl of Warren and the barons who were in his company recovered the town of Berwick-upon-Tweed, which William Walleys, and other enemies of the king, had seized'.[3]

On 18 October the Scots crossed the Tweed and entered Northumberland. The inhabitants, who had but recently witnessed the astonishing spectacle of their invincible army heading south in disarray, had plenty of warning of the imminent invasion and a stream of refugees fled for the walled protection of Newcastle, taking their cattle and their household property with them. The Scots vented their spleen on the deserted cottages and farmhouses by consigning them to the flames. Realising that the Northumbrians had vanished before them, the Scots now turned westwards and invaded Cumbria. This was not so much an orgy of wanton destruction as the systematic looting and stripping of the county. Scotland was desperately short of foodstuffs, thanks to the very scanty harvest that autumn, and apart from teaching the hated Southrons a bitter lesson the object of the invasion was to exact reparations. Anything and everything of value was removed and shipped over the border. The whole of Cumbria, from Inglewood Forest to Cockermouth, was meticulously ravaged. During this prolonged raid the Northumbrians, believing that the danger had passed, returned to their farms and villages. When this was reported to Wallace by his scouts, he ordered a rapid and unsuspected return to the district so recently visited. The Forest of

Rothbury, midway between Berwick and Newcastle, became the headquarters of the flying columns that roamed at will over Northumberland, rounding up the wretched inhabitants and robbing them before putting them to the sword. Northumberland was now even more thoroughly pillaged than before, and what could not be removed was promptly burned to the ground.

The Northumbrians, in effect, were being made to suffer for the sack of Berwick the previous year. They had had little or nothing to do with that atrocity, but they now paid the grim penalty for just happening to be the nearest Englishmen available. Hemingburgh's terse comments on this calamity summed up the dreadful situation:

> In that time the praise of God ceased in all the monasteries and churches of the whole province, from Newcastle-upon-Tyne to Carlisle. For all the monks, the canons regular, and the other priests, the servants of the Lord, with almost the whole population, had fled from the face of the Scots. Thus the Scots had liberty for fire and rapine from Saint Luke's Day [18 October] until Martinmas [11 November], and there was none to stop them, save for a few of our men who were in the castles of Alnwick and other places and who sallied out sometimes and cut off a few stragglers.

Indeed, the castles of the two northern counties remained in English hands. The Scots lacked the necessary engines to assault them and Wallace wisely refused to get bogged down in futile sieges. This was a lightning war of movement, the sort of campaign in which he excelled by experience and inclination, and it was no part of his remit to occupy the northern counties with a view to permanent subjugation. The sole exception to this policy was Carlisle Castle which, it may be remembered, had been governed by the elder Robert Bruce. Ironically, the son of the Competitor and father of the future king was removed from his command on 13 October, only five days before the Scottish invasion of Northumberland, because of the suspect loyalty of his son. Bruce had handed over the castle to the Bishop of Carlisle and presumably withdrew across the Solway to Annandale thereafter. Towards the end of the campaign, about the middle of November, the Scottish army entered Carlisle and sent forward a priest with a message from their commander:

> My Lord William, the Conqueror, commands you to have a care for your lives and to yield this town and castle to him without bloodshed; and he will grant to you your lives and limbs, and all your beasts. If you will not do this, he will immediately attack you and destroy you utterly.[4]

Someone cried out from the battlements, 'Who is this Conqueror?'

'William,' answered the priest, 'whom you call Walays.'

According to Hemingburgh the English garrison returned a dignified defiance and prepared to defend the walls. The castle was very strong and housed over a hundred men-at-arms, and under normal circumstances Wallace would not have persisted in his attempt to take it. But Carlisle was the western gateway to Scotland, a formidable barrier to any future Scots incursion into Cumbria as well as the main supply base for English invasions of Dumfriesshire and Galloway. A large force was therefore left behind to invest the castle, but no serious attempt was made to attack it.

Meanwhile, a second force was despatched south to invade County Durham. This was a much richer province than the northern counties and, moreover, it was the see of the hated Antony Bek. Bishop Bek, however, is said to have invoked the powers of St Cuthbert, patron of the diocese. At any rate divine intervention, in the form of a severe snowstorm on the Octave of St Martin (8 November), halted the Scots in their tracks. The importance of this storm has probably been exaggerated by the English chroniclers. The Scots had come as far south as they dared and, taking the storm as a portent of an early and harsh winter, deemed it more prudent to head for home. Hemingburgh would later reveal that it had been a close-run business. So severe had been the panic about the coming of the Scottish army that he doubted whether Bishop Bek could have mustered more than a hundred horse and three thousand foot to withstand the onslaught.

One other episode from this invasion deserves mention. During the first week of November, before the Scots turned their attention on Cumbria, they came upon Hexham where the priory, devastated in April 1296, still lay in ruin, abandoned by all except three canons who had returned to rebuild the oratory. When the Scots were observed approaching the monks took refuge in the ruined building but the soldiers pursued them and at spear-point demanded the treasures of the church. One of the monks defiantly replied, 'It is not long since you and your people carried off everything to your own country as if it were yours, and you know best where you hid it. We have gathered little since then, as you now see.'

At this juncture Wallace himself entered the chapel and rebuked his followers. Then he turned to the monks and asked them to celebrate mass. One of them began the service and everything went smoothly until the moment of elevating the host. At that point William reverently withdrew from the chapel to lay down his weapons, but as soon as he was out of sight the soldiers grabbed the celebrant and stripped him of his robes, chalice, candlesticks and crucifix, even the missal itself. A few moments later Wallace re-entered and found the trembling priest alone. Instantly he ordered that the perpetrators of this sacrilege be hunted down and decapitated. Hemingburgh, who reported this incident, comments that, naturally, the robbers were not apprehended, 'for they only pretended to search for them'. Wallace tried to protect the monks, telling them to stay close to him and admitting that he had little control over his men. Over the next two days, while his army was busy looting the surrounding countryside, Wallace kept the three monks close by him and when he left Hexham he granted a document to the priory giving it protection in the name of himself and Andrew de Moray, together with a safe-conduct pass for a canon of Hexham, his squire and two servants. These two documents were quoted verbatim by Hemingburgh and are of considerable interest, on account of the language in which they were couched and the terminology used:

> Andreas de Moravia and Willelmus Wallensis, Leaders of the army of the kingdom of Scotland, in the name of the excellent prince, Lord John, by the grace of God, the illustrious king of Scotland, with the consent of the community of the same kingdom, To all men of the said kingdom, to whom these present

letters shall come, Greeting: Know ye that in the name of the said king, we have taken the prior and convent of Hexceldsham in Northumberland, their lands, their men, and whole possessions, with all their goods, moveable and immoveable, under the firm peace and protection of the said lord the King, and ours; Wherefore we strictly forbid you to do them any hurt, mischief or injury whatsoever, in their persons, lands or goods, under penalty of forfeiture of your own goods and estates, to the said lord the King; or to kill them or any of them, under pain of losing life and members: These presents to remain in force for one year to come and no more. Given at Hexceldsham the seventh day of November.[5]

The safe-conduct follows much the same formula, enjoining everyone to 'bring them under safe custody unto us, so that no one of them, in their persons or their goods, may be in any way molested'. Interestingly, from that time onwards Hemingburgh drops his customary epithet of *ille latro* ('that brigand') when referring to Wallace.

Continuing to rove eastwards again, Wallace's marauding army advanced on Newcastle. On the march they came to the little town of Ritton whose inhabitants, believing themselves safe because they were on the south bank of the river, taunted the Scots with jeers and catcalls. A number of Scots, however, caused consternation by swimming the river and chasing off the foolish villagers before razing their houses. The people of Ritton fled southwards screaming, 'The Scots are coming!' and this spread the panic even further. The English of the northern counties were by now so thoroughly demoralised and in such abject terror that few men were prepared to remain behind to offer resistance. One of the exceptions was the garrison of Newcastle which marched out to do battle with the Scots, but wisely Wallace gave the castle a wide berth before turning north for home.

A lament, composed by the Prior of Alnwick shortly after the Scottish invasion, sheds some light on the devastation caused. It names the Northumbrian nobles slain in the course of the campaign (Vescy, Morley, Summerville and Bertram) and describes the burning of Alnwick in graphic detail. It also singles out Willelmus de Wallia as the leader of the army.[6]

According to Wyntoun and Bower, Wallace remained in England until Christmas, but the Lanercost Chronicle is probably more correct in stating that he and his troops recrossed the frontier on St Cecilia's Day (22 November). Their operations in England had netted a vast amount of booty of which, says Hemingburgh, 'they gave the Galloway men their share'. The western army continued to invest Carlisle Castle until 8 December, by which time they were running short of provisions and were glad to cross the Solway without realising their objective.

Shortly afterwards, however, the failure to reduce this English stronghold became painfully evident. A few days before Christmas, Sir Robert de Clifford launched a revenge attack from Carlisle on Annandale. This was a large operation by all accounts, involving several thousand men (though Hemingburgh's figure of twenty thousand was probably an exaggeration). These foot soldiers were a northern levy and were fundamentally untrained, although their ranks were stiffened by some hundred men-at-arms from Carlisle Castle. As soon as they had crossed the Solway this host was given a free hand to plunder at will, each man keeping booty for himself. There was a massacre of 308 Scots who were driven by cavalry into the swamp known to this day as the Lochar Moss, where they were cut down by the infantry. Ten towns and villages were burned before Clifford's men took a brief Christmas break.

Then they crossed the border again, resumed their depredations, and sacked the town of Annan in February 1298, even destroying a church in the town which was a daughter establishment of Gisburn (Walter of Hemingburgh's own church) which the Bruce family had presented to the monks. The Annandale incursions were intended as retaliation for Wallace's attack, but they may also have been designed to teach the Bruces a lesson. This vindictive action reinforces the view that the young Earl of Carrick at least had been in arms against England, though not involved at Stirling Bridge or in the subsequent operations in the northern counties of England. The destruction of the Gisburn church at Annan was as barbarous as anything perpetrated by the Scots at Hexham or elsewhere. Strangely enough, the Annandale raid has been either ignored by historians or brushed aside. One suspects that the atrocities committed on that occasion were every bit as horrendous as anything the Scots did in Cumbria or Northumberland, the sole difference being that there was no Scottish counterpart of Hemingburgh or the Lanercost Chronicle to put the matter in perspective. By the cruel and indiscriminate usury of war, the people unfortunate enough to inhabit these Border districts suffered out of all proportion.

8

GUARDIAN OF
SCOTLAND

To sla he sparyd noucht Inglismen;
Til Scottis he dyd gret profyt then;
The grettest lordis of oure land
Til hym he gart them be bowand:
Willy, nilly, all gart he
Bowsome till hys byddynd be;
And till hys byddyng, quha were noucht bown,
He tuk and put them in prisown.

WYNTOUN

SHORTLY after his triumphal return to Scotland, probably at Christmas 1297, William Wallace received the accolade. This much is stated by Fordun, adding that he was knighted by 'a certain distinguished Earl of the Scottish nation', without specifying who actually performed the ceremony. In the Middle Ages anyone of the nobility, from the king himself down to the humblest knight, could knight another, but in practice it was confined to royalty and the great magnates. There has been considerable speculation as to who knighted Wallace. James the Steward or Malcolm, Earl of Lennox, have been suggested; even the elder Earl of Carrick, although this seems less likely. One recent writer has stated the younger Earl of Carrick as a matter of fact.[1] By a process of elimination, only the future King Robert could have performed this ceremony. The Earl of Fife was a minor; Angus and March supported King Edward; Caithness, Ross and Sutherland were too remote; while Atholl and Menteith were serving with the English army in Flanders. This narrows down the possibles to the earls of Buchan, Strathearn, Lennox and Carrick. While the claim advanced for Lennox is usually based on his early friendship with Wallace (from his northern campaign), the ambivalent attitude of this magnate before and during the battle makes his role in conferring knighthood unlikely. Buchan and Strathearn, no matter which side they were currently on, were tainted by their pro-English collaboration in the months prior to the battle and their outlook thereafter was ambiguous. This left only the younger Earl of Carrick. It could be argued, of course, that his own position had been pretty ambivalent, but he had now come out firmly on the Scottish side. Besides, he was actually related to William Wallace. Wallace's Uncle Richard was married to the young earl's aunt and the link between the Bruces and the Wallaces was continued in the next generation by the marriage of Sir Duncan Wallace (a first cousin of the patriot) to Eleanora, Countess of Carrick, widow of Alexander Bruce, Earl of Carrick.

At any rate, the point is not material. Some of Wallace's detractors have questioned whether he was knighted at all, but this suggestion can easily be brushed aside. Documents and charters issued by Wallace from early in 1298 onwards append the Latin word *miles* to his name, while even English documents describe him by this title, and there is the evidence provided by a contemporary English political ballad which mentions the knighthood bestowed on him when he returned from England. Matthew of Westminster uses the *miles* epithet in describing Wallace's invasion of Northumberland and King Philip of France addressed Wallace as a knight in a missive of that year.

The earliest document still extant, in which William used the title himself, was the charter granted at Torphichen to Sir Alexander Scrymgeour on 29 March 1298. The Scrymgeours had been hereditary standard-bearers to the kings of Scotland since the reign of Alexander I, and the present knight had been one of Wallace's most loyal supporters since May 1297, distinguishing himself at the siege of Dundee, the town of which he was now formally appointed constable. The Latin charter speaks for itself. The preamble styles the grantor as 'Wilhelmes Wallays, Knight,

Guardian of the Kingdom of Scotland and Leader of its armies, in the name of the illustrious Prince, Lord John, by the Grace of God King of Scotland, by consent of the Community of that Kingdom'. The charter goes on to say that, 'by consent and assent of the nobles of the said kingdom' (*per consensum et assensum magnatum dicti regni*), six marks of land in the territory of Dundee were given to Scrymgeour, as well as the constabulary of the castle 'for faithful service and succour given to the said kingdom, in carrying the Royal Banner in the army of Scotland'. It ends 'In witness of which thing the common seal of the foresaid Kingdom of Scotland is affixed to the present writ.'[2] This charter is of such a nature that only the sovereign, or his representative, could pretend to issue, because it deals with the declared property of the crown and constitutes a right of constabulary which required a royal writ. It clearly states that Wallace was acting with the consent and assent of the magnates; previously he claimed to be acting on behalf of the community of the realm, so this marks a shift in power.

Blind Harry avers that Wallace was formally elected sole Guardian of Scotland at a council held at Perth, the very council which the Earl of March refused to attend. This would place the election immediately after Stirling Bridge and before the invasion of England; but Fordun and Wyntoun, the earliest authorities on the subject, claim that the election took place later, following the return from England. Bower, admittedly a much later authority, asserts that the election took place at a council convened in the Forest Kirk, identified as the Cistercian monastery near Carluke. Significantly, there are no hard and fast details regarding these councils, and it seems improbable that anything like a representative assembly, attended by the magnates, prelates and leading burgesses of the realm, could have been summoned in the chaotic circumstances of the period. And even if such a council had been convened, it is hard to imagine that the nobility of Scotland, far less the great magnates, would have been unanimous in electing such a young man, only recently knighted, as their sole ruler. Burton concluded that Wallace's elevation had 'the consent in some shape or other of the burghs and other portions of the Estates', but Lord Hailes summed up the situation admirably: 'That he deserved the office is certain. How he obtained it, must remain for ever problematical.' The truth may be that, being the right man in the right place at the right time, Wallace simply took the reins of government into his hands, and with a triumphant army backing him solidly, there was no one, magnate or otherwise, who dared oppose him.

Be that as it may, we have incontrovertible evidence that Wallace was issuing documents as joint leader of Scotland (without reference to the King himself) from 11 October 1297, then as joint leader in the name of King John (7 November), and now as Guardian. There were no references to Andrew de Moray after the document of 7 November, and it is presumed that he died about that time. If Barron is correct in his surmise that the wounded leader was borne back to Moray to die, he may have been dead already by 7 November; news from Moray would not have travelled very fast to northern England, especially with Wallace conducting a campaign of such rapid movement. All that can be said with certainty is that, sometime between November 1297 and March 1298 Wallace took, or obtained, the title of Guardian, whether by formal election or common consent cannot be determined. One thing is certain, however; he now had possession of the great seal of Scotland, for the Scrymgeour charter was thus appended. Incidentally, the grant to Scrymgeour was later confirmed by Robert Bruce, who alluded to his predecessor as *Lord* William Wallace, a title which Wallace himself never assumed.

That Wallace was no longer merely the leader of the army but supreme governor of Scotland soon became evident. Officially he was styled *Gardein du Reaume* in Norman French or *Custos Regni* in Latin. Wyntoun refers to him as *Wardane* of Scotland. Technically he was a regent or viceroy, always scrupulous in claiming to act on behalf of King John (still enjoying easy captivity in the south of England); in fact he had dictatorial powers, and he needed them badly if he was to achieve his political goals as well as consolidate his military gains.

This is arguably the most important phase in Wallace's turbulent career; unfortunately it is also the least known, due to a paucity of archival material. In default of any transactions or deliberations of a council, we can only look at the circumstances of Scotland at the beginning of 1298. We have a young man, a giant of a man in spirit as well as physique, the man who has not only trounced the most formidable army in Europe but also carried the war into the territory of one of the most powerful nations of the period. He has just taught the enemy a bloody lesson and, more to the point, he has returned laden not only with the material riches of the northern counties but large stocks of grain, cattle and other foodstuffs — manna from heaven to a nation on the brink of starvation. This is a young man whose innate modesty shines forth, a selfless patriot manifestly working solely for the good of his people.

In stark contrast is the self-serving, double-dealing nobility, some of whom had changed sides so often that it is difficult to keep track of their momentary allegiance. These earls, barons and knights, whom the common people had become accustomed to regard as their natural leaders, had been thoroughly discredited over the past decade. Some of them, like Sir William Douglas, Sir Andrew de Moray of Petty and the Earl of Ross, were in English prisons; others, like Sir Alexander Comyn, brother of the Constable of Scotland, had been conscripted into the English army now fighting in Flanders; some, like the Black Comyn, were at liberty but living under close supervision in England, or, like the Red Comyn (his son) afraid to step out of line on account of their closest relatives held hostage in England. There were those Scottish magnates, like Patrick, Earl of March, and the constable himself, who chose to support Edward of their own volition, and there were those magnates who were, in fact, more English than Scots anyway. In this category came the elder Earl of Carrick who, despite his marriage to a Celtic heiress, Marjorie of Carrick, was probably born at Writtle near Chelmsford, the son of a great magnate whose lands in Annandale were insignificant compared to his vast estates in Essex and Yorkshire. Gilbert de Umfraville, the Earl of Angus, was the son of a Northumbrian knight, had been the ward of Simon de Montfort, Earl of Leicester, and became a powerful English baron.

All of these men had sworn fealty to Edward, not once but several times. Indeed, their oaths had been given, and broken, so often that one wonders what reliance could be put on them. By contrast, William Wallace was the one outstanding figure in the Wars of Independence who had never taken the oath of fealty to Edward; his assertion to that effect was all that he managed to utter at the farce of a trial held in 1305, yet it was as a traitor that he was tried and condemned.

Apart from the fact that Scotland's natural leaders had been hamstrung by their position in regard to Edward, they were also divided among themselves. The powerful Comyn family were closely related to King John, but if they ever wavered in their allegiance to him it was to further their own claim to the empty throne. For this reason the Comyns and the Bruces were seldom able to co-operate. The wheeling and dealing between these factions and those who supported now one, now the other, are positively Byzantine in their complexity; but when they were not conniving and conspiring against each other they were undermining the one effective ruler the Scots now possessed. Fordun has a chapter entitled 'Regarding the Conspiracy of the Magnates against the Guardian' in which he represents the magnates as saying 'We will not have this man to reign over us', and denounces the 'stupid folly of the foolish' and their 'insidious envy' with many biblical parallels. 'So, through envy was brought about the downfall of the clergy, the ruin of the people, and the destruction of the people.'[3]

Given such a pernicious background, it is nothing short of a miracle that Wallace was able to govern his unruly country and achieve as much as he did in the pitifully brief space of time allotted to him. In his political dealings he was to exhibit that same decisiveness and ruthlessness that had marked his military career. He had precious little time for feudal factiousness and scant respect for rank and precedence. Fordun has a most revealing passage which probably explains why only the most altruistic of the magnates gave him their support:

> So Wallace overthrew the English on all sides; and gaining strength daily, he in a short time, by force and by dint of his prowess, brought all the magnates of Scotland under his sway, whether they would or not. Such of the magnates, moreover, as did not thankfully obey his commands, he took and browbeat, and handed over to custody, until they should utterly submit to his good pleasure.

Even if this account of Wallace's treatment of the magnates were only partly correct, it would well explain why not one of the Scottish earls ever gave him wholehearted support. Jealousy alone estranged them from him. In Lord Hailes's words, 'His elevation wounded their pride; his great services reproached their inactivity in the public cause.'

Nevertheless, it is significant that, when the magnates of Scotland were summoned, in the name of King Edward, to a parliament at York on 14 January 1298, not one of them heeded the command. Failure to turn up to that assembly led to their automatically being branded as public enemies. That the negative response of the magnates to Edward's command was so all-embracing seems further evidence of the grip which Wallace had on Scotland at this time. The euphoria of Stirling Bridge had been reinforced by the successful campaign through northern England and it has been suggested that the magnates sensed a new power growing up around them which they had to take into account. Edward, on the other hand, was still on the Continent, and seemed the lesser of two evils. But if the magnates failed to attend the York parliament it was only as part of their temporising policy. For the moment they would play a waiting game.

On the appointed date the magnates of England assembled at York which, for the duration of the ensuing war (a period of six years), would remain Edward's temporary capital, the Exchequer and Bench and other departments of state being transferred there. The Earl of Surrey seems to have taken the chair, as Edward's representative, but all the great earls and barons of the country were present on that august occasion, and included the Earl of Gloucester (Edward's son-in-law), the Earl Marshal, the great Constable, the earls of Arundel and Warwick, the redoubtable Henry Lord Percy who had taken the Scottish surrender at Irvine, and such rising stars as John de Wake and John de Segrave, who would play a prominent part in the execution of Wallace seven years later. It is only fair to point out that it was with the greatest difficulty that English magnates were persuaded to attend. Although they put up the impression of solidarity at York they were, in fact, seething with discontent at the heavy burdens placed upon them by Edward's foreign adventures, and were only won round when Edward sent confirmation of Magna Carta and the Charter of the Forest from Flanders.

While Edward was absent on the Continent the regency was nominally in the hands of the sixteen-year-old Prince of Wales. Young Edward lacked the moral strength of his father and was already showing evidence of those traits and character defects that would eventually topple him from his throne. In what was virtually a power vacuum, the rebelliousness of the barons came dangerously close to open revolt. King Edward's two principal lieutenants, the Constable Hereford and the Earl Marshal Norfolk, openly defied their master and denounced their fealty. The Church refused to pay the tax levied by Edward for the prosecution of his foreign wars — half a year's income — and also repudiated its corporate fealty.

Edward was in no position to do much about Scotland, although certain measures were taken which indicate the situation. Orders were given for the replacement of the Scottish prelates by Englishmen, evidence of the complicity of the Scots clergy in the resistance movement. The dismissal of the Lord of Annandale from the governorship of Carlisle in October 1297 has already been mentioned. His successor, the Bishop of Carlisle, subsequently received orders from Westminster, promulgated on 14 November, to prepare to receive the young Earl of Carrick into the King's peace, but there is no evidence that Robert Bruce complied with this and, indeed, Clifford's raid into Annandale demonstrates the opposite. Meanwhile, there were further imposts and levies with a view to raising the money for the forthcoming expedition against the Scots. On 8 December 1297 a writ was addressed to the Archbishop of York for raising funds in his province for 'an immediate expedition against the Scots, our enemies and rebels',[4] and two days later a writ was addressed to the people of Wales for the levying of troops. On the same date Earl Warenne was reappointed commander of the army, by a writ addressed to all the earls, barons, knights and others 'beyond the Trent'. Further writs, dated 13, 18 and 19 December, made arrangements for the payment of the Welsh troops going into Scotland.

The *Scotichronicon* is the sole authority for a curious story that Edward even sent a furious letter to Wallace himself at this time, saying that 'if the king himself had remained in his kingdom, Wallace would not have dared to make such an attempt' — an allusion to the audacious raids into northern England — and warning him of dire reprisals if he should invade England again. Bower has Wallace retorting cheerfully that he intended to be back in England again after Easter. This anecdote seems highly unlikely, given the character of the protagonists. Edward would surely never have deigned to communicate with a man whom he regarded contemptuously as an outlaw and a brigand; nor would Wallace have so flippantly made such a challenge, especially at a time when he must have been only too well aware of the prodigious preparations being made to invade Scotland.

When the Scots magnates failed to attend the York parliament, the assembly was put back for eight days to enable the recalcitrant earls to change their mind. The second assembly was summoned to appear at Newcastle, with a view to assessing the potential strength of the army required for the invasion. On 22 January, therefore, the English magnates reassembled and estimated that the army now consisted of 'two thousand chosen horsemen, armed cap-a-pie, of other horsemen more than twelve hundred, and of foot soldiers, including Welsh, more than a hundred thousand, while, as they advanced to the frontier, every day added to the numbers both of horse and foot.' With this formidable army, the largest so far to take the field against the Scots, Earl Warenne, atoning for his precipitate flight from Stirling the previous September, mounted a counter-offensive. He crossed the border and made straight for Roxburgh which was on the brink of capitulating. The castle had been under siege for several months, but now that the Scots had brought up some kind of giant catapult it was no longer so impregnable. At the approach of the English army, however, the besieging Scots melted away. Warenne made a cautious and leisurely advance as far as Kelso; but there, for some inexplicable reason, he came to a halt. It has been suggested that Wallace, with a hand-picked force of light cavalry, hovered round the extended lines of the English army in such a manner as deterred Warenne from pushing forward into the hills.

Instead, the English army followed the Tweed down to Berwick early in February, intent on dislodging the troops under Henry de Haliburton. As at Roxburgh, the Scots vanished at the approach of the army; Warenne relieved the garrison of the castle which had withstood a three-month siege and which, starving and diseased, had been on the point of surrendering to the

Scots. It was there that a letter from King Edward caught up with Warenne, saying that he intended to return to England shortly and directing the earl to take no further action against the rebellious Scots until he arrived to take over the supreme command. It is probable that Edward had grave doubts about Warenne's ability to defeat the brilliant young general who had so soundly beaten him a few months previously. The costs of maintaining such a vast army in the field, especially in the depths of winter, must have been exorbitant, so Warenne stood down the levies from the northern shires, retaining only the troops from the more distant counties, as well as the Welsh contingent.

During the winter of 1297–98 Wallace had also been busy with administrative matters. First and foremost, he organised Scotland into military districts and devised a plan for raising levies of all able-bodied males over the age of sixteen. Over every four men was set a fifth known as a quaternion; over every nine was set a tenth (decurion); over every nineteen was set a twentieth; and so on, in hundreds (centurions) and thousands (chiliarchs), so that a proper chain of command was established. This system, with its terminology derived from classical Rome and Greece, cut right across the previous feudal arrangement and was clearly intended to limit the power of the landowning classes — a matter which could not have endeared him to the so-called 'natural leaders'. Bower also states that Wallace caused a gallows to be erected in every town, burgh and village as a mute threat to those who failed to comply with the conscription regulations. That this was no mere threat was demonstrated by the fact that when Wallace discovered that some burgesses of Aberdeen had not turned up, he paid a flying visit to that town with a small body of hand-picked men, 'and at Aberdeen and in its neighbourhood punished with a hanging those who had stayed away from the army without excuse'. Bower adds, 'He returned to the army more quickly than you would believe,' to get on with the business of carrying the war into the enemy's own country.

Some attention was also given to drilling the foot soldiers, so that large bodies of men could move in close order without colliding. At this time Wallace invented the schiltrom, forerunner of the square which was to dominate British infantry tactics till the end of the nineteenth century. His foot soldiers were armed with formidable spears, twelve feet in length, and the men were drilled until they were able to form a compact mass with spears bristling outwards in all directions, a fearful obstacle to the English cavalry. That the Scots infantry were able to manœuvre in close order in a perfectly drilled manner and keep their formation was put forward by Bower as the reason why the English army, confronted by this well-disciplined force at Stainmore in Cumbria, chose to back down and withdraw as best it could without putting the matter to the test. When the Scots wished to charge the retreating English, Wallace forbade this on pain of death,

> saying that in the course of other struggles between the kingdoms it was the prepared plan for a splendid victory to wait until the arrogant king of England along with his royal forces and fearsome commanders turned tail before a few commons and patriots of Scotland on land which he claimed as his, although the sword had not yet been drawn on the other side.

Wallace also made a valiant attempt to overcome the insurmountable problem of feudalism, a concept which was essentially alien to the Scottish temperament. The power of the magnates and knights derived from their military service, but from their ranks were also drawn the sheriffs and constables, the officials and administrators, while many of the higher clergy were recruited from the lower echelons of the nobility. Now Wallace began appointing base-born men, and the sons of minor gentry like himself, purely on their own merits.

So too in matters spiritual, he engineered the appointment of William de Lamberton to the powerful see of St Andrews. This cleric belonged to a family which had settled in Berwickshire towards the end of the eleventh century and had taken its name from the hamlet in the parish of Mordington near Berwick. In 1292 Lamberton was chancellor of Glasgow Cathedral and was thus a protégé of Robert Wishart. Although he swore fealty to Edward in 1296 he was one of the first clerics to come out in open support of Wallace the following year. This support was now repaid by Wallace nominating Lamberton to the bishopric left vacant by the death of the pro-English William

Fraser. On Fraser's death, however, another strong adherent of Edward, William Comyn, brother of the Earl of Buchan, had been nominated by the Culdees to the bishopric and had actually set out for Rome in person to seek confirmation from Pope Boniface VIII. Wallace, exerting all his diplomatic skills, succeeded in overturning Comyn's nomination and getting his own man elected instead. The Pope subsequently confirmed Lamberton's appointment and he was consecrated at Rome on 12 June 1298. These facts were recounted to the Pope in 1306 by none other than King Edward himself, when seeking to have Lamberton's appointment nullified.[5] Incidentally, the Pope's confirmation of this election was, on 17 June 1298, addressed cautiously to 'his dearest son in Christ ———— illustrious King of Scotland', the name of the monarch being left blank.[6]

Having secured the appointment of his own nominee, Wallace made a clean sweep of the Scottish church, ejecting all the English priests whom Edward had presented to Scottish benefices. This ecclesiastical purge received the heartiest endorsement from the Scottish clerical historians, but naturally was vociferously condemned by the monkish chroniclers of England who accused Wallace of the murder of priests and nuns (a charge specifically raised against him at his trial in 1305). It is not improbable that many English clergy were forcibly ejected, and that some of them were murdered in the heat of the moment, but this was an unfortunate aberration and no part of Wallace's official policy.

Most of Wallace's energy in the early months of 1298, however, went into the direction of the war. Once invasion was imminent Wallace gave orders for the destruction of the towns in Berwickshire and the Lothians. The population of this vast area was evacuated north of the Forth and the countryside laid waste. This scorched-earth policy was ruthlessly calculated to deny shelter and sustenance to the invader. King Edward returned from Flanders, landing at Sandwich on 14 March, and lost no time in going to York to take over the personal supervision of the invasion plans. Nothing was to be left to chance, and Edward's planning was meticulous. Organising an expedition on the scale he envisaged took some time; but it is clear that there were diversionary raids and skirmishes, testing the strength of the Scottish defences and the will of the people to resist, before the main onslaught. During the lull before the storm, for example, Sir Aymer de Valence, Earl of Pembroke, with Sir John Siward, son of the Earl of March, crossed directly from Flanders with a substantial force and landed in Fife with the intention of splitting the Scots in two. This expedition at first met with little opposition and laid waste a great deal of Fife before it ran into Wallace and his army on 12 June, in the forest of Blackironside or Blackearnside, near Abernethy. From the nature of that locality it appears that the engagement was something of a running fight rather than a pitched battle, but the result was the annihilation of the invaders.

On this occasion the Scots suffered some grave losses. Sir Duncan Balfour, Sheriff of Fife, and perhaps Sir Christopher Seton, were among the casualties.[7] Sir John Graham was badly wounded, and one of Blind Harry's tenderest passages describes how Wallace, instead of taking a much-needed rest from the fighting in the fierce heat of a summer noon, carried water in his helmet from a nearby stream for the relief of his wounded men.

The actual invasion of Scotland was scheduled for 25 June. From the middle of March onwards, elaborate plans were set in train. Realising the problems of feeding such a large army, while fighting over terrain which the Scots had denuded, Edward set up a depot at Carlisle where provisions were to be brought over from Ireland. A large quantity of shipping was stationed at ports along the east coast of England for the purpose of bringing supplies to Berwick and Edinburgh as and when these towns fell into English hands again. A parliament was held at York on 25 May and again the Scottish magnates were summoned but 'neither came nor sent'. Two days later Edward issued orders to the sheriffs to have the county levies mustered at Roxburgh no later than 23 June. On 28 May he appointed Patrick, Earl of March, as captain of Berwick Castle. During the days immediately before launching the invasion Edward, in a rare show of piety, visited the shrines of St John of Beverley and other local saints, invoking the support of God in what he now perceived as almost a crusade.

Edward reached Roxburgh on 24 June. By this time, according to Hemingburgh, the English army consisted of three thousand heavy cavalry, four thousand light horse and eighty thousand foot. Interestingly, the vast majority of the infantry consisted of paid troops recruited in Ireland and Wales, rather than feudal levies from the English counties. Riding at the head of this vast army, Edward advanced through the Lothians to Kirkliston. As he went, he beheld only scenes of devastation, the burned-out ruins of farms and villages, bereft of crops and live-stock. Already, as may be imagined, the English columns stretched back towards the Borders and were vulnerable to the hit-and-run tactics in which the Scots delighted. Moreover, the English army was frequently assailed by flying columns based in the castle of Dirleton near the coast of East Lothian, together with Tantallon between the Lammermoor Hills and the sea, and Hailes north of the Tyne. Dirleton's twelfth-century stronghold was to impede the progress of another English invasion, 350 years later, until it was demolished by Oliver Cromwell. On the earlier occasion, however, the task of taking out this thorn in the English flank was deputed to Bishop Bek. This time the storm-troops of St Cuthbert's were no match for the gallant defenders who fought off the attack. Dirleton and Tantallon were formidable fortresses and, without siege-engines, the warrior-bishop had little hope of reducing them. The situation was exacerbated by the fact that Bek's troops were short of provisions and were obliged to scavenge for peas and beans in the ruined fields. In desperation Bek sent one of his lieutenants, Sir John Fitz-Marmaduke, back to Edward asking for reinforcements. According to Hemingburgh the King addressed Sir John sarcastically, 'Go back and tell the Bishop that in so far as he is a bishop he is a good man, but that his goodness is out of place for this task.' Edward's implacable hatred of the Scots was chillingly illustrated in the orders to Fitz-Marmaduke:

> You are a cruel man, and I have several times rebuked you for being too cruel, and for the pleasure you take in the death of your enemies. But go now and exert all your frightfulness, and I shall not even blame you, but praise you. And mind you do not see my face again until these three castles are burnt.

Faced with such uncompromising earnestness, Sir John enquired, 'And how am I to do this, my lord King, since it is so exceedingly difficult?'

'Go,' replied Edward with mounting exasperation. 'You will do it by doing it [*quia faciens facies*], and you will give me your promise that you will do it.'

With this not particularly helpful answer ringing in his ears, Sir John rode back to the bishop. Fortunately for Bek's forces, three English supply vessels called at nearby Dunbar and the troops, their bellies full, renewed the onslaught. After two days of fierce hand-to-hand combat, they forced the Scots to surrender on condition that their lives would be spared. The other castles were then attacked, but were found to have been abandoned, whereupon they were consigned to the flames as Edward had commanded.

While Bek's men tackled the three castles on their flank, Edward's army rested for several days at Kirkliston, a village ten miles west of Edinburgh on the banks of the River Almond which separates West Lothian from Midlothian. The English were now virtually in the heart of Scotland and could strike in any direction at will, once it became apparent where Wallace and his army were to be found. Further advance was hampered by lack of provisions. Edward's supply ships on the east coast had been held up by contrary winds and until vital provisions could reach them the vast army was on short rations. It is significant that, on 20 July, shortly before the confrontation of armies near Falkirk, the Scots attacked the great supply base at Carlisle with the intention of rupturing the flow of provisions from Ireland. The Scots besieged Carlisle Castle for two weeks and devastated the surrounding town. The blockade of Carlisle had the desired effect, for thereafter Edward was to get no supplies from that source.

As usual, Wallace was having to rely on the common people for the bulk of his support. Hemingburgh attributes the lukewarm attitude of the Scottish magnates to the fact that Wallace 'was deemed base-born', despite his recent knighthood. Nevertheless, among his adherents could be numbered Macduff of Fife. The position of James the Steward was as ambivalent as ever, although Edward's doubts regarding his loyalty led to one of the Steward's castles being seized on 31 August and handed over to Sir Alexander de Lindesay as a reward for his services. On the other hand, the Steward's younger brother, Sir John Stewart of Bonkill in Berwickshire, contributed a contingent of

archers from the Borders, together with a company of foot soldiers from the Stewart lands in Bute. Such cavalry as Wallace
could muster was under the command of John the Red Comyn,
nephew of Balliol and destined to dubious immortality as the
man whom Bruce slew at Dumfries in 1306. Sir John Graham,
having recovered from wounds sustained at Blackearnside, was
back in the saddle in time for the main attack. Sir Robert Boyd
had raised a sizable force from the Kilmarnock and Loudoun
area. There was also Sir Nichol de Rutherfurd, a knight with
substantial estates in Northumberland as well as Berwickshire.
His English lands had been seized by Edward in 1296 and thereafter Rutherfurd had adhered to the Scottish cause. Last, but by
no means least, there was the young Earl of Carrick whose loyalty was not something that either Wallace or Edward could rely
upon. But in addition to harrying the Annandale estates of the
elder Bruce the previous winter, Edward now foreclosed on
Bruce debts which went back to the time of the young earl's
grandfather, and seized over six hundred and fifty pounds
worth of goods from his Essex estates, in retaliation for Bruce's
failure to hand over little Marjorie as a hostage.[8] The sequestration of his Essex property seems to have been the last straw, for
now Bruce threw in his lot with Wallace and held the castle of
Ayr for the Scots. From this stronghold he could control shipping in the Firth of Clyde and prevent supply vessels from
Ireland getting to Greenock and Glasgow.

It must be emphasised, however, that Wallace's support
came from the grass-roots — the squires and bonnet lairds, the
yeomen, farmers, cottars and peasantry, the burgesses, craftsmen and labourers of the towns and villages, the little people
who answered the call to arms not because of some great magnate's bidding but because a nobler cause was at stake, the freedom to live without alien interference. It has been surmised that
the bulk of Wallace's support came from Lothian and the
Borders, whose populace had been displaced by the English
advance, and who therefore had most to gain from a Scottish
victory. Hemingburgh frequently makes a distinction between
Scots and Gallovidians, *Scoti et Galwalenses*. The similarity
between the Latin name for the latter and Wallace's own surname in that language leads one to suppose that the term was
loosely applied to the people of the south-west of Scotland gen-

erally, rather than to Galloway in particular, even although ethnically there was little now to distinguish between the Strathclyde people of Cymric stock and the rest of the inhabitants of Scotland.

Hemingburgh's fine distinction between Scots and Gallovidians is echoed in the metrical chronicle of Robert de Brunne, who says that Wallace's army was composed of troops from Scotland, Galloway, the March and the Isles. In this context the March signified the area around Dunbar and hence probably the Lothians in general, while the Isles may have been a reference to John Stewart's Butemen. Thus Scotland implied the central regions bounded by the Forth and Tay. Some of the Highlanders whom Andrew de Moray commanded at Stirling may have continued in Wallace's service, and the men of Fife, by and large, rallied under Macduff; but in general the Scottish army that took the field in the summer of 1298 was recruited south of the Highland line.

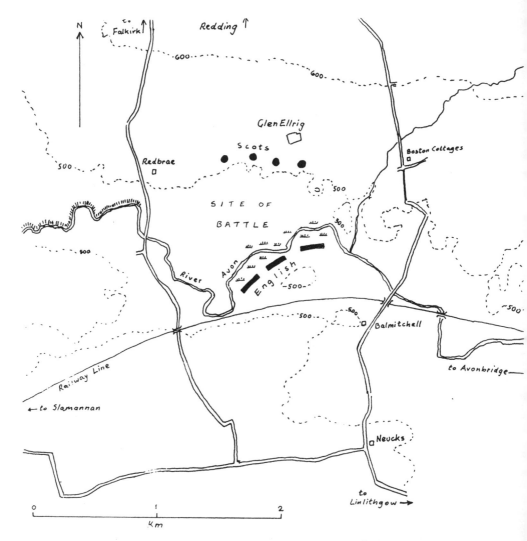

N

to Falkirk

Redding ↑

600

600

Glen Ellrig

Scots

Boston Cottages

Redbrae

500

500

500

SITE OF

BATTLE

River Avon

English

500

500

500

500

500

Balmitchell

Railway Line

← to Slamannan

to Avonbridge

Neucks

to Linlithgow →

0   1   2

Km

FALKIRK   1298

9

FALKIRK

He was an ogre of unspeakable depravity who skinned his
prisoners alive, burned babies and forced the nuns to dance
naked for him.

ECCLESIASTICAL PROPAGANDA AGAINST WALLACE IN THE SUMMER OF 1298,
IN *FLORES HISTORIARUM*, II, 578

OPINIONS differ as to the size and composition of the English
army which now turned northwards to engage the Scots in
what was hoped would be the final showdown. The traditional
view, based on contemporary chronicles, places Edward at the
head of 87,500 men. Hemingburgh's estimate of seven thousand horse of all kinds is probably not far out, while Wallace
could barely muster a thousand horse, and probably much less.
Sir Charles Oman (1898) considered, however, that the size of
the infantry had been greatly exaggerated and put their total at
little more than the horsemen. This reduced figure was based
on the assumption that the infantry was composed almost
entirely of Irish and Welsh volunteers, attracted by the prospect
of plunder, and that Edward had not considered the expedition
important enough to call out the levies from the English counties. This view is strangely at variance with the figures reported
by historians writing close to the event itself, not to mention the
documentary evidence of writs summoning those very levies.
Bishop Bek took the field with a force of at least fifteen hundred

men, many of them well mounted. In addition, both Hemingburgh and the anonymous writer of the Harleian manuscript make specific mention of an additional contingent from Edward's French fief of Gascony. This contingent, almost all on horseback, was well armed and battle-hardened, and was considered a valuable addition to the task-force. The various figures were confined to fighting men and took no account of the vast throng of camp-followers, sutlers and smiths, baggage-masters and mule-drivers which accompanied the host. In Edward's wake trailed an immense baggage-train bringing everything imaginable, from the latest siege-engines and heavy artillery, devices for bridging rivers and scaling walls, endless wagons bearing arms and ammunition and an abundance of war materials of all kinds.

The one thing which seems to have been in short supply that summer was food. Either Edward's planners had misjudged the quantities required to feed such a large army, or they had miscalculated the ability of this army to live off the land. As they penetrated deeper and deeper into the heart of Scotland they found to their dismay scarcely a blade of grass to feed the horses, far less anything to sustain the troops. More and more, therefore, Edward had to depend on his supply ships and these, from bad weather and Scottish privateers, were few and far between. When Bishop Bek and his troops caught up with the main army at Kirkliston they found the soldiery desperately short of food and beginning to suffer as a consequence. When a few ships succeeded in entering the Firth of Forth it was found that they had brought only a small quantity of food, but two hundred casks of wine. In a desperate bid to boost the morale of his troops Edward ordered that the wine be distributed among the men. The Welshmen, imbibing on empty stomachs, got roaring drunk and went on the rampage during the night. There was no love lost between the Welsh and the English and a violent brawl ensued. When the corps of chaplains tried to separate the combatants no fewer than eighteen priests paid with their lives. The English men-at-arms avenged the clerics by attacking the Welshmen with such ferocity that eighty of the latter were killed and the rest of the contingent driven out of the encampment. In the cold light of dawn the whole camp clamoured against the drunken Taffies, and Edward was informed that the mutinous Welsh were about to desert to the Scots.

'What do I care if my enemies join my enemies?' asked the King contemptuously. 'Let them go where they like; with God's help I shall be revenged on both of them in one day.'

The Welshmen did not desert, but their loyalty was sorely tried and the English treated them with suspicion thereafter. There was no doubt that, if there was a repeat of Stirling Bridge, the Welsh would desert to a man. This ugly incident did nothing for the morale of the army as a whole. Gloom settled over it and there was angry muttering in the ranks. Such an experienced warrior as Edward no doubt sensed the mood of his men and now even he had doubts about the venture. For the first time in his long military career he began to lose heart, and in this depressed state he ordered a withdrawal to Edinburgh until stores could be replenished.

Things looked bad for the English. They had had a long and fatiguing march from the Borders through a ruined countryside, they were starving and baffled by the non-appearance of the Scottish army which seemed to melt away before the advance. As the process of demoralisation intensified, time was clearly on the side of the Scots. All that Wallace had to do, it seemed, was to wait. The further the English were drawn into the centre of Scotland, the longer would become their supply lines. Eventually they would be starved into retreating, and then the Scots could fall upon them, picking off the stragglers at will. It was the tactic for which Wallace was best suited. He was well aware of the parlous state of the enemy; if he bided his time, famine and the collapse of morale would defeat the English for him.

At dawn on 21 July a scout, sent out by the Earl of March, returned to report that Wallace's army was only eighteen miles away, in the Forest of Selkirk and making ready to attack the English as soon as they showed the first sign of retreating. This was the first positive sighting of the elusive Scots and it filled Edward with elation. 'God be praised!' he cried, 'who has brought me out of every strait! They shall have no need to fol-low me, for I shall go to meet them, and on this very day.'[1] The troops were ordered to buckle on their equipment and strike camp immediately. Edward mounted his destrier and personal-ly exhorted the men. By nine o'clock that morning the entire army was on the move in the direction of Falkirk. The destination was kept secret from the rank and file and there was a great deal of conjecture as to the King's intentions. The army moved slowly, for the infantrymen, proceeding at less than three miles an hour, set the pace. Night was falling as they approached Linlithgow and bivouacked in the fields some way south of that town, remaining in combat readiness with their arms at their sides and using their shields as pillows. The horses were not picketed in lines as was the normal practice, but each was tethered by its master and, as fodder was lacking, 'tasted nothing but hard iron' in Hemingburgh's colourful words, alluding to the bits.

Edward's page fell asleep and therefore failed to control his master's great war-horse which, restless from lack of fodder, trampled on the sleeping monarch. This is the generally accepted story, although the chronicler Walsingham says that a false alarm that the Scots were mounting a night attack panicked the King's horse as he was trying to mount it, and a hefty kick broke two of his ribs. Hemingburgh, on the other hand, states that the alarm was raised by the King's cries of pain, and spread by the rumour that Edward had been seriously injured. Both chroniclers agree that the tumult was only quelled when King Edward courageously mounted the high-backed saddle and gave immediate orders for the advance to continue, although it was still dark. He appreciated that positive action was the only way to relieve the tension.

The army skirted Linlithgow before dawn broke and then continued on about six or seven miles. A brief glimpse of spears glinting in the early morning sun betrayed the presence of a Scottish cavalry patrol on a far-off ridge, but by the time the lightly armed skirmishers reached the spot the Scots had vanished. Edward deduced that the Scottish army could not be far away, and called a halt to give his troops a chance to catch their breath. It was the Feast of St Mary Magdalene and Edward, who was always great on the outward show of piety, had a portable altar set up so that the Bishop of Durham could celebrate mass. By the time this drum-head service was concluded the sun was well up, and now it became clear that the Scottish army was deployed in battle order, on the lower slope of a hillside about a mile ahead.

Why, oh why, when his guerrilla tactics had worked so well until now, did Wallace stand and offer pitched battle to such a large and well-armed army? It seems clear that this was never Wallace's intention, but his plans were gravely upset by the night advance of the English. Whether, in spite of this, the Scots might still have withdrawn as the English advanced, is a matter for speculation. In the more open country around Falkirk, however, the opportunity to make an orderly withdrawal was very limited. The retreat in good order of the Scottish army, composed largely of foot soldiers, would have been exceedingly difficult in the immediate presence of a greatly superior force, with powerful cavalry which might easily have pursued and run them down. This probability would have occurred to Wallace and for this reason he reluctantly gave orders to deploy his troops in battle formation. Although this decision had to be taken hurriedly, the ground was well chosen and, in the circumstances, surprisingly well prepared for the expected onslaught.

If the precise location of the Battle of Stirling Bridge has been the subject of some debate, then the site of Falkirk has been much more controversial. Despite the name by which it is commonly known, the battle was some distance from the town. The majority of chroniclers speak of a battle at or near Falkirk: 'a field called Fawkirke' or 'on one side of Fawkirke'.[2] Only Matthew of Westminster placed it specifically 'on the plain which is called Falkirk',[3] but even this has been variously interpreted by more recent historians. The featureless carse around the town contained none of the prominent landmarks which pinpointed the battles of Stirling Bridge and Bannockburn. Some speak rather vaguely of a site between Linlithgow and Falkirk, but the traditional view was that the location was north of the medieval town. The compiler of the Falkirk section in the first *Statistical Account*, for example, says that the battle took place 'somewhat more than half a mile north from Falkirk', adding that the moss which covered the Scottish front was now drained by the Forth and Clyde Canal. Sir Charles Oman, however, put it about two miles *south* of Falkirk, with Darnrig Moss as the marshy ground protecting the Scottish front. This supposition was based on Blind Harry's statement that the English camp on the night before the battle was on Slamannan Muir, 'south from Falkirk, a little above the toun'.

The ridge on which the Scottish horsemen rode when the English army first saw them was traditionally supposed to be at Redding, about three miles south-east of Falkirk, where a large rock was known locally as Wallace's Stone. Similarly, the land on the north side of the town, between the railway station and the Forth and Clyde Canal, was known for centuries as Campfield and Graemesmuir, the former in allusion to the battlefield and the latter in tribute to Sir John Graham who fell in the battle. Today this district is known as Grahamstown in his memory. Before this area was extensively developed in the middle of the nineteenth century the ground was very marshy, and therefore accorded with the morass or bog that protected the Scottish front. Similarly Bainsford, another part of the modern town, is said to have derived its name from the English knight Sir Brian de Jay who, in one version of the battle, was killed when he tried to traverse the extreme right of this morass. Inevitably, old inhabitants could point to a couple of ancient yew trees on the east side of Graham Street which, according to hallowed tradition, marked the very spot where the good Sir John was slain. This was apparently confirmed by the English chronicles which stated that many of the Scots were drowned in a river as they fled from the battlefield, and the River Carron does, indeed, flow not far to the north. From all this circumstantial evidence and scraps of tradition it was generally concluded that the battle had been fought over what is now Grahamstown.

This tradition was more or less accepted until the late 1930s, when it was challenged by James Fergusson who conjectured that the battle took place about four miles south of Falkirk, on the River Avon, at a point midway between the modern villages of Slamannan and Avonbridge, the likeliest spot seemingly just below the house of Glenellrig.[4] This conjecture was based on Hemingburgh, who derived his account of the battle from eyewitnesses. Hemingburgh states that the Scots were drawn up *in campo duro, et in latere uno cuiusdam montiscilii juxta Fawkirke* (on hard ground and on one side of a hillock near Falkirk). In itself, this is too vague, but taken in conjunction with other evidence the location becomes clearer. When Edward hesitated before attacking, the barons objected on the ground that it was unsafe, there being 'nothing between the two armies but a very small stream' (*non est nisi torrens permodicus*). When the knights charged they found what they had not noticed before, that the ground along the waterside was boggy and impassable — Hemingburgh's pithy expression was *lacus bituminosus*. They therefore wheeled off to the flank to find a way round, the first line to the west and the second to the east. Fergusson was the first historian to take these details into account. They proved that in front of the Scots as they stood in battle array were, first hard sloping ground, then a small river, running east and west, with a deep moss on its southward bank (and perhaps on both banks), with good ground for cavalry beyond, on which the English arrayed themselves before their attack. The Scots therefore faced south, and the English army's advance was roughly northwards.

As the phrase *near Falkirk* could mean anything from one to ten miles from the town, Fergusson deduced that the Avon, rather than the Carron, was the river which separated the two armies. The Avon runs west to east about four miles south of Falkirk, but after it passes Avonbridge it turns to the north-east and then runs almost due north to reach the Forth between Grangemouth and Bo'ness. As it does not flow eastwards after a point about a mile below Avonbridge, Hemingburgh's description is accurate. For this reason Fergusson concluded that the west-to-east stretch of the Avon had to include the battle-site. By examining the actual terrain, moreover, he narrowed down the battlefield to the area just north of Glenellrig where the ground perfectly fitted Hemingburgh's description. Here, he argued, were Wallace's schiltroms. From a distance, the Avon, meandering between fields, does not seem much of a defence, but when one descends the gradual slope towards the stream on the south side the marshy nature of the water meadows becomes readily apparent. It is still prone to become waterlogged, but in earlier times it must have been very swampy indeed, before the area was substantially drained in the eighteenth century.

The only objection to this theory is that it would have entailed a very considerable southward diversion from Linlithgow. Here again, however, many historians supposed that the English advanced *through* that town whereas Hemingburgh states quite unequivocally that 'night overtook them on this side of Linlithgow, and at dawn the next day they passed the town'. If they had actually entered the town, the starving, half-mutinous troops would have broken ranks in search of food and plunder, or there would have been some mention of its having been laid waste by the Scots or otherwise offering no temptation to the English. Fergusson's view that the line of advance was more to the south, close to Torphichen, is confirmed by Blind Harry who has the English march to Slamannan Muir begin from Torphichen. If we bear in mind that the English intelligence was that Wallace was 'near Falkirk in the Forest of Selkirk' or 'in the forest of Falkirk', Edward could not have had any precise notion of where his enemy was encamped.

The controversy over the site of the battle, however, is as nothing compared with the arguments that continue to rage over whether Wallace should have fought it at all. Poor Wallace has often been blamed for risking everything on a pitched battle; it is always easy to find fault in a lost battle, and if nothing succeeds like success, then equally no credit is allowed for failure. The only accurate account of what happened was written by Hemingburgh who naturally gives us an English view of events. The Scottish accounts are very brief, mainly written long after the event, and sidetracked by the need to pin the blame on some factor such as Sir John Comyn's supposed treachery or cowardice, or even some entirely imaginary assistance given to the enemy by Robert Bruce. The latter theory is easily rebutted, for Bruce was in Ayr Castle at the time, more than fifty miles away. And the conduct of Sir John Comyn would not only have been out of character but can also be explained quite rationally.

Furthermore some critics, notably Evan Barron, have argued that the tactics which lost Falkirk were the direct antithesis of the tactics which won Stirling Bridge. This argument is put forward with the implication that success at Stirling was due to Andrew de Moray, and that without his genius as a strategist Wallace was bound to lose Falkirk. This is a specious argument not supported by the facts. Apart from anything else, no general would use the same tactics in two battles fought on quite different ground and against quite different opponents. Yet there were similarities in these battles. In both, Wallace relied heavily on infantry armed with spears against a foe whose strength lay in his heavy cavalry. At Stirling the spearmen were used offensively, to seize the bridgehead; at Falkirk they were employed defensively, on well-chosen ground sloping against a cavalry charge, the front defended by such natural obstacles as a small river and an extensive marsh, with a forest (the Torwood) not far off into which, if the worst came to the worst, infantry could withdraw and cavalry would be hampered in pursuit. In each case the ground was chosen with great skill. There is also the evidence of one chronicler (the compiler of the Cottonian manuscript) that the Scottish front was protected by an open palisade of long, sharp stakes driven into the ground at an angle, and laced with stout ropes.[5] Such an elaborate defence work gives the lie to the canard that Wallace was taken by surprise.

According to Hemingburgh the Scottish infantry was drawn up in four close masses or clumps called schiltroms, circular in form and each consisting of a double rank of men facing outwards. The front rank crouched or sat on the ground with their twelve-foot spears slanting upwards, while the rear rank stood with their weapons inclined over their comrades' heads. 'Their spears point over point, so sair and so thick, and fast together joint; to see it was marvellous,' commented Robert de Brunne poetically. The spaces between the schiltroms were occupied by the Border bowmen commanded by Sir John Stewart. To the rear were the cavalry, ready to give chase when the enemy broke ranks.

This strategy has often been criticised, although Fergusson shrewdly points out that it was exactly the strategy used by the Duke of Wellington at Waterloo when the French cavalry broke on the British squares. The main difference between these two great battles, half a millennium apart, is that the French artillery of 1815 was not as accurate or deadly as the English archery of 1298. As it happens, Waterloo was 'a damned close-run thing' and the round-shot and grape of the French cannons did far more damage than the successive charges of Napoleon's cavalry. In 1298 it was not the heavily armoured destriers that broke Wallace's schiltroms, but the Welshmen and Lancastrians armed with the longbow. This was a relatively new weapon, so deadly and capable of upsetting the tenets of medieval chivalry that it was at first condemned as illegal and regarded with the horror reserved, in a later age, for poison gas. Had it not been for the deadly accuracy of the longbowmen Edward would have been foiled by those forests of spears and forced to retreat, a retreat which Wallace would have turned into a headlong rout. Then

Wallace would have been hailed as the greatest general of the age, and not be unfairly relegated to the role of a guerrilla leader whose ability to handle troops in a pitched battle was debatable.

As the English host deployed in battle order on the far side of the stream Wallace cried out to his men those immortal words: 'I have brought you to the ring; dance the best you can.'[6] By now the enemy had not eaten for almost twenty-four hours. When Edward saw the Scots arrayed before him he decided that his men should have a square meal before engaging in battle, reckoning that what supplies were left might as well be used up. This was a commonsense approach; but his staff officers were anxious to avoid delay, fearing that the Scots might attack while they breakfasted. This folly was compounded by the fact that, for once, the English army had failed to send scouts to spy out the land. For this reason the barons thought that they had a plain field in front of them at last and could therefore deploy the cavalry to best advantage. This cardinal error might well have cost them the battle.

For once Edward allowed himself to be swayed against his better judgment. In mitigation, he was now fifty-eight years of age, quite elderly in medieval terms, and we must suppose that the shock and pain of his broken ribs were taking their toll. With a pious invocation to the Holy Trinity he gave way to his barons, although instead of ordering the cavalry to charge he sent the unreliable Welshmen forward first. The Welsh, still resentful over their rough handling less than forty-eight hours earlier, flatly refused to be treated as spear fodder. All the threats and promises in the world would not budge the sullen archers. There was nothing for it, therefore, but to send in the cavalry after all. The first wave, commanded by the Earl Marshal and the earls of Hereford and Lincoln, charged with considerable panache — straight into the marsh which had hitherto been undetected. The lush greenery of the meadow concealed a viscous swamp which brought the clattering knights to an unseemly halt. In a state of confusion bordering on farce, which must have given some grim amusement to the Scottish schiltroms on the opposing slope, the heavy cavalry extricated itself from the bog and wheeled off westwards to the left to seek a way round.

The second line was a glittering spectacle in which the banners of thirty-six barons and the pennons and guidons of innumerable knights provided a blaze of colour. It advanced at a wary trot, commanded by Bishop Bek who, having perceived the mess the first line had got itself into, led his horsemen diagonally towards the eastern side of the moss with the intention of striking the Scots on their left flank. This tactic worked, and Bek's cavalry crossed the stream in good order, then halted to wait for the third line to get into position. The third echelon was commanded by King Edward himself and he, no doubt suffering from his broken ribs, was having considerable difficulty in remaining upright in the saddle. Consequently, the third wave was much slower in deployment. Meanwhile some of the barons in Bek's regiment were becoming increasingly irritable at the delay. When Bek tried to calm them down, Sir Ralph Basset told the bishop to go and sing mass and leave the fighting to them. With that, Basset, followed by most of the other knights, swept Bek aside and flung themselves at the schiltrom on the extreme left of the Scottish line. Shortly afterwards the Earl Marshal's ragged line, having finally got around the other side of the moss, launched a similarly impetuous but disorderly attack on the Scottish right.

Now Wallace's incessant and wearisome drilling of his men paid off handsomely. The schiltroms stood firm. The spearmen showed a courage and resolution which did them credit; against those wicked steel points all the gallantry and dash of English chivalry came to grief. Not one infantryman wavered as the huge war-horses with their heavily armoured riders bore down on them. Sadly, the same could not be said for the Scottish cavalry under the Red Comyn. Although the horsemen were held in reserve at the rear of the schiltroms, they wavered as the English charged the schiltroms, then wheeled about and galloped off the field without striking a single blow. Fordun says that the Scottish horse deserted Wallace treacherously 'on account of ill-will, begotten of the spring of envy'. The story was embroidered at great length by Blind Harry who imputed to Comyn sinister motives. Comyn's sister was the wife of the Earl of Dunbar, one of Wallace's arch enemies, but such ties of kinship seem to have counted for very little in the thirteenth century. According to Harry, Comyn tried to foment a quarrel between Wallace and Sir John Stewart on the grounds that the latter, by birth and social status, had the right to command the

Scottish army.[7] There is, however, absolutely no evidence to support this contention.

It is more likely that, in the heat of the moment, Comyn was swept along by the stampede of his men, or he may have galloped after them in a vain attempt to rally them and check their flight. At worst, the case against Comyn is not proven; but in default of any hard evidence to the contrary he cannot be charged with treachery. The argument that he took fright at the sight of the heavily armoured English cavalry hardly merits examination, for Comyn had fought fearlessly, almost recklessly, at Dunbar only two years earlier, and nothing before or since Falkirk should lead us to suppose that he had lost his nerve since that battle.

Only a handful of horsemen, including Wallace and his immediate staff, remained, riding up and down beside the schiltroms exhorting the spearmen to stand firm. Sir John Stewart's archers, armed with the Scottish shortbow, did not have the skilled marksmanship of their English counterparts. The latter, moreover, had a far superior weapon, whose range and velocity easily outmanoeuvred the Scots. The English cavalry, having failed to make much impression on the spearmen, turned their attention on the archers and rode them down. When Sir John Stewart tried to rally them, he was thrown from his horse and slain, according to John Major, though both Wyntoun and the *Scalacronica* say that he had already dismounted, the better to fight on foot among the common soldiers at his command. His archers closed ranks around his fallen body and sold their lives dearly — 'men of handsome form and tall stature' says Hemingburgh admiringly, echoing the Flowers of the Forest of a later, and even more tragic, encounter. The same chronicler, describing the schiltroms, likened them to a thick wood. A hundred and eleven English horses perished on that deadly and impenetrable hedge,[8] and the field became a chaotic welter of baffled knights swirling around and between the implacable masses of spearmen.

Despite the headlong flight of the Scottish cavalry, the battle could still have gone either way; but now Edward committed the main body of his infantry to the attack. This force appears to have consisted almost entirely of English levies and Irish volunteers, for two of the English accounts are emphatic that the

Welshmen continued to stand back until they saw that the Scots were beaten.[9] There was, however, a considerable body of Lancastrian longbowmen among the infantry and it was their deadly hail of arrows which succeeded where the armoured cavalry had failed. This onslaught was backed up by the shower of missiles thrown by the foot soldiers as they advanced over ground littered with stones and rocks. At this crucial point, even a squadron of well-trained cavalry could have worked wonders, just as they did at Bannockburn sixteen years later, but the assault of the English infantry was unchecked on this occasion. As the hail of arrows and stones decimated their ranks, the schiltroms wavered and finally broke, enabling the cavalry at last to charge in and despatch the spearmen as they turned and ran. At close quarters twelve-foot spears were useless, while swords and dirks had little effect on the armour of the knights and their great chargers. The *coup de grâce* was administered by Bishop Bek, whose cavalry had worked its way round to the rear and now charged downhill to slaughter the spearmen as they tried to escape. Before defeat turned to utter rout, the Welshmen at long last joined in the butchery.

Wallace, with the battered remnants of his army, withdrew to the north. The open rolling countryside of the present day was, in fact, densely wooded in the late thirteenth century, so that pursuit by the English cavalry was severely handicapped. Nevertheless, the slaughter of fleeing foot soldiers was cruel and relentless. Those who managed to escape the vengeful lances of the cavalry had to get across the River Carron and no doubt many of them drowned in its treacherous tidal waters. The more impetuous English knights pursued the fleeing Scots as far as Falkirk itself. Among them was Sir Brian de Jay, Master of the English Templars, who rashly pursued Wallace into the wood of Callendar where his horse became bogged down and he himself was killed, perhaps even by Wallace himself.[10] By a strange coincidence, the only other man of note who fell on the English side was Sir Brian's colleague, the Master of the Scottish Templars.

The Scottish infantry was virtually annihilated that day, the most conservative estimate of the slain being put at ten thousand. Among them were Sir John Stewart, Sir John Graham and Macduff of Fife. Graham and Stewart were subsequently interred in the churchyard of Falkirk where their tombs may be seen to this day. Graham's is marked with two epitaphs, the earlier in Latin and the other, of much later vintage, in the vernacular which was twice restored in the eighteenth century when the stone weathered badly:

> Heir lyes Sir John the Grame, baith wight and wise,
> Ane of the chiefs who rescewit Scotland thrise.
> Ane better knight not to the world was lent,
> Nor was gude Grame of truth and hardiment.

His memory was perpetuated by one of the most moving passages in Blind Harry's epic, the verses being rendered in the form of a panegyric by Wallace lamenting his fallen comrade.

The Battle of Falkirk was a much more devastating blow than Dunbar. The loss of men was far greater and there must have been few families in southern Scotland which did not suffer as a consequence. More importantly, this defeat brought to an end the three hundred days of Wallace's government, and with it the hopes of ridding Scotland of the foreign yoke. Wallace's career declined from that day; he left on that battlefield not only the flower of his army but his reputation as a leader. A quarter of his life yet lay before him, but never again was he to exercise any meaningful influence on the course of affairs.

10

DIPLOMATIC MANŒUVRES

Gud men (he said) I was your Governour;
My mynd was set to do yow ay honour,
And for to bring this realme to rychtwysness;
For it I passit in mony paynfull place,
To wyn our own, myself I nevir spared;
At the Fawkirk thay ordand me reward.
Off that reward ye hear no more throu me;
To sic gyfts God will full weill haiff ee.

BLIND HARRY

FOR all that Falkirk was a major blow to the Scots, it was in no sense a decisive victory for the English. The infantry had borne the brunt of the English attack but the cavalry, the officer corps, got away unscathed to fight another day, redeem the slur on its character and organise resistance in the remoter districts, especially north of the Tay and in the hills of Galloway. The people who had been cowed into submission after Dunbar were not the people whom Edward defeated at Falkirk. They were tempered by the fire of battle and found a new resilience, making them more determined than ever that they would not be subjugated. But defeat at Falkirk meant the end of Wallace's rule and shortly afterwards he gave up the guardianship; whether voluntarily or not is immaterial. His position had become increasingly untenable in face of the jealousies of his high-born rivals, and it is interesting to speculate that, sooner or later, he might have been removed from office, even if the Battle of Falkirk had been successful.

Immediately after the battle he marched north to Stirling where he ordered the destruction of the town and its castle, with the intention of denying the enemy its most precious objective. In any case Edward was in no immediate position to follow up his victory; his troops were exhausted and starving. When a supply ship managed to dock at Leith two days after the battle there was only sufficient food to succour the Edinburgh garrison itself, with nothing left over for the famished soldiers at Falkirk. The English army tightened its belt and marched forward, and on 26 July Edward entered the ruined town of Stirling. The only building left standing and tolerably habitable was the Dominican convent which, for two weeks, became Edward's headquarters. Here he recuperated from his injury and gave orders for the hurried repair to the castle walls. Meanwhile a punitive expedition had been sent into Fife to lay that county waste because of Macduff's support of Wallace in the battle. The Irish troops found St Andrews deserted by its inhabitants and vented their spleen by razing it to the ground. Wallace's men retreated as Edward advanced but had ample time to destroy Perth by burning, so that the enemy gained nothing from occupying it.

If Wallace, still nominally Guardian of Scotland, was now on the defensive, the campaign was not entirely lost. It seems likely that the young Earl of Carrick, operating from Ayr, took command of the irregular forces operating in Galloway that summer and was responsible for the siege of Carlisle which continued as late as 2 August. By the middle of that month Edward had had enough of campaigning against an elusive enemy and, after leaving a company of Northumbrians to garrison Stirling Castle, he headed south with his army. Some time was spent in and around Edinburgh before Edward moved westwards through the Forest of Selkirk, crossing Peeblesshire and Lanarkshire and reaching Ayr on 26 August. Hemingburgh records that Edward found both town and castle 'empty and burnt', the Earl of Carrick having systematically destroyed them after evacuating the inhabitants into the hilly and densely wooded districts of his earldom. Ayr was doubly disappointing; not only did the destroyed town afford little in the way of shelter as summer came to an end, but the supply ships expected from Ireland and the west of England failed to materialise. 'For fifteen days there was a mighty famine in the camp,' says Hemingburgh.

At the beginning of September Edward left Ayr but there was no thought of giving chase to the wily Bruce. By now many of the horses were dying (though this presumably provided the soldiers with a desperately needed source of protein). The chastened army now proceeded by Cumnock and Sanquhar into Nithsdale. On the evening of 2 September Edward reached Treskuer (Troqueer) on the west bank of the Nith overlooking the town of Dumfries, and inspected the Castledykes site south of the town itself. The following day he was at Dalgarno and Tibbers where he must have seen the stone castle erected by Sir Richard Siward. On 4 September he stayed at Lochmaben where his troops occupied the Bruce mote-hill by the church. The Bruce castle of that period stood on an eminence between the Kirk and Castle lochs dominating the main road north and south. As at Dumfries, King Edward spent some time inspecting the existing fortifications in great detail, his object being to establish military strongpoints for the control of Scotland against further outbreaks of rebellion. In Wales Edward had built massive fortresses of stone, designed for the permanent subjugation of that principality. In Scotland, however, he seems to have been concerned with a less permanent form of occupation, and for that reason felt that wooden peles were sufficient. Stockaded peles were subsequently erected at Selkirk and Dumfries, and a similar structure at Lochmaben — but not on the site of the then existing castle of Annandale, the traditional Bruce stronghold.

Instead, the wooden pele was erected at the southern end of the Castle Loch on the site of an Iron-Age fort, Sir Robert de Clifford being left in charge of the construction gang. The work progressed sufficiently well for Robert de Cantilope to be appointed as constable on Christmas Day. The progress of the building is well documented: on 28 December forty-eight labourers from Cumbria were hired at twopence a day to assist in the work. On 2 February 1299 Clifford wrote to the King's Treasurer at Carlisle asking that, as he had ordered the crossbowmen to remain at Lochmaben, they should receive fifteen days' pay in advance, along with further crossbowmen coming from Carlisle, with threepence daily each owing to 'the great dearness in the country'.

This pele was attacked in August 1299 by Scottish forces commanded by the Earl of Carrick, operating from the great Border castle of Caerlaverock. The attack was beaten off and Robert de Conynghame, Constable of Caerlaverock, was killed in the assault. His severed head was subsequently displayed on a pole from the great wooden tower. Steps were taken to reinforce the original wooden structure with stonework. In the ensuing century this was to form the nucleus of a great stone castle, strategic key to the western Borders of Scotland, and even today its ruins are an impressive reminder of its former importance. Today it is known as Bruce's Castle, though ironically its only connection with the future king was his abortive raid of 1299.

Having made elaborate arrangements for the garrisoning of strongpoints, Edward crossed the River Sark on 8 September and re-entered England, reaching Carlisle later the same day. The third invasion of Scotland in less than three years had achieved very little. The spectacular success of Falkirk was more apparent to some nineteenth-century historians than it really was, and certainly Edward did not regard it as one of his greatest achievements. The campaign of 1298 closed on a disappointing note as Edward ruefully counted the costs at Carlisle. His men had won a victory, to be sure, but losses through illness and disease probably far exceeded those slain in battle. In time-honoured fashion the Scots had harried the rearguard and picked off the stragglers at will. It is recorded that few of Edward's horses made it back to Carlisle; that alone must have been a grievous loss, given the value of a fully trained battle-charger.

Edward had sojourned in Scotland barely two months and had led his starving and mutinous troops on an uneasy and exceedingly costly march through the Lowlands. He had defeated a formidable enemy but failed to destroy it, he had not managed to penetrate the Highlands at all, and his hold on the Lowlands was proving illusory; he had restored the chief castle of central Scotland but had left its garrison so isolated that within half a year it would be forced to surrender; he had found that all his good work of two years ago had been utterly undone and his strongholds destroyed. Edward consoled himself by dividing among his principal followers the estates of the Scottish barons who had failed to respond to his summons, and restoring the English clergy who had been summarily ejected from their benefices.[1] It is ironic that the number of priests restored to their livings far exceeded the number of troops making up the garrisons left behind to keep the Scots in check. In real terms, however, this had little effect other than to alienate the Scottish magnates who, now that their formidable johnny-come-lately had been discredited, were beginning to discover a sense of patriotism at long last.

That Edward, despite his great victory, had achieved absolutely nothing, is shown by the fact that, as early as 9 August 1298, Sir John de Kingston, then deputy constable of Edinburgh Castle, wrote an urgent despatch to the Lord Treasurer saying:

> The Earl of Buchan, the Bishop of St Andrews and other great earls and lords, who were on the other side of the Scots water [the Firth of Forth] have come to this side. Today they are in Glasgow. They intend to go towards the Border, as is reported among them and their people who are in the Forest . . . They of the Forest have surrendered themselves to the Scots.[2]

Even worse, a band of Scots had had the effrontery to march right up to the gates of Edinburgh Castle and had done considerable damage, capturing the constable Sir Thomas d'Arderne in the process. If the Scots could behave thus with impunity, it makes a mockery of Edward's latest pacification of Scotland. This interesting report concluded with some very disturbing news, casting doubts on the loyalty of Sir Simon Fraser who had, until that time, been one of Edward's most ardent supporters. Fraser had accompanied Edward to Flanders and had fought with great distinction there, with the result that the King had restored his estates in both Scotland and England. After Falkirk Fraser's continuing devotion to the English cause led to his appointment as Warden of Selkirk Forest, superintending the activities of the outposts which Edward had established throughout this vast wilderness. Now, however, Kingston was warning Edward that Fraser 'I fear is not of such good faith as he

ought to be' and begging His Majesty and his council to beware.
Furthermore:

> Whereas Sir Simon Fraser comes to you in such haste, let me
> inform you, Sire, that he has no need to be in such a great
> hurry, for there was not by any means such a great power of
> people who came into his jurisdiction but that they might have
> been stopped by the garrisons if Sir Simon had given them
> warning. And of this I warned him eight days before they
> came; and before they entered into the Forest, it was reported
> that there was a treaty between them and Sir Simon, and that
> they had a conference together, and ate and drank, and were
> on the best of terms. Wherefore, Sire, it were well that you
> should be very cautious as to the advice which he should give
> you.

If someone as loyal as Fraser was now changing sides, it
showed how counter-productive the recent campaign had been.
The Scots might have been thrashed in a pitched battle, but they
had seen how Edward's proud host had slunk back across the
border, their tails between their legs, and this alone must have
put new spirit into the people of the Lowlands, a spirit that communicated itself all the way to the highest leaders.

Meanwhile Edward was soon making plans for yet another
expedition against the tiresome Scots. On 26 September, less
than three weeks after he returned to Carlisle, he addressed a
fresh summons to the Earl Marshal and a great number of other
magnates (including the earls of Angus and March). This document has a curiously modern ring, Edward justifying his aggression against a smaller and weaker neighbour in the kind of
language which Hitler reserved for the Czechs in 1938 and the
Poles in 1939. The eve of Pentecost (24 May 1299) was fixed for
the muster of what promised to be an even larger force than
before, 'to go forward in the Scottish business upon the enemies
of the crown and realm of England, and to put down their disobedience and their malice which purpose nothing else but to
subdue the said crown, and the estate of the said realm of
England, to their power.'[3]

On 12 December Edward issued orders to various sheriffs
and other officers in England to forward provisions to Berwick,

and their Irish counterparts were instructed to send supplies to the great base at Skinburness near Carlisle, in each case by 6 June 1299. Edward was in a vehement mood, determined to attack the rebels the following summer with as much power as he could muster, and then to annihilate them utterly. Again, the extreme language of his writs is difficult to reconcile with the character of justice and compassion painted by the English chroniclers. Otherwise, this was a period of comparative tranquillity and Edward indulged his penchant for shows of piety by making pilgrimages to the tombs of St John of Beverley and other local saints, 'thanking God for his victory, as was his custom after such affairs'.[4]

John de Kingston replaced Walter de Huntercombe as Constable of Edinburgh Castle on 25 November, but his warnings about Sir Simon Fraser were either unheeded or unfounded, for that knight continued in the post of Warden of Selkirk Forest and was commanded to give his assistance in forays from Berwick and Edinburgh against the unruly Scots during November and December. On 19 November Patrick, Earl of March, was appointed commander of the forces and castles on the east coast of Scotland south of the Forth. All this is evidence that Edward had some hold on the south-east of Scotland, together with his proud stockade at Lochmaben in the south-west; but in truth the English were only hanging on by their fingernails.

Meanwhile, there had been an inevitable change in the government of Scotland. Even if the Scottish magnates had not demanded his resignation, Wallace's guardianship was no longer tenable. Fordun claims that he 'chose rather to serve with the crowd, than to be set over them, to their ruin, and the grievous wasting of the people. So, not long after the Battle of Falkirk, at the water of Forth, he, of his own accord, resigned the office and charge which he held, of Guardian.' Wyntoun repeats this in substance, adding a comment about Wallace's devotion and consideration for 'the leal commons of Scotland'. To Wallace this was the only honourable course. Lesser men might have been content to withdraw completely from public affairs, or succumb to the blandishments offered by the King of England, but Wallace never gave up the struggle. Henceforward he would wage war by whatever means, limited though they might be, and even attempt diplomacy if that course helped to free his country.

According to the Rishanger Chronicle Wallace went into hiding after Falkirk, together with his brother Sir Malcolm, the Earl of Atholl and a number of other knights. This has been interpreted as Wallace, finding open warfare no longer feasible, reverting to his earlier guerrilla tactics.

By 2 December 1298, if not earlier, Robert Bruce, younger Earl of Carrick, and John Comyn the Red were joint Guardians of Scotland.[5] This was a remarkable turn of events, for the government was now in the hands of the two principal rivals for the throne. Hitherto they had acted mainly, if not entirely, from selfish motives. It is significant that Carrick was the only Scottish earl elected to this prestigious position, reflecting his standing in regard to the other earls. Indeed, when one considers the rest of the magnates, this choice was inevitable.

The younger John Comyn of Badenoch, nephew of King John, represented the Balliol faction. Robert Bruce, Earl of Carrick, now twenty-four years of age, represented the Bruce faction. While there was an immediate threat from England the two Guardians co-operated well enough, and the day-to-day administration of Scotland continued reasonably smoothly. Sheriffs held their courts in many parts of the country, taxes were collected and parliament of a sort continued to meet, perhaps irregularly and in some rather unconventional locations, so that acts were passed for the good governance of the country.

The dual guardianship functioned for about a year, and it has been suggested that something of Wallace's selfless statesmanship must have rubbed off on the two young noblemen; but as the threat of invasion receded the old rivalries came to the surface once more. In the course of 1299, however, there was some evidence of solidarity. Even the earls of Buchan and Menteith cast their lot with the Guardians, while the Earl of Angus, the English-born and bred Ingelram de Umfraville, changed sides once more and espoused the Scottish cause. On 20 February 1299 Edward had him publicly denounced as an enemy and a rebel and granted his estates in Northumberland to that rising star, Henry de Percy. The earl's right-hand man, Sir David de Brechin, who had fought on the English side at Dunbar but who married the widow of Sir John Stewart of

Bonkill after Falkirk, was another defector to the Scottish side. Sir John de Soulis, a brave and energetic knight whom Fordun curiously describes as 'simple-minded and not firm enough', joined the inner council advising the Guardians.

Interestingly, as William Wallace's star waned, that of his elder brother Malcolm was in the ascendant. Remarkably little is known about this knight, who seems to have kept his head down in the previous decade. He was probably much older than William and after his father's untimely death in 1291 was no doubt preoccupied with running the family estate. Now, however, he came to prominence. One account suggests that it was he who delivered William's resignation to the council of magnates; and certainly in the ensuing period he provided the liaison between his brother and the ruling junta.

Sir Robert de Keith, Sir David de Graham and Sir William de Balliol, as well as that enigmatic figure, James the Steward, now assumed leading roles in the conduct of Scotland's affairs. One must assume that many other earls, barons and knights lent their tacit support to the Guardians. Defeated in battle he may have been, Wallace was nevertheless the catalyst which led to the revival of national interest among the traditional ruling classes. He had shown his betters that courage and determination could defeat the mightiest army in Europe. His record in pitched battles might be debatable, but it was he who showed the Scots that their own indomitable will could make the English subjugation of their country unworkable. If only the Scots had the guts to make a stand against Edward, and stand together for their common good, then they could not be conquered.

The year 1299 marked the nadir of Wallace's fortunes and, indeed, the rest of his life looks like an anticlimax. One recent historian, in fact, has dismissed the last seven years of his life in a few lines, as a period of obscurity, 'harrying the English whenever he could with bands of fearless men, or acting as messenger to the King of France or His Holiness the Pope for his friend William Lamberton, Bishop of St Andrews.'[6] This conceals a great deal of activity, though the story can only be constructed from tantalising scraps in the chronicles and contemporary documents. Wallace had pulled strings to secure the election of William de Lamberton to the bishopric of St Andrews, and Lamberton never forgot this. He continued to regard Wallace as a close friend, and was later to entrust him with several diplomatic missions of the utmost importance. Lamberton had a much broader view of Anglo-Scottish relations than the rest of his peers, for he had spent much of the time since his nomination to the see out of the country. After his consecration at Rome in 1298 he went to France and pleaded the Scottish case at the court of Philip IV to such good account that King Philip gave him a letter, dated 6 April that year, which he personally took to the Guardians. This missive praised 'their constancy to their king and their shining valour in defence of their native land against injustice'. Philip described himself as 'not unmindful of the old league between their king, themselves, and him, and carefully pondering ways and means of helping them'.[7]

Having delivered this encouraging, though not particularly helpful, letter Bishop Lamberton returned to France in the company of Sir John de Soulis and the abbots of Jedburgh and Melrose. They remained there until July when King Edward succeeded in making his peace with Philip and alienating him from the Scottish cause. From Paris, however, Lamberton wrote to the Guardians, urging them 'to carry on the war vigorously, until the Bishop and the other lords in France could return to Scotland'. At the same time he wrote a letter to William Wallace, praying that 'for the love you have of me, you will do all possible hurt and damage to the King of England'.[8] Another letter went to the canons of St Andrews instructing them to employ a portion of his own provisions for the sustenance of Wallace. Oddly enough, the substance of these three letters was repeated in a letter which King Edward wrote to Pope Clement in 1306, indicating that the bearer was captured on his way from France and the letters impounded. Edward was certainly aware of this diplomatic correspondence and the imminent return of the Scottish envoys from France; between 10 June and 20 August 1299 he sent urgent orders to various shipmasters in the Channel ports of Rye and Winchelsea to intercept, and capture if possible, 'the Bishop of St Andrews, the abbots of Melrose and Jedburgh, Sir John de Soulis, and other Scottish enemies in Flanders' whom his network of spies had informed him 'will embark at Dam or thereabouts'. It seems unlikely that the letters ever reached their proper destination, but at least they are strong evidence of Lamberton's tireless efforts abroad and his continuing support for the erstwhile Guardian.

In spite of the vigilance of English ships, Lamberton and his companions got back to Scotland without mishap. While it may be argued that Philip's letter, warm and generous though it might be, did not amount to actual support in men and *matériel*, the French ruler's attitude was enough to keep Edward's attention focused firmly on the Continent. The mobilisation of English forces, originally planned for 6 June, was therefore put back until August, and then cancelled for that year, so the diplomatic mission won for the Scots a valuable breathing space.

This does not mean that hostilities came to an end. In mid-July a force of twelve knights and three hundred men-at-arms was mustered at Carlisle for a raid into Annandale, and a week or two later there were reports that, in retaliation, the Earl of Angus and Sir William de Balliol were harassing Edward's outposts in the vast Selkirk Forest still under the nominal command of Sir Simon Fraser. To this period also belong the guerrilla raids referred to by John the Marshal, bailiff of the Earl of Lincoln in the barony of Renfrew, when he sent an urgent appeal to the King for assistance. Wallace, with three hundred men-at-arms and a multitude of foot soldiers, had been lurking in Galloway but had now advanced on the bailery of Cunninghame, seized the King's bailiffs and other officers, 'made a fine for their heads and had totally rebelled against their late fealty'. Unless he got immediate help, John felt he could not defend his barony. To the same period probably belong the undated petitions to the King from the abbots of Sweetheart (near Dumfries) and Dundrennan, couched in similar alarming terms and confirming the activities of Wallace throughout Galloway.

Cracks were now beginning to appear in the Scottish solidarity. Sir Robert de Hastings had a mole in the Scottish council and his eye-witness account of an extraordinary incident formed the basis of the report which Hastings wrote to King Edward from Roxburgh on 20 August. Until the previous month, Hastings had been Edward's warden of the west march, but when it seemed likely that the Scots might lay siege to Roxburgh Castle, he was sent there to conduct its defence. According to Hastings, Angus and Balliol had been joined by the 'great lords of Scotland with all their power', but when they learned that Roxburgh was too strongly garrisoned to be attacked, they had 'kept quiet till Wednesday next after the Assumption of Our Lady [19 August] on which day I had my spy among them'.[9]

On that fateful day the Scots held a council of war at Peebles, attended by all the leaders except Wallace. In addition to both Guardians, there were James the Steward, the Earl of Buchan, Bishop Lamberton, the Earl of Menteith and several knights, including Sir Malcolm Wallace. The immediate business was the conduct of the war in the Borders area, but one of the knights, Sir David de Graham, turned the discussion into a very heated argument when 'he demanded of the council the lands and goods which were the property of Sir William Wallace, since he was going out of the kingdom without the will or leave of the Guardians'. It appears that this was news to the council as a whole, although the probability is that Wallace's action had been undertaken with the encouragement, if not under the direct order, of Bishop Lamberton. Not surprisingly, Sir Malcolm Wallace deeply resented Graham's outburst and pointed out that his brother's lands and goods could not be expropriated until it was proven 'whether he went out of the kingdom for profit of the kingdom or against it'. This cutting remark was doubtless intended to shame Sir David into silence and remind him of the younger Wallace's impeccable record of selfless devotion.

Malcolm's interjection, however, far from putting the matter in perspective, provoked an unseemly brawl. Hastings described the ensuing fracas in vivid terms:

> Upon that, each of these knights gave the lie to the other and drew their knives; and the Earl of Buchan and Sir John Comyn thought, because Sir David de Graham is with Messire John Comyn, and Messire Malcolm Wallace with the Earl of Carrick, that some quarrel was begun with the intention to deceive them, and Messire John Comyn leaped on the Earl of Carrick and took him by the throat, and the Earl of Buchan upon the Bishop of St Andrews, and they held them fast, because treachery or treason was planned, until the Steward and others went between them and stopped this scuffle.

The violent quarrel was abruptly quelled by the arrival of a messenger with a despatch stating that Sir Alexander Comyn and Lachlan MacRuari, captain of the West Highland gallow-glasses, were burning and devastating Argyll and northern Dunbartonshire. The squabbling subsided and some semblance of order was restored to the meeting. Bruce and Comyn were confirmed as Guardians, but Lamberton was appointed as an additional Guardian and significantly entrusted 'as principal chieftain' with control of all the castles in Scottish hands. Once more the Guardians of Scotland represented the three classes of the Establishment — the earls, barons and the prelates. Dissension among the leaders was probably due to military inactivity, always bad for morale in wartime. Consequently Lamberton, exhibiting great diplomacy and tact in handling the touchy magnates, devised a plan of campaign for the autumn which would effectively keep the mutually antagonistic factions apart. The Earl of Carrick was despatched to Galloway to attack the English garrisons at Annan and Lochmaben; he left the gathering accompanied by Sir David de Brechin and probably also Sir Malcolm Wallace. The Earl of Buchan and his kinsman John Comyn went north, while the Steward and his cousin Menteith headed for Clydesdale, and Keith, Angus and Lamberton remained in the Borders. Sir Ingelram de Umfraville, Earl of Angus, was appointed Sheriff of Roxburgh and Keith appointed Warden of Selkirk Forest. Noting that Keith had been given a hundred knights and fifteen hundred foot soldiers, Hastings concluded his report grimly that 'they have it in command from the said Guardians to do the worst they can upon our marches. The thing, Sire, seems more true, because each great lord has left a part of his troops in the company of the said Sir Ingram.'

While the collective leadership of Scotland was wrangling and almost coming to blows, William Wallace was quietly getting on with the business of fighting King Edward with every means at his disposal. Shortly before the council at Peebles, Wallace had been in central Scotland, ambushing English supply trains and effectively starving the garrison at Stirling of provisions. When the castle fell to Sir John de Soulis a few months later, the ninety-strong garrison was on the verge of starvation, the men having already eaten their horses. At a court of enquiry, convened later to examine the losses which John Sampson, the Constable of Stirling, had sustained in King Edward's service, he mentioned an attack by Wallace on St Bartholomew's Day (24 August) when he had seized all of their supplies.[10]

From the complaint of Sir David de Graham, it would appear that Wallace must have left Scotland a few days later. One English chronicler states that he set sail with five knights to solicit the aid of King Philip, although this account places the incident shortly after the Battle of Falkirk.[11] On the other hand, the report from Hastings makes it clear that late August 1299 was the date of Wallace's departure.

From the time of John Major in the early sixteenth century it was fashionable to ridicule the notion that Wallace had made at least one visit to the Continent, and Blind Harry's lengthy account of his hero's wanderings and adventures was dismissed as pure fable. The principal argument against such exploits was the lack of any reference to them in the French chronicles. The more scientific approach to the study of history, beginning in the mid-nineteenth century, however, soon turned up concrete evidence of Wallace's diplomatic missions. Apart from the circumstantial evidence furnished by the Hastings report and Lamberton's recent return from France, there was an account in the earliest manuscript version of Fordun that 'Wallace sailed for France, where he exhibited such bravery, as well against the pirates on the sea as against the English on the land, that he acquired great renown, that he was greatly honoured by the king of France, and promised extensive lordships, but that he was drawn again to his native land by natural affection.'[12] Admittedly, by saying that Wallace went to France after the Battle of Roslin, Fordun places this incident in 1303 and not 1299, but Harry claims that Wallace made two trips to Europe, so Fordun may have assumed that only one mission took place at the later date.

The facts, however, are clearly set out in the Cottonian manuscript:

> At this time Wallace, with five knights, betook himself to France, asking and requiring assistance from the king of that country. And when he had reached the city of Amiens, straightway it was announced to the king of France that an enemy of the king of England had arrived there; immediately the king ordered him to be detained in prison, which, gratefully and

joyfully the people of that city, namely Amiens, did comply with, because they so greatly esteemed the English king. Then the king of France sent a letter to the king of England, saying that if he would accept of William Wallace the Governor of Scotland, he should be sent him; to which the king of England replied with many thanks, and with most urgent requests that Wallace and his attendants should be surrendered to him at Amiens, and everything belonging to him sequestrated, which was accordingly done.[13]

This account has to be treated with a certain amount of caution. While it is obvious that Wallace and his comrades must have gone to France, it is hard to believe that Philip the Fair would have seriously considered such a breach of diplomatic etiquette as handing over to his implacable enemy the man who had just been fighting in alliance with France. The people of Amiens, capital of Picardy, could hardly have had much esteem for the Plantagenet monarch who had fought over their territory to their grievous loss. They are more likely to have welcomed Wallace with open arms. Equally suspect is the tradition that Edward replied to Philip declining the offer but requesting that the French monarch keep the Scot in custody. In view of the strenuous efforts made by Edward in the ensuing years to get his hands on Wallace, it is hard to believe that he would have rejected such a golden opportunity as this, had it presented itself.

Any doubts regarding Wallace's arrival in France, let alone his courteous treatment by King Philip, should be dispelled by the letter which the French sovereign gave to his distinguished visitor before Wallace left his court to travel on to Rome:

Philip, by the grace of God, King of the French, to my loved and faithful, my agents, appointed to the Roman court, greetings and love: We command you to request the supreme Pontiff to hold our loved William the Waleis, of Scotland, knight, recommended to his favour, in those things which with him he has to despatch. Given at Pierrefonds, on Monday after the feast of All Saints.[14]

This remarkable document appears to have been found in

215

Wallace's possession at the time of his arrest in 1305. At that time he also had several letters of safe-conduct, not only from Philip but also from Haakon of Norway, and also a letter of credentials from King John Balliol which indicates that Wallace had a meeting at some stage with his sovereign. These and other documents were delivered to King Edward at Kingston by Sir John de Segrave and were deposited in the Treasury at Westminster. Most of them subsequently disappeared, though their existence is known from the *Kalendar of Treasury Documents*, an inventory compiled by Bishop Stapleton about 1323, which has survived. The letter to the Pope was discovered by the Revd John Stevenson in 1841 while employed as Sub-Commissioner of Public Records to sift through the unsorted mass of documents which had been preserved in the Record Office in the Tower of London. The letter is written on parchment in the handwriting, with contractions and symbols, peculiar to the period. It was first published by Stevenson and was subsequently photographed and translated for publication in the *National Manuscripts*.[15]

Interestingly, this document bears the intriguing endorsement *Quarta lra Re ffanc* (fourth letter by the King of France). When or by whom was this annotation made? The answer might have enormous significance. Did Wallace possess other letters from Philip? If so, to whom were they addressed and what did they contain?

Much of the ninth book of Blind Harry's epic is devoted to Wallace's first visit to France, which the minstrel placed before the battles of Blackearnside and Falkirk. The middle of the tenth book deals with Wallace's resignation and subsequent departure for France. It may be that there was only one such visit, as many of the details Harry gives for both trips are similar. According to Harry, the first trip took place in the month of May, and he was accompanied by fifty men (which, if this described his retinue as a whole, would not be out of line with the Cottonian manuscript's reference to five knights); but there is no reason to question the ensuing statement, that he had gone without the knowledge or consent of 'the lords of Parliament', knowing full well that they would not allow him to leave the country. The departure was also kept a closely guarded secret to prevent interception by English patrol vessels. Harry names his travel-

ling companions as 'the two Wallaces who were his near kinsmen, and William Craufurd and Kneland who also were held
dear by him'.

The ship sailed from Kirkcudbright, an odd choice of embar-
cation since it would have entailed a long and hazardous voyage
either round the northern coasts of Scotland, or through the
Irish Sea and Bristol Channel, but probably the latter. They were
two days out when they ran into a flotilla of pirate ships commanded by Thomas de Longueville, the Red Rover, for sixteen
years undisputed master of the seas. Inevitably the leading ship
catches up with the Scottish vessel and first to jump aboard is
the pirate chief; but Wallace seizes him by the throat and pins
him to the deck. Longueville pleads for his life and Wallace
addresses him in Latin, 'I have never taken as a prisoner any
man who was my foe; for God's sake, I grant thee thy life.'
Having disarmed the pirate, Wallace makes him swear on the
sword never to do him injury again. Longueville keeps his
word, but as Wallace's prisoner he is compelled to order his fleet
to sail to La Rochelle and surrender to the French authorities.

In true feudal fashion, Longueville offers to become
Wallace's man and take service with him, but Wallace refuses,
saying that his friendship would be good enough. Thus, in triumph over the scourge of the seas, Wallace lands at La Rochelle
to a hero's welcome and the pirates are taken into custody.
Longueville journeys with Wallace to Paris to make his peace
with King Philip, Wallace interceding with the monarch on the
pirate's behalf. The pirate is not only pardoned, but knighted (or
rather restored to his lands and title). Significantly, Harry inter-
jects a note that this was recounted 'according to my author', i.e.
Master John Blair who presumably accompanied Wallace on his
French mission. Longueville later renounced his French lands
and title to a kinsman and settled in Scotland where he became
Lord of Kinfauns near Perth and progenitor of the Charteris
family.

Tiring of inaction at the French court, Wallace volunteered
for service in Philip's campaign in Guienne, a province which
Philip had seized from Edward in 1294 and which the English
king was now intent on regaining. Wallace is said to have mustered some nine hundred Scottish exiles for the French service.
During this campaign Wallace is alleged to have led his Scots

brigade to victory at Chinon and taken part in the capture of Bordeaux. A knight named Guthrie was despatched to France to recall Wallace. He sailed from Arbroath to Sluys, and having eventually caught up with the knight errant, brought him back to Paris, whence they journeyed together to Sluys and took ship back to Montrose. According to Harry, Wallace was out of Scotland for four months, from 21 April to the end of August, but these dates are impossible to reconcile with his known movements, either in 1298 or 1299.

The second visit is placed by Harry immediately after Wallace's resignation of the guardianship. On this occasion Harry has him departing from Dundee with eighteen companions. Again he meets with an adventure at sea; this time he encounters an English pirate named John Lynn off the Humber estuary. As before, he sends the captain and crew into the hold for their own safety, while his eighteen comrades take on 140 pirates (incidentally, this number 'seven score' recurs frequently in Harry's descriptions of Wallace's skirmishes with the English). This time he slays the pirate. Landing at Sluys, he travels through Flanders to Paris, where Philip offers him the lordship of Guienne, but he declines. Again he proceeds to Guienne; again he captures Schenoun (Chinon) and besieges Bordeaux. It is not improbable that Wallace did fight in Guienne — the circumstantial details concerning Chinon and Bordeaux have an air of verisimilitude — but it would be stretching coincidence too far to suppose that history should repeat itself so soon and so closely. On this occasion, however, he discovers treachery in France as well as back in Scotland. Summoned by Philip, Wallace remains at his court for two years and even here he discovers traitors at work. He will tarry no longer. Philip gives him letters from Scotland urging him to return home, loads him with presents and reluctantly bids him farewell. With Longueville, Wallace sails from Sluys and, passing up the Tay, disembarks at the mouth of the Earn.[16]

The two visits are so similar in incident that it is highly likely that they were one and the same. The story of Wallace's capture of the Red Rover was certainly well established by Harry's time, and a variant of it, from an independent source, was used by Sir Walter Scott in *The Fair Maid of Perth* 'given by an ancient and uniform tradition, which carries in it great indications of truth, and is warrant enough for its insertion in graver histories [than this historical romance]'. The anonymous author of *Muses' Threnodie*, believed to have been composed early in the fifteenth century, lamented:

> I marvell our records nothing at all
> Do mention Wallace going into France.
> How that can be forgote I greatlie scance;
> For well I know all Gasconie and Guien
> Do hold that Wallace was a mightie Gian
> Even to this day; in Rochel likewise found
> A towre from Wallace' name greatly renown'd.

There are tantalising references to long-lost ballads by the French troubadours, but nothing has so far come to light in support of this claim. Consequently, Blind Harry is our only source for Wallace's exploits and activities. Conversely, Harry makes no mention of any trips to Norway or Rome, though both are suggested by the documents which were in Wallace's possession at the time of his arrest. It should be remembered that Norway, at this time, extended as far as the Pentland Firth and it would have required no more than a short ferry trip from Thurso to Stromness or Kirkwall to be technically in Norway. The fact that one of these documents was issued by King Haakon V suggests a visit to Europe later than 1299, for he succeeded his brother Eirik II in that year. Haakon, uncle of the late Maid of Norway, probably retained more than a passing interest in Scottish affairs. It will also be remembered that the widower Eirik had married Isabel Bruce, sister of the younger Earl of Carrick, in 1293, and it is interesting to speculate whether Isabel, still Queen of Norway in 1299, may have communicated with her brother using Wallace as an intermediary.

Wallace's journey to Rome is more probable, to judge by the actions of Pope Boniface who was singularly well disposed towards the Scots at this time. As early as the summer of 1298, as a result of Lamberton's pleading, the Pope had written to Edward rebuking him in general terms for his behaviour towards the Scots. This was followed on 5 July 1299 by a papal bull addressed to Edward, and entrusted to Winchelsea, Archbishop of Canterbury, to deliver into the King's hands personally. Winchelsea later recorded that he went to considerable lengths, and a great many inconveniences, chasing after Edward, with the result that the missive was not served on Edward until he was at Caerlaverock near Dumfries in August 1300. The doughty archbishop was not content merely to hand over the document, but added a few admonishing words of his own: 'Jerusalem would not fail to protect her citizens, and to cherish, like Mount Sion, those who trusted in the Lord.' Edward is said to have fallen into a rage, shouting, 'I will not be silent or at rest either for Mount Sion or Jerusalem; but as long as there is breath in my nostrils, will defend what all the world knows is my right.'[17]

The bull claimed that Scotland from ancient times had been and still was a fief of the Holy See, and was not now or ever a fief of the English sovereign. Boniface ordered the immediate release of Bishop Wishart and other Scottish ecclesiastics who were languishing in English prisons, and demanded the surrender of the castles, abbeys, convents and monasteries in Scotland. Such was the power of the Church that Edward dared not treat the papal bull with the contempt he felt. In the end he sent a fairly anodyne reply, saying that, in a matter of this gravity, he would have to consult his council and would, by their advice, transmit his determination to his 'superior and revered father' by special messengers. The bull was discussed at great length in the parliament held at Lincoln on 12 February 1301, but 104 barons assembled there voted to reject it in the most absolute terms. In the interim, Edward, ever scrupulous in maintaining an outward show of legality and respect for the law, had the monasteries scoured for information on the subject, and took lengthy counsel of the learned doctors of civil law at Oxford and Cambridge. The result of this frenetic activity was an elaborate restatement of Edward's claims and the assertion of his absolute and indefeasible title to the realm of Scotland. The letter sent in reply to the Pope, dated 7 May 1301, was a supreme example of solemn diplomatic tomfoolery, in reckless defiance and omission of essential facts. The rebuttal sent to the Pope by the Scottish envoy, Baldred Bisset, dealt with Edward's claim point by point and systematically exposed the falsity of the King's assertions. Edward's only firm ground was conquest, and the conquest of Scotland was the one point now in practical dispute.

Whether Wallace was in Rome while this weighty matter was being discussed has never been ascertained, and all searches through the extensive medieval archives in the Vatican have so far yielded nothing to substantiate this tradition. On the other hand, continuing papal interest in Scotland and the Scots at the turn of the century places such a presence at the Papal Curia by the personable young Scottish knight within the bounds of probability.

11

THE COMYN WARS

The Scots wist that wele, and schewed him the vis,
Ther side was ilk a dele in poynt to wynne the pris.
Boldely they bed bataile with visage full austere,
The King's side gan faile, for he had no powere.
Further mot he noucht, Scotland for to se,
That time no thyng he wrought, but spendid his moné.
The marche under wardeyn he left it as before,
Unto the south again he went, and did no more

PETER OF LANGTOFT

A T the time when Wallace and his five belted knights slipped out of the country on their diplomatic mission, Bishop Lamberton's strategy was put into effect. Bruce made his abortive attack on Lochmaben from the Maxwell stronghold of Caerlaverock. The Comyns adopted guerrilla tactics in the north, while the Steward and the Earl of Menteith attacked English strongpoints in Clydesdale and the west. Lamberton remained in the Forest, with his headquarters at Stobo near Peebles. In November 1299 the three Guardians came together again in the Torwood during the last phase of the siege of Stirling Castle. The English garrison, as previously noted, was being starved into submission and Edward, who had mustered a host at Berwick intent on raising the siege, was powerless, on account of bad weather and the recalcitrance of his nobles, to take the field against the Scots at that time of year. By now Wallace's diplomatic efforts were beginning to pay dividends; on 13 November the Guardians wrote to Edward saying that Philip of France had offered to mediate on their behalf and arrange a truce. Edward, however, refused to agree to this and some sporadic fighting went on through the ensuing winter without anything decisive being achieved. The Guardians went their separate ways again, leaving Sir John de Soulis to receive the surrender of Stirling Castle soon afterwards. This time the Scots were determined to hold on to this key position and a garrison under Sir William Oliphant was then installed.

The events of the winter months of 1299–1300 are obscure, but some time between November and the following May the Earl of Carrick resigned as Guardian. There was a clash of personalities among the Guardians and it seems that young John Comyn was the troublemaker — at one point he declared vehemently that he would not serve with Bishop Lamberton. The Steward and the Earl of Atholl interceded on behalf of the bishop, but in the end it was Bruce, not Comyn, who resigned from the regency. His place was filled by Sir Ingelram de Umfraville, one of the Comyn faction and a relative of the Balliols. Bruce was undoubtedly soured by this turn of events; from this period dates his disillusion with and disaffection from the patriot cause.

This change of heart was compounded by military operations in the south-west, the traditional Bruce country. The Earl of Buchan, who was also Sheriff of Wigtownshire, campaigned in Galloway early in 1300 with the hope of winning over the Gallovidians, always men of an independent turn of mind, whose chief enemy was not the King of England but (as they saw it) the Earl of Carrick, whose territories in Annandale and Ayrshire tended to encircle them.

In July Edward's long-awaited invasion of Scotland got under way. Angered at the temerity of the Scots in attacking his newly founded pele of Lochmaben the previous autumn, Edward concentrated his energies first on reducing the great castle of Caerlaverock at the mouth of the Nith, some ten miles south of Lochmaben. The splendidly photogenic structure which nowadays dominates the Solway coast south-east of Dumfries was largely built by the Maxwells in the fifteenth century, and the stronghold of Edward's time was a much more modest affair. Edward's attack on this fortress merited no more than a single line in Langtoft: 'A poure hamlet he toke, the castelle of Karelavrock', but an eye-witness of the affair was Walter of Exeter, a Franciscan friar of Carocus in Cornwall, who was inspired to write a lengthy ballad in Norman French describing the siege in loving detail. According to this ballad, written during or soon after the siege, the castle was lightly held by about sixty men. Siege-engines were brought in by sea and soon made short work of the defences. According to one account, the defenders were permitted to leave on certain terms; another states that the constable and twenty-one of his men were imprisoned at Newcastle and Appleby, while the Lanercost Chronicle says merely that many of the defenders were subsequently hanged. At any rate, the surrender of the castle was an amusing diversion for Edward and his new bride, living symbol of the Treaty of Provins between England and France. Peace between these two adversaries had been negotiated in 1299 and sealed by a dynastic marriage. Edward's first wife, Eleanor, had died in 1290; now he took as his bride Marguerite, the seventeen-year-old sister of King Philip.

Meanwhile even more elaborate preparations than ever before were put in hand for the latest attempt to subjugate the Scots. These preparations were not lost on the Scots and some peace feelers were put out. Bishop Dalton tried to parley with Edward but was brushed aside. At Kirkcudbright Edward met John Comyn and the Earl of Buchan and received the Scottish peace proposals: the restoration of King John and the English estates forfeited by the Scottish magnates. Edward regarded these reasonable proposals as impertinent and brought the two-day parley to an abrupt close. The English army now moved slowly forward through Galloway. While Edward tarried at Twynholm, his scouts engaged a party of Scots on the Cree estuary and captured Sir Robert Keith, the Marischal.

The following day the main body of the English army advanced to the Cree and paused at a point midway between the present-day village of Creetown and Newton Stewart, where the river winds and loops through mud-flats to the sea. On the Wigtownshire bank the Scottish army was drawn up, under the command of the Earl of Buchan, with a sizable force of cavalry. At low tide the English foot soldiers forded the river and engaged the Scots at close quarters. Edward intended to hold back his cavalry but through some breakdown in communication the Earl of Hereford led his brigade forward and charged into the Scots. Edward felt obliged to follow, against his better judgment, and the entire English cavalry crossed the tidal river. At this the Scots were thrown into panic and confusion and fled in disarray. Edward did not press home his advantage, so the actual Scottish losses were light, and the English army recrossed the Cree without having achieved much.

Desultory fighting continued in Galloway throughout the summer, but then, on 30 October, Edward granted a truce until the following Whitsun (21 May 1301) and returned to England without achieving anything beyond the seizure of Caerlaverock.

This flurry of English military operations is deceptive, for Scotland continued to exist in its curiously semi-independent state. Even in those limited areas under English control there was a duality of authority, not unlike the situation in southern Ireland in 1918–21, where the rebels maintained their own system of law and order and collected their own taxes. Inevitably, the triumvirate of Lamberton, Comyn and Umfraville was no more successful than the previous arrangements. Somewhere between December 1300 and Whitsun 1301 the guardianship of these three was dissolved and a single ruler was appointed. According to Fordun this appointment had the personal blessing of King John, now living in style on his ancestral estates at Bailleul. In this it is possible to see the hand of Wallace, who is believed to have met King John and discussed the problems of the regency. Equally, however, it is not improbable that Wallace was sadly disillusioned when he eventually met the man in whose name he had waged war and administered Scotland, and it has been suggested that, having met and taken the measure of Toom Tabard, his unswerving allegiance diminished thereafter.

At any rate, Sir John de Soulis occupied a position midway between the Comyn–Balliol faction and the Bruces. He was related to the Comyns by marriage, but his family, with lands in Eskdale and Liddesdale, were neighbours and ancient allies of the Bruces. Though Bishop Lamberton was no longer a Guardian he worked closely with Soulis in 1301–2, and between them they succeeded in rallying the moderates to the patriotic cause.

Shortly before Whitsun 1301 Edward's lawyers completed the task of preparing the brief in answer to the Pope's strongly worded letter of the previous summer and this set out at great length, with numerous dubious, fanciful and downright mythical references to Brutus the Trojan, King Arthur and Athelstan, the case for Edward's superiority over Scotland. In modern parlance, this document was worthy only of a shyster; even English historians of later generations had to concede that this was one of the most extraordinary state papers to be found on record. Edward, sometimes dubbed the English Justinian in allusion to his legal reforms, appears to have been well satisfied with this monumental exercise in chicanery. The brief was despatched to Rome and Edward went north again.

In May 1301 Scottish and French delegations were supposed to confer with Edward's commissioners at Canterbury with a view to securing a lasting peace in Scotland. Early the previous month, however, Edward, intent on clinching the matter, warned his northern barons to be ready as soon as the truce expired at Whitsun 'to resist the attacks of the Scots, if necessary'. Once again, we have the curious spectacle of the aggressor shifting his aggression to his victims. And Edward was not content to wait until the truce expired; on 12 May he issued orders for a levy of 12,000 men. In the event he took the field with no more than 6,800 men, all on foot with the exception of their officers and a few hobelars (light horse).

This time he summoned his barons and feudatories to meet him at Berwick on 6 July. Mindful of the lessons learned on previous campaigns, he arranged this time for an impressive fleet of seventy ships to keep the expedition well supplied with provisions. With such attention to the material, Edward did not neglect the spiritual, devoting much valuable time to further pilgrimages to the shrine of St Thomas à Becket and other holy places. The invasion was launched in July, the English forces being divided into two armies commanded by the King and the Prince of Wales respectively. Edward advanced from Berwick on 18 July and made a very leisurely progress through the Borders and the Lothians as far as the Forth. He was in Peebles for twelve days (2–14 August) and entered Glasgow a week later where he remained a fortnight (21 August to 4 September). Between 27 September and 27 October he was mainly encamped at

Dunipace, where Wallace's uncle had been priest, but he also paid a lightning visit to Stirling. A large contingent was despatched to strike westwards into Clydesdale where siege was laid to Bothwell Castle in August. That great fortress fell to the English a month later. As usual, the Scots melted away before Edward's advance, contenting themselves with snapping at his heels, harrying the lengthy supply lines and cutting off the stragglers. This time, though, Edward was determined to stay in Scotland and by Christmas he had established his headquarters at Linlithgow, where he built a pele. It was here that another truce, negotiated through the good offices of King Philip, was declared on 26 January 1302, covering the period till St Andrew's Day (30 November). Edward remained at Linlithgow till the worst of the winter had abated, then recrossed the border on 19 February 1302. The main fact recorded by the English chroniclers is the loss of those few horses which had been brought on the expedition, through want of forage and the severity of the winter.

Meanwhile the Prince of Wales had less success, never venturing inland from the Solway coast and grinding to a halt near the present-day town of Stranraer. The Scots dominated the south-west and harried the Prince's army on the flanks without letting up. Soulis and Umfraville made an assault on Lochmaben pele early in September but only just failed to capture it. The Scots mustered their forces near Loudoun Hill and prevented Edward and the Prince of Wales from uniting their armies on the Clyde coast as planned. To be sure, the Prince's troops later managed to take Turnberry Castle near Girvan, but he was unable to quell resistance in Carrick as a whole and was forced to withdraw before the onset of winter and join his father at Linlithgow. In Matthew of Westminster's telling phrase, 'he achieved nothing important or even worthy of praise'.

In truth, the expedition of 1301–2 achieved absolutely nothing. Although conducted on a much smaller scale than Edward's previous Scottish campaigns, the losses sustained were proportionately greater and far outweighed even the temporary advantages. The Scots carefully avoided the English army, but if they had no wish to engage in pitched battles they were every bit as active as in previous campaigns. In September 1301 Sir Robert de Tilliol, castellan of Lochmaben, confessed that he was in dire straits. To Edward he wrote:

> And we give you to understand as a certainty that John de
> Soulis and the Earl of Buchan, with their power, are lying at
> Loudoun; and Sir Simon Fraser at Stonehouse, and Sir
> Alexander de Abernethy and Sir Herbert de Morham. If Your
> Majesty would only send a hundred armed horse, with a good
> leader, tomorrow the latest! But be informed that all the coun-
> try is rising because we have no troops to ride upon them.[1]

On 7 September, probably no more than a day or two after this letter was written, Soulis and Umfraville, with a large force estimated at seven thousand and growing by the day, burned Lochmaben town and assaulted the pele, and made a second attempt to reduce it the following day; but sustaining heavy losses they drew off and turned away towards Nithsdale and Galloway. Tilliol sent a further message that the Scots were seducing those who had accepted the King's peace. People in their droves were joining the enemy and Sir Robert was con-vinced that an invasion of England was imminent. Perhaps Edward's own propaganda was having its effect. At any rate, Sir Robert Hastings and his troops sallied out of Roxburgh Castle in search of these Scottish invaders. On 3 October the Constable of Newcastle-on-Ayr wrote to Edward that the Scots were in Carrick, 'before the Castle of Turnberry, with four hundred men-at-arms and within these eight days had wanted to attack Ayr Castle'. He begged for reinforcements as he and 'the other loy-alists' could not withstand such an attack. In February 1302, despite the truce having just come into effect, the castle at Ayr was besieged by the Scots.

The truce meant that the English were unlikely to resume the offensive until the spring of 1303 at the earliest, although it is doubtful how effective such an agreement would have been. Criticism of Soulis and Umfraville is invidious, but one cannot help thinking that if William Wallace had a force of seven thou-sand at his disposal, ranged against Edward's army which was allegedly rather smaller, Lochmaben pele would not only have fallen but the English would have been cleared out of the Lowlands altogether.

Doubtless this thought occurred to Edward also, for, only

four days after recrossing the Tweed, he changed his mind and tarried at Morpeth. Here he gave his magnates a pep talk. The truce was unlikely to produce any lasting benefits. Nothing less than an all-out invasion of Scotland would settle the matter once and for all. This time he directed his remarks particularly towards the high officials in Ireland who he felt were not pulling their weight.

Two things, not unconnected, happened in 1302. Robert Bruce, Earl of Carrick, was rapidly becoming disenchanted with his fellow magnates. Despite his success in waging war on the enemy in the south-west, he was excluded from the regency and relegated to a minor role. He had been exasperated by Comyn and then Soulis, but the last straw was probably the news from the Papal Curia of the transfer of John Balliol from the custody of the Abbot of Cluny to King Philip in the summer of 1301 and the strong rumour that Philip was now sending him back to Scotland with a French army. The restoration of King John was the last thing Bruce wanted, fearing that his own position would be threatened.

Some time after the truce of January 1302 came into effect, Bruce surrendered to Sir John de St John, the English governor of Annandale and Galloway. On 28 April Edward put his seal to a document which spoke of 'his liege Robert de Brus, Earl of Carrick'. After a preamble stating that the King accepted the submission of Sir Robert Bruce the younger for the sake of the good service which Robert's ancestors and family had rendered, the document went on to promise that if Bruce were to lose his lands or suffer any disadvantage as a result of any truce or papal ordinance, the King would grant reasonable maintenance 'as is proper for him'. Of special favour he restored to Bruce's tenants their lands in England lately taken for their rebellion. Edward granted to Patrick de Trumpe the younger and his aunt Matilda de Carrick, two of these tenants, certain lands in the manor of Levington in Cumbria, to which they had fallen heirs. This extraordinary document also promised that, in the event of the throne being restored to Balliol or his son, Bruce was to be permitted to pursue any claims to his inheritance in the English courts. 'If, by chance, it should happen that the right must be judged elsewhere than in the King's court, then in this case the King promises Robert assistance and counsel as before, as well as he is able to give it.' It has been argued that the right referred to here was Bruce's claim to the throne, inherited from his grand-father the Competitor, but Edward would hardly concede such a right to one who had so recently been a rebel.

In May Bruce set the seal on his defection by taking up the English appointments of Sheriff of Lanark and Governor of Ayr. About the same time he remarried, taking as his second wife Elizabeth de Burgh, daughter of the Earl of Ulster (an associate of the Turnberry Band of sixteen years before). The earl was one of Edward's most loyal lieutenants and this marriage may have been intended to harness Bruce more closely to the English interest. Elizabeth, however, was also the niece of Egidia, wife of the Steward, and thus the ties between the Bruce and Stuart families were strengthened. It was the marriage of Bruce's daughter Marjorie to Walter the Steward which was to found the Stuart dynasty 'that cam wi a lass'.

If Bruce's defection was a severe blow, it was softened to some extent by success on the diplomatic front. If, as has been suggested, Wallace was in France again in 1301–2, this may help to explain the success of a visit paid by Bishop Lamberton to the French court. At any rate, he returned to Scotland with a letter from Philip dated 6 April, addressed to 'the Guardians, the mag-nates and the whole community, his dear friends' to whom he wished 'health and hope of fortitude in adversity'. This letter seems to have confirmed Bruce's worst fears. In it, Philip:

> received with sincere affection their envoys John, Abbot of Jeddwurth, and John Wissard, Knight, and fully understands their letters and messages anxiously expressed by the envoys. Is moved to his very marrow by the evils brought on their country through hostile malignity. Praises them for their con-stancy to their King and their shining valour in defence of their native land against injustice, and urges them to persevere in the same course. Regarding the aid which they ask, he is not unmindful of the old league between their King, themselves, and him, and is carefully pondering ways and means of help-ing them. But, bearing in mind the dangers of the road, and dreading the risks which sometimes chance to letters, he has given his views by word of mouth to W[illiam], Bishop of St Andrews, for whom he asks full credence.[2]

These fine words were taken to mean that Philip was considering helping King John to regain his throne. At the very least it seemed that he would send troops to help the Scots, or perhaps renew hostilities with Edward on the Continent. But larger factors were now in play. Philip had quarrelled with Pope Boniface and the latter, as a counterweight to the obstreperous French ruler, now drew closer to Edward. Then, on 11 July, the flower of French chivalry was hammered by the despised Flemish burghers at Courtrai using Wallace's schiltrom tactics. The battle was virtually a replica of Falkirk with one vital exception: the French lacked the longbow and proved no match for the close ranks of Flemish spearmen. The Swiss at Morgarten and the Scots at Bannockburn were later to demonstrate that the age of chivalry (in the strict sense) was over. Philip cut his losses and a truce was made between England and France.

The first evidence of the growing *rapprochement* between the Papacy and England came on 13 August 1302 when Boniface sent strongly worded bulls to Bishop Wishart and the other Scottish prelates. The Pope who had, only three years earlier, rebuked King Edward for his treatment of the Scots and had subsequently taken Scotland under his protection, now admonished the clergy with scarcely concealed threats if they did not make their peace with Edward. Bishop Wishart was singled out for a special ticking-off, being likened by His Holiness to 'a rock of offence and a stone of stumbling'. Boniface was at that juncture ingratiating himself with Edward whom he also urged to resume war against France. But Edward, his 'dearly-beloved son in Christ', managed to temporise, making just the right noises to keep Boniface happy, and in return the Pope relaxed the modicum of restraint he had exercised on Edward's aggression against the Scots.

The truce between Scotland and England expired at the end of November 1302. Although it was too late in the year for an all-out invasion, Edward decided that some show of force was needed immediately. He himself did not take the field, but entrusted the expedition to that rising star, Sir John de Segrave. On 29 September Segrave was ordered to join forces with Sir Ralph de Manton and strike at the very heart of Scotland as soon as the truce ran out. This punitive expedition, which advanced by Kirkintilloch (near Glasgow) and struck at Stirling, soon ran into difficulties. By the end of the year Segrave was reporting back that 'certain the Scots rebels, in increased force, have broken into the lands there in his possession, occupied certain castles and towns, and perpetrated other excesses; and, unless checked, they may soon break into England as usual.' The threat of a Scottish invasion of England was, no doubt, exaggerated; but in response to this plea Edward despatched Sir Ralph Fitz-William, the King's Cofferer or Paymaster, on 20 January 1303 with a large contingent of knights and men-at-arms. Thus augmented, Segrave's army, which was arrayed in three divisions of ten thousand men each, began a fresh advance through Lothian. The first division was encamped near Roslin south-east of Edinburgh when it was suddenly attacked at dawn on 24 February by a large force, estimated about eight thousand strong, under the command of Comyn and Sir Simon Fraser, who had marched through the night from Biggar. The English were routed, Segrave himself being seriously wounded and taken prisoner. The second division coming up was ambushed and annihilated, but the soldiers of the third division, who had been delayed by their devotions, avoided the trap and partially retrieved the situation by repulsing the Scottish attack and liberating some of the captives, including Segrave. The English chronicles made light of the affair, but the Scots claimed it as a great victory. Certainly it was a master-stroke, the main forces of the English army being destroyed and Sir Ralph de Manton being among those who fell in battle that day.

Interestingly, the Rishanger Chronicle attributes this marked reversal in English fortunes to the reappointment of William Wallace as captain of the Scottish army. As Rishanger was alone in making this assertion it has always been treated with caution, the feeling being that Wallace would not have supported Comyn at this time. But Sir John Comyn, even if he harboured ambitions of gaining the throne for himself, was still nominally regent on behalf of his kinsman King John, and Wallace had been consistent in fighting for the liberation of Scotland in John's name. In default of references to Wallace in the chronicles of the period we must reluctantly fall back on Blind Harry as the only source of material giving a clue as to the patriot's activities after his return from France.

It will be recalled that Wallace landed at the confluence of the Tay and the Earn. By night he made his way to Elcho where his 'dear cousin named Craufurd' lived. William Craufurd concealed Wallace and his men in his barn for four or five days, but when the food ran out Craufurd journeyed to Perth to purchase fresh supplies. The English, suspicious of his buying more foodstuffs than usual, seized Craufurd and interrogated him closely in prison. Craufurd said that the food and wines were required for a kirking feast, so he was released; but the English were convinced that he was harbouring the notorious outlaw. Young Butler (the son and grandson of James and John Butler slain by Wallace a few years previously) raised a force of eight hundred men and set off in pursuit. Craufurd warned Wallace of what had transpired, and by the time he and his men (numbering nineteen in all) were combat-ready, Butler's troops were approaching the building. The Scots managed to escape into Elcho Park, a dense woodland where Wallace had constructed a tiny stronghold; but when it became apparent that Butler intended burning down Craufurd's house, with his wife and family inside, Wallace rushed out into the open and drew off the English in hot pursuit. Wallace retreated into his 'strength' and a desperate hand-to-hand skirmish ensued in which a number of the attackers were killed. The English withdrew momentarily to consider the situation and Wallace divided his slender forces into three groups under Longueville, William Craufurd and himself. Butler split his forces into three in order to attack the wood from different directions. Wallace turned to confront the party led by Butler himself and ambushed them as they reentered the wood. The first seven Englishmen were slain on the spot, but Butler himself escaped and withdrew the rest of his group. As night fell, Butler left patrols to watch the wood while the remainder returned to their camp.

The English governor of Perth, whom Harry names improbably as the Earl of York, sent orders to Butler not to attack again until he came up with a much larger force. Butler, who had strong personal reasons for seeing Wallace slain, did not wish to see this prize fall to his superior officer. Harry has him parleying with Wallace and proposing single combat at dawn the following morning. At daybreak, however, the Scots tried to slip away through a thick mist and in the ensuing mêlée Craufurd was wounded and young Butler slain by Wallace's own hand. In the resulting confusion the Scots made good their escape to Methven Wood, Wallace allegedly carrying his wounded kinsman all the way. On the way they encountered Ellis of Dundas and Sir John Scott, who had been on the point of submitting to the English but who now, seeing Wallace, decided to join forces with him. Harry claims that Wallace and his growing band went to Birnam near Dunkeld, where they were joined by Squire Ruthven, and then on to Atholl and Lorn in search of food, 'the district having been made bare both of wild and tame animals'. Later they replenished their supplies by attacking the English outpost at Rannoch Hall. As his forces increased Wallace attacked Dunkeld, slaying all the English there and plundering the cathedral, before advancing on Perth and laying siege to the English stronghold. These and other events, occupying a large part of Book XI (lines 330–790), were no doubt muddled and confused, being derived in large part from the oral traditions of a later century, yet the substance was probably not far removed from Wallace's exploits during the period prior to his betrayal.

After Courtrai, Philip began patching up his quarrel with Edward. Sensing that France and England were now drawing closer together, the Scots tried to secure their position. Early in May 1303 a powerful delegation of Scottish leaders visited France with a view to securing effective aid from Philip. The delegation consisted of Lamberton, Bishop Crambeth of Dunkeld, the Earl of Buchan, James the Steward, Sir John de Soulis, Sir Ingelram de Umfraville and Sir William de Balliol. They were treated with Gallic charm but given the run-around, and returned with chagrin to report on 25 May to Sir John Comyn that a treaty of peace had been signed five days previously at Paris between France and England — a treaty from which the Scots were expressly excluded. It was small consolation to be told smoothly by Philip that they should not be alarmed at this omission. The French King promised that he would immediately follow up the treaty by sending envoys to Edward urging him to pull back from war against the Scots. This, it was hoped, would lead to a truce pending a peace conference attended by the three monarchs (John now being included). Philip explained the exclusion of the Scots from the treaty on the grounds that their case could be more easily settled between Edward and himself once they were united in friendship and affinity. This last was an allusion to the fact that the bonds of marriage between the two royal houses were to be further strengthened; part of the treaty included the betrothal of the Prince of Wales and Princess Isabella of France. Finally Philip urged them not to do anything to provoke Edward further, although he added in the same breath that the fame of the late conflict had spread over the entire world, and he was confident that, if Edward refused to make peace, they would act with resolution. Philip's remarks, as reported back to Comyn, were jumbled and confused and may have become garbled and distorted in the telling, the envoys being anxious to put as fine a gloss on matters as possible, but one is left with the impression that the Scots were naïve and gullible.

At the same time, friction between Scotland's former allies, King Philip and Pope Boniface, erupted into open war, resulting in the capture of the Pope by the French and his subsequent death. Effectively the Treaty of Paris, by bringing hostilities between France and England to an end, merely enabled Edward to turn his attention once more to the Scots. Ironically, the treaty was ratified by Edward from his headquarters at St Johnston (Perth) on 10 July 1303.

After the defeat at Roslin Edward was in no mood to leave the campaign to his subordinates. On 9 April he issued writs for the levy of almost ten thousand men from the English counties, and simultaneously ordered his new ally, Robert Bruce, to bring a thousand men from Carrick and Galloway. About the same time Sir Richard Siward was summoned with three hundred men of Nithsdale. The size of Edward's army has not been computed but it included large contingents from Ireland, Wales, Gascony and even Savoy (whose Count commanded in person). By 16 May Edward was at Roxburgh, where he stayed till the end of the month, then he advanced by Edinburgh and Linlithgow, and reached Perth on 10 June. This was his headquarters for about seven weeks, and from Perth attacks were made on the surrounding countryside. The advance was resumed at the beginning of August, through Brechin and Aberdeen and thence by Buchan to Banff, Cullen and Elgin. The limit of the advance was Kinloss in Moray, where Edward remained from 13 September to 4 October. By 6 November he had withdrawn to Dunfermline where he made his headquarters in the majestic abbey and spent the winter.

Only two strongholds offered resistance. At Brechin the English advance was somewhat delayed by the heroic defence of the castle by Sir Thomas Maule. Matthew of Westminster says that he cheered on his men and mocked the attackers from the battlements, making a great show of wiping the dust of the wall where it was struck by the rocks hurled by Edward's siege-engines. Unfortunately for the doughty Thomas, one of the missiles he derided struck him down, but with his dying breath he exhorted his men to fight on. The garrison held out for forty days before capitulating. Sir William Oliphant put up a courageous resistance at Stirling Castle which defied Edward right through until 24 July 1304, and then only surrendered when the starving garrison could no longer withstand the pounding from the thirteen giant siege-engines which were arrayed against it.

Hemingburgh says that the expedition through Scotland in the summer of 1303 was marked by wholesale conflagration and devastation, although it is not clear exactly who did the burning. Edward's apologists have often pointed out that such wholesale destruction was contrary to his policy: it was against his interests to destroy what was, after all, his own property. Nevertheless, there is the chilling evidence presented in an order by Edward from Dunfermline dated 18 November 1303, directing his Chancellor to issue a pardon in favour of Warin Martyn. Martyn was the commander of the Welshmen in Edward's army, and he was now being held accountable for sundry murders, robberies, arson and other atrocities committed by the men under his command. Edward shrugged this off, taking the pragmatic view that such things were inevitable in wartime.

From the fact that Edward over-wintered at Dunfermline, on the north shore of the Forth, and had penetrated further north than any previous expedition, it seems that Scottish resistance was on the verge of disappearing altogether. To be sure, a former trusted lieutenant, Sir Simon Fraser, continued to hold out, but the submission of the Earl of Carrick was an important coup for Edward. Furthermore, as the implications of the Treaty of Paris sank in, the Scottish leaders realised that no help would be forthcoming from France after all. They now lost heart and in December Comyn began tentative negotiations with Edward, culminating in the peace made at Strathord on 9 February. The terms of capitulation were remarkably lenient, probably because Edward was in an indulgent mood; the rebel leaders were merely rapped over the wrist, being sentenced to various terms of banishment. The full terms of this punishment belong more properly to the next chapter, for they have a direct bearing on the fate of Wallace.

William Wallace alone did not enter the King's peace. Harry is silent on the matter, but there is no reason to doubt the word of Robert de Brunne who alleges that, while Edward was at Dunfermline, Wallace (who was then in the Forest of Selkirk) asked his friends to seek terms on his behalf. But Edward was 'full grim' and would offer nothing but a reward of three hundred marks to the man who would bring him Wallace's head. On receipt of this unyielding resolve Wallace fled and continued 'to dwell in moors and marshes'. Edward's response, in view of his subsequent treatment of Wallace, is fully consonant with Brunne's account. It is possible that some of his former comrades, during their own negotations with the King, raised a plea on his behalf; but if it were entered, such a plea was unlikely to have been at Wallace's request. He was every bit as implacable as Edward himself and he had shown, time and time again, that he would never submit to the King of England. He never had, and he never would; that was his forthright message. This is confirmed by Bower:

> For the noble William was afraid of the treachery of his countrymen. Some of them envied him for his uprightness, others were seduced by the promises of the English, and others with tortuous machinations and infinite care prepared traps for him, hoping thereby for the favour of the King of England. In addition, persuasive arguments were offered to him by his immediate close friends that he like the others should obey the King of the English, so that they might thus obtain peace. Besides, others were sent by the King himself to persuade him to do this, promising him on the same King's behalf earldoms and wide possessions in England or in Scotland, to be chosen by himself and held by his successors for ever. He despised all these approaches, and speaking for the liberty of his people like a second Matthias he is reported to have answered: 'Scotland, deso-

late as you are, you believe too much in false words and are too
unwary of woes to come! If you think like me, you would not
readily place your neck under a foreign yoke. When I was
growing up I learned from a priest who was my uncle to set this
one proverb above all worldly possessions, and I have carried it
in my heart,

> I tell you the truth, freedom is the finest of things;
> Never live under a servile yoke, my son.

And that is why I tell you briefly that even if all Scots obey the
King of England so that each one abandons his liberty, I and my
companions who wish to be associated with me in this matter
shall stand up for the liberty of the kingdom. And (may God be
favourable to us!) we others shall obey no one but the King [of
Scots] or his lieutenant.[3]

These stirring words have the ring of truth, entirely consonant with all that we know of Wallace's character. He remained
what he had always been, Edward's indomitable and unyielding
foe, the only Scottish leader who never wavered in his allegiance to his country and its king. John had been enthroned at
Scone, and Wallace's actions, whether as Guardian or guerrilla,
had been carried out in that king's name.

For his part, Edward was just as obdurate. During the preliminary negotiations in December 1303, when draft proposals
for peace were put to John Comyn, Edward made his views
crystal clear: 'With respect to William le Waleys, the King intends
that he shall be received to his will and as he shall ordain.'[4] At
Strathord the following February Edward's attitude was even
more explicit: 'And as to Messire William le Waleys, it is agreed
that he shall give himself up to the will and grace of our Lord the
King, as it shall seem good to him.'[5]

One of the friends of Wallace who interceded on his behalf
was Sir Alexander de Abernethy, who made a formal submission
to Edward at Strathord. Abernethy was immediately appointed
by the Prince of Wales as Warden between the Mounth and the
Forth, with the task of watching the fords across the river, lest
the guerrilla leader should try to leave the Forest and escape
into the Highlands. Abernethy sought clarification: what terms
should be given to Wallace if he tried to surrender? On 3 March

1304 King Edward wrote unequivocally to Abernethy from Kinghorn in Fife:

> In reply to your request for instructions as to whether it is our pleasure that you should hold out to William le Waleys any words of peace, know that it is not at all our pleasure that you hold out any word of peace to him, or to any other of his company, unless they place themselves absolutely (*de haut en bas*) and in all things at our will without any reservation whatsoever.[6]

In other words, nothing short of unconditional surrender would suffice.

Ironically, Wallace's chief ally after the wholesale capitulation of Scottish leaders at Strathord was Sir Simon Fraser. From the fact that Abernethy's patrols were operating in Strathearn and Menteith it appears that Wallace and Fraser were roaming the district around Stirling, probably harassing the besieging forces and helping to bring clandestine aid to Oliphant's garrison.

In March 1304 Edward moved out of Dunfermline Abbey. Although the remains of his own sister, as well as her husband Alexander III and their sons, were interred there, Edward had no compunction about ordering the abbey's destruction. Most of the English chroniclers, clerics to a man, could find no excuse for such an atrocity. Dunfermline Abbey, founded by the English princess St Margaret in the eleventh century and as sacred to the Scots as Canterbury was to the English, was the most magnificent of the medieval ecclesiastical structures to be found north of the border. The chroniclers described its destruction as atrocious, barbarous or 'unscrupulous and vindictive'. Matthew of Westminster alone sought to justify Edward's vandalism. The abbey was spacious enough to lodge at one and the same time three mighty kings and their retinues. But there was an accursed taint on the place. Its size had rendered it suitable for the Scots nobles to hold their meetings there; and there they had devised machinations against the English King; and thence, in time of war, they issued as from ambush, to harry and murder the English. What then? The King's army, therefore, perceiving that the temple of the Lord was not a church but a den of robbers, a thorn in the eye of the English nation, fired the buildings.

The chapel and a few cells for monks were all that was spared. Even today, however, enough remains of the once-splendid edifice to remind us of the great abbey that was once so admired.

Some time during that month the guerrilla band led by Wallace and Fraser was defeated in a bloody encounter at Happrew near Stobo in Peeblesshire by a large English force led by Sir William de Latimer, Sir John de Segrave and Sir Robert de Clifford.[7] A portent of things to come was the fact that Wallace was tracked down on this occasion by a fellow Scotsman, John of Musselburgh, who received ten shillings from Edward's own hand as a reward. It was Wallace's last fight. Blind Harry makes no mention of this battle at all; but as the minstrel's account of this period is thoroughly unrealistic (maintaining that, on the eve of his betrayal, Wallace had rid the country of the hated Southrons) this omission is immaterial. Soon Wallace would be on his own, the only Scotsman of any note to continue the struggle. His would be the only banner of resistance still fluttering beyond the battered walls of Stirling Castle. On 5 May Wallace's old friend and staunch ally, Bishop Lamberton, submitted to Edward at Stirling while the siege of the castle was still in progress, and shortly afterwards Sir Simon Fraser also surrendered.

Wallace, with no more than a handful of faithful adherents left, was powerless to prevent the all-out assault on Stirling Castle. The powerful fortress which had so often been fought over in the past decade had resisted all attempts by the English to dislodge its resolute constable and his garrison since the previous summer. On 1 April 1304 King Edward commanded the earls of Strathearn, Menteith and Lennox to blockade the castle, preventing the people of Stirling from slipping in and out with much-needed provisions. Five days later several great siege-engines were shipped from Edinburgh and Berwick. The greatest artillery in the British Isles was slowly converging on the beleaguered fortress. On 16 April Sir John Botetourte was ordered to give assistance to the Earl of Carrick in forwarding 'the frame of the great engine of Inverkip' which Bruce had just reported as unmanageable. Five days later Sir Robert de Leyburne, Constable of Inverkip Castle, was reprimanded for his inefficiency and ordered 'to arrest at Glasgow all the iron and great stones of the engines there and forward them to Stirling, without any manner of excuse or delay', for by his inaction 'the siege is greatly delayed'. Meanwhile, on 12 April the King had ordered the Prince of Wales 'to procure and take as much lead as you can about the town of St John of Perth and Dunblane, and elsewhere' for use in molten form as horrific ammunition. The Prince's men were to strip the lead off all the church roofs, though the sanctimonious Edward was careful to stipulate that sufficient lead was to be left to give some covering to the altars.

During the first half of April King Edward himself had spent some time before the walls of Stirling, assessing the situation and looking for weak points. On 22 April he returned to Stirling and took personal charge of the siege operations. These were on a scale hitherto unimaginable. Ranged before the walls were at least thirteen of the most powerful engines yet devised, capable of hurling a stone projectile of three hundred pounds or a heavy twelve-foot dart more than a thousand yards. There were other specialised machines, such as a kind of jib crane of great height on a movable platform which was used to hoist a cage containing twenty men-at-arms to the top of the walls. A long spar with a wicked steel claw at the end served to pull down the upper parts of parapets and overhanging galleries. Giant 'rats', up to sixty feet long and containing huge beams shod with steel, were used to ram walls and gates, while 'tortoises' (armoured shelters) enabled engineers to approach moats and fill them with rocks and earth. The enormous artillery pieces, the catapults and ballistae with their oaken wheels twelve feet in diameter, had not materially changed since they were invented by the Romans a thousand years earlier, but on this occasion Edward was equipped with a fiendish new device known as the War Wolf, which apparently was having teething troubles.

The defence was not entirely passive either, for both Rishanger and Hemingburgh record that the garrison killed many of the besiegers with engines of their own. Grapnels were lowered from the walls by cranes to overturn the rats and tortoises, while molten lead and pitch or boiling oil and water rained down on the attackers with deadly force. King Edward appears to have supervised the siege with great zest. His enjoyment of the action was hardly diminished when, one day as he was riding about and directing his men, a Scottish archer shot him. The steel-tipped arrow lodged in his armour but did not wound him, and Edward ebulliently shook his fist up at the battlements, threatening the bowman with a good hanging.

Although conditions inside the castle were becoming desperate by midsummer, the situation was not much better outside. One correspondent admitted that the King's horses had nothing to eat but grass and there was 'the utmost need of oats and beans'. In another letter, written the same day to Sir Richard de Bremesgrave, the recipient was urged to 'send all the King's stores he can find in Berwick, in haste by day and night, to Stirling, for they can find nothing in these parts'. Edward himself was continuing to summon reinforcements and field engineers.

Sir William Oliphant offered a spirited and resolute defence. Every day Edward's troops filled in the ditches with logs and tree-branches, and every day the garrison set fire to them. Next Edward tried filling the ditches with rubble and earth so that he could move the scaling turrets right up to the walls. This tactic led to desperate hand-to-hand combat and many times Edward's shock-troops were repulsed. But the end was inevitable; the starving garrison was now short of water and Sir William offered to submit if he and his men were granted their lives. Edward, however, insisted on absolute and unconditional surrender. At last, on 20 July 1304, the garrison gave in. There were said to be seven score defenders, but by the time of the capitulation it appears that only Sir William and twenty-five others (including two friars) were still alive. Before the defenders were permitted to come out of the castle, Edward insisted that they submit to a curious field trial, partly as a scientific experiment and partly for the entertainment of the ladies of the court, including young Queen Marguerite. No one was permitted to enter the castle until it should be bombarded by the War Wolf which, at long last, was ready for action. Those within might defend themselves from *le Loup de guerre* as best they could, for the diversion and amusement of the Queen and her ladies-in-waiting. The result of this savage bombardment is not recorded, but at length Oliphant and the remnant of his garrison were allowed to emerge. Oliphant, who had been captured at Dunbar and confined at Devizes Castle until September 1297, was now sent south in chains and lodged in the Tower of London. The rest of the gallant garrison were despatched to various English castles. In triumph Edward returned to England towards the end of August.

The fall of Stirling Castle was the last act in a drama which had lasted for four years. This period of continual warfare, often known as the Comyn Wars from the principal protagonist on the Scottish side, had not advanced the cause of independence. Nevertheless, it had demonstrated to Edward that Scotland was a much tougher nut to crack than he could ever have envisaged. Indeed, there must have been times when he wondered whether these annual campaigns in the north would ever achieve his goal. The cost in lives and resources to England alone must have been considerable, but one shudders to think what effect this war of attrition was having on the Scots. Langtoft said of Comyn and his men in 1304 that they 'have nothing to fry, or drink, or eat, nor power remaining wherewith to manage war', but when they submitted at Strathord Edward himself must have felt only relief, rather than jubilation.

It is idle to speculate that Wallace, the one leader who consistently showed courage and resourcefulness, would have fought the English far more resolutely than Comyn and his confederates, and would have used the available forces to much better advantage. Whenever Wallace commanded, the Scots showed their old mettle, but by 1304 he lacked the mandate to wage war on a large scale. Nevertheless, with the submission of Comyn and his colleagues in February that year, Wallace re-emerged as the one leader standing between Edward and his long-cherished goal, the one great patriot determined never to yield so long as he breathed.

12

BETRAYAL AND DEATH

Mors justi rapida quam precessit bona vita
non minuit merita si moriatur ita.

The sudden death of a just man after a good life
does not lessen his merits if he dies thus.

PROVERB QUOTED IN THE *SCOTICHRONICON*, XII, CAP. 8.

A FTER Strathord in February 1304 Sir William Wallace was the only Scottish leader left at large to carry on the armed struggle. Wallace was now reduced to what he had been before 1297, an outlaw heading a band of desperate men. They roamed the countryside, relying on the wildness of the terrain and the help of those Scots who were still sympathetic or well disposed to the patriot cause. As Edward's grip on Scotland tightened, with a military and administrative occupation more thorough than at any time since 1296, Wallace must have had problems enough just to stay alive and elude his pursuers, let alone engage in any major military operations.

The terms offered to the Scottish leaders by Edward, and which they accepted at Strathord, were comparatively lenient. Sir John Comyn, who had latterly been the rebel chief, got off lightly if ignominiously, being forced to make a grovelling submission which turned into a humiliating public spectacle. James the Steward and Sir John de Soulis were let off with two years' banishment in the southern half of England. Sir John alone of all the magnates refused to abide by these terms and went abroad to spend the rest of his life in France. Sir Simon Fraser, who had been one of Edward's most trusted and loyal supporters till 1301 when he changed sides, and who had then been one of the last to surrender, was more harshly dealt with, being sentenced to three years' banishment from Scotland, England and France. That he did not pay with his life for his treachery is explained by the fact that he was a doughty warrior who had compelled the grudging respect of his adversaries and former allies. The lenient treatment of Comyn and Fraser, who had so recently defeated a large English army three times in a single day at Roslin, is a measure of Edward's conciliatory attitude towards the Scots. So too, Bishop Wishart, now well on in years, was sentenced to two or three years' exile 'because of the great evil he has caused' but this was soon mitigated, for the bishop was brought into the scheme for reorganising the government of Scotland which was eventually promulgated in the Westminster parliament in September 1305.[1] Incidentally, this ordinance gave prominence to the Steward's kinsman Sir John Menteith who had, in fact, been Constable of Dumbarton Castle for the English since 1304.

The various terms of banishment imposed at Strathord were, at best, only loosely enforced. Before long, sentences were remitted, lands and property restored, and the self-same rebel leaders gradually brought into Edward's scheme for the reorganisation of Scottish government. Only one man was excluded from the terms of Strathord, and that was Sir William Wallace. When other and far greater men had demonstrated their perfidy and treachery, not once or twice but many times over, and yet were accepted into the King's peace, Edward's hatred for the younger son of an obscure knight seems obsessive to put it mildly. We have already seen how Edward referred to Wallace uncompromisingly as someone to whom unconditional surrender was the only course left open. On 25 July 1304, the day after the formal surrender of Stirling Castle, Edward held a ceremony at which he commanded fourteen of his leading barons to settle how they and others who had given long and valuable service in the Scottish campaign should be rewarded. This roll of magnates, however, also contained a paragraph which shows that, even at such a euphoric moment, Wallace was niggling in the back of

Edward's mind. This dealt with the terms offered to the Scottish leaders who had recently submitted to him and indicated that they were now being enlisted in the hunt for the arch-enemy.

According to Langtoft, Edward had previously put a price of three hundred marks on Wallace's head; now nothing so crude as a blood price was stipulated, but the terms were clear enough. The Scottish leaders, Wallace's former comrades-in-arms, were recruited to hunt him down, and on their success in this project would depend the severity or leniency of their own punishment. Sir John Comyn, Sir Alexander Lindesay, Sir David Graham and Sir Simon Fraser, all lying under sentence of banishment, were now enjoined to do their utmost 'between now and the twentieth day after Christmas' to capture Wallace and to hand him over to the King:

> The King will see how they bear themselves in the business, and will show more favour to the man that shall have captured Wallace, by shortening his term of exile, by diminishing the amount of his ransom or of his obligation for trespass, or by otherwise lightening his liabilities. It is further ordained that the Steward, Sir John de Soulis and Sir Ingram de Umfraville shall not have any letters of safe-conduct to come into the power of the King until Sir William Wallace shall have surrendered to him.[2]

To their everlasting credit not one of these men appears to have complied with this extraordinary bargain. No doubt they agreed to it at the time but never took it seriously. That Edward continued to harbour a vindictive grudge against Wallace, even though he was now a fugitive, is shown by the fact that, on 28 February 1305, he gave orders for the release from custody of Ralph de Haliburton. This knight had been one of the handful of survivors from the obstinate garrison of Stirling Castle. After the siege he had been imprisoned in England, but seven months later was released into the care of Sir John de Mowbray, one of the Scottish quislings now working assiduously for King Edward, and taken by him back to Scotland for the express purpose of hunting down the outlaw Wallace. The records indicate that Sir John and others gave security to re-enter the said Ralph at the parliament summoned at London three weeks after Easter

(18 April 1305) 'after seeing what he can do'. So far as can be ascertained, this miserable renegade was unable to achieve his objective. Murison, however, speculates whether Ralph de Haliburton was the 'Ralph Raa' at whose house, four months later, Wallace was captured.[3]

The terms of Strathord had been confirmed and ratified by a parliament held at St Andrews in March 1304. This assembly, packed by Edward's nominees, time-servers and collaborators, had agreed to Edward's demand that Wallace, Fraser and the garrison still holding out in Stirling Castle should be branded as outlaws, and on this shameful matter the parliament dutifully legislated. For more than two years Scotland groaned under the mailed fist of the conqueror. English sheriffs, provosts, sergeants, constables, tax-gatherers and a whole host of other officials, backed by large bodies of troops, busied themselves with the repair of castles, the refortification of burghs and the restoration of law and order throughout the land. In doing their dirty work, the Anglo-Norman régime relied heavily on a large army of paid spies and informers recruited from the native population. The comparative docility of the Scots, especially after the fall of Stirling Castle and the submission of Simon Fraser (both occurring in July 1304), probably paved the way for the settlement of September 1305 whereby Scotland, no longer a realm but merely a 'land', was to be gradually assimilated.

In such a climate it is nothing short of a miracle that Wallace and his small band remained at large as long as they did. The Scots had been worn down by years of devastation, often wrought by their own leaders. They were war-weary and probably came to the conclusion that, no matter which side won, they would still be under the yoke of an alien, Norman administration. The struggles and hardships of scratching a living from poor soil in a harsh climate were bad enough without bothering much about the King to whom they paid their taxes, or the laws by which their lives were governed. There is good ground for suspecting that the erstwhile national hero was, at best, an embarrassment, and at worst the cause of considerable English reprisals, to those Scots unfortunate to live in areas where the Wallace gang were believed to be hiding. The temptation to desert from the shrinking band of guerrillas must have been enormous, and Wallace himself went to great lengths to prevent this.

This is vividly exemplified by the story of Michael de Miggel (Meigle in Perthshire). Michael had done homage to King Edward at the mass assembly of 14 March 1296, but had immediately forsworn himself, for he was one of those Scottish knights taken prisoner when Dunbar Castle capitulated six weeks later. For a year and a half he was incarcerated in Nottingham Castle, evidence that he was regarded by the English as a dangerous prisoner requiring close supervision. He had been repatriated in the autumn of 1299 in exchange for James de Lindesay, an English knight whom the Scots had held captive in Bothwell Castle. On 1 September 1305, at an enquiry held in Perth, there was raised the case of Michael de Miggel who was charged with having been a confederate of Wallace. The sworn deposition of his interrogators was

> that he had been lately taken prisoner forcibly against his will by William le Waleys; that he escaped once from William for two leagues, but was followed and brought back by some armed accomplices of William, who was firmly resolved to kill him for his flight; that he escaped another time from said William for three leagues or more, and was again brought back a prisoner by force with the greatest violence, and hardly avoided death at William's hands, had not some accomplices of William entreated for him; whereon he was told if he tried to get away a third time he should lose his life. Thus it appears he remained with William through fear of death, and not of his own will.[4]

Luckily for Michael, his story was believed and he was set at liberty. Although this statement was imprecise, 'lately' has been interpreted as referring in all probability to the early summer of 1305 when Wallace and his band were still at large.

After his defeat at Happrew near Peebles, Wallace is believed to have moved north, perhaps with the forlorn hope of somehow relieving the beleaguered Stirling Castle. After the castle fell, however, a brigade of cavalry and three hundred archers, under the command of Sir Aymer de Valence, was detached from the main English force to go after Wallace, for there is mention of a running fight with the guerrillas 'under Earnside' in Stirlingshire. Once more, though heavily outnumbered,

Wallace's men used their knowledge of the terrain so skilfully that the Anglo-Scottish task-force was beaten back and heavy losses inflicted on both men and horses by the guerrillas before they made good their escape.[5]

It has been surmised that Wallace continued to enjoy what little protection could be offered by Bishop Lamberton. Although the Bishop of St Andrews had formally submitted to King Edward at Strathord and been let off more lightly than the others, there is evidence that he had not entirely given up hope of resisting the English. On 11 June 1304, only five weeks after he had sworn fealty to Edward, he was intriguing with the Earl of Carrick, negotiating a secret bond of mutual assistance. It has been suggested that Wallace may even have had a hand in arranging this deal,[6] although it might be supposed that the guerrilla had more pressing matters on his mind at that time. Such a combination, of Bruce and Lamberton, was all the more remarkable in view of the fact that the former had been appointed by King Edward to assist Sir John de Segrave, the new Warden of Scotland south of the Forth, in hunting down the last obstinate rebel. Writing to 'his loyal and faithful Robert de Brus' in March 1304 to express pleasure at the diligence with which the earl had served him, Edward concluded, 'As the robe is well made, you will be pleased to make the hood.' Bruce, however, may have been playing a double game, and the lack of real success in hunting down Wallace in the summer of 1304, by powerful forces led by Segrave, Clifford and Latimer (to whose staff Bruce was then attached), may have been due to warnings which the wily Bruce managed to get to the guerrillas.

On the other hand, although Wallace and Lamberton had been very close since the latter's nomination to the diocese of St Andrews in 1297, if not earlier, there is no evidence to suggest that Wallace was well disposed towards Robert Bruce. For one thing, Wallace had invariably upheld the cause of King John who represented for Bruce the head of the rival faction. So long as Wallace regarded John Balliol as his rightful monarch, he could not have supported Bruce; and the latter's frequent compromises, political trimming and downright unreliability would not have endeared him to such a man of principle as Wallace. But by 1304 the situation had changed. Balliol was a pathetic exile, resigned to ending his days in France, and although he had not formally renounced his throne, the prospects of his restoration were exceedingly remote. Fergusson argues that Sir John Comyn, the leader of the Balliol faction in Scotland, 'had proved, in spite of his great services, an ultimately unreliable champion of the national cause', the inference being that Wallace would not have looked on him as the future source of national redemption; but in 1304 Comyn was no more or less reliable than the slippery Bruce had been. Bruce's personal redemption would not emerge till much later. In 1304–5 the probability that Wallace was beginning to regard the Earl of Carrick as a potential king seems very small. To be sure, Bruce had the strongest claim to the throne after Balliol, but he had been the first Scottish magnate to submit to Edward, and even if he had shown himself to be a capable soldier, his deviousness and total lack of faith in anything but his own ambitions would hardly have recommended him to Wallace.

Nevertheless, the possibility that Wallace was, in sheer desperation, beginning to see Bruce as a potential saviour of his country cannot be entirely ruled out. The agreement between Bruce and Lamberton was real enough, and Lamberton, next to Wishart, had never lost sight of the eventual restoration of independence as a goal to be devoutly wished. At the time of his arrest Wallace was found to be in possession of various papers which included 'confederations and ordinances made between Wallace and the magnates of Scotland'. What this documentary evidence of a conspiracy amounted to we can only guess, for the documents themselves, like most of the others in Wallace's possession, have long since vanished without trace; but they may have implicated both Lamberton and Bruce, and possibly others, in some plan to renew the struggle. Certainly it is a matter of record that Bruce was under suspicion by 1305, and fled from London when he was warned that his arrest was imminent. Furthermore, there is ground for thinking that the manner in which Wallace met his death was the last straw for Bruce and precipitated his final breach with King Edward.[7]

Interestingly, Blind Harry has an extensive passage in his last book, dealing with negotiations between Wallace and Edward Bruce, younger brother of Robert, who had been campaigning in Ireland. The tale of the younger Bruce's landing at Kirkcudbright with fifty gallowglasses, and his subsequent exploits in Galloway, may have some grain of truth, despite the obvious error when Harry claims for Wallace unqualified success in clearing the Southrons from the south-west of Scotland. This could scarcely have been further from the truth at this time. But there may have been some substance in Harry's assertion that Wallace invited Robert Bruce to return to Scotland and take the throne. According to the poem, Bruce sent word to Wallace by means of the ever-faithful Jop, suggesting a meeting on Glasgow Moor on 1 July 1305. In view of the incriminating documents found on Wallace at the time of his arrest, there may well be some truth in this story.

If we are uncertain what Wallace thought of Bruce, there are some indications of how Bruce regarded Wallace. In the first place, Sir Malcolm Wallace became one of Bruce's staunchest adherents, and the youngest brother, Sir John Wallace, also stood high in Bruce's service, paying dearly as a result. We know also that Malcolm sided with the Earl of Carrick at that stormy meeting in Peebles in August 1299 when the magnates came to blows. If, as has been surmised, it was the Earl of Carrick who knighted Wallace shortly after Stirling Bridge, then this must be taken as a sign of the respect and admiration which Bruce felt for the Guardian. On 5 December 1303, at a time when Bruce was in Edward's peace, he confirmed to Alexander Scrymgeour the lands which Wallace had given to him in 1298. Such a confirmation alone might be taken as proof that Bruce was sympathetic to Wallace's past actions; but this was immeasurably strengthened by Carrick's reference to the former grant having been made not by plain *William Wallace*, nor even by *William Wallace, Knight*, but by *Lord William Wallace*. In the Latin document the formula was *de dono Domini Wilhelmi Wallays*, the style usually reserved for a baron or considerable landowner, neither of which Wallace was. This charter is all the more remarkable in view of the fact that it was drawn up at a time when Wallace's fortunes were at their lowest and his influence in Scottish affairs negligible, and Bruce himself was in the King's peace.

Things were getting too hot for Wallace in Perthshire and Stirlingshire so he moved south and west. The story, recounted by Blind Harry, of the meeting of Sir Aymer de Valence, Edward's lieutenant in the south-west, and Sir John de Menteith at Rutherglen Kirk may be entirely fanciful, but something not unlike this must have taken place. Menteith's background and career were not untypical of the period. A close relative of the Steward, he was the son of that Walter Stewart who had held the earldom of Menteith in right of his wife. He thus came from one of the most powerful Norman families in Scotland. He had been taken prisoner at Dunbar and had then, without compunction, changed sides, serving with Edward's army in Flanders. In 1298 he returned to Scotland and espoused the national cause in which he was certainly active in October 1301, when he was described as 'the King's enemy', and continued on the Scottish side until September 1303. He subsequently joined Edward once more and six months later was promoted in the King's service. According to Harry, Sir John was chosen for the task of apprehending Wallace because he was on intimate terms with him. Harry tries to mitigate Menteith's treachery with a speech in which he protests to Valence that Wallace has endured many severe struggles, 'not for himself but for our heritage; to sell him in such a manner would be a great outrage'. Valence points out that Wallace has spilled the blood of Christian men and put souls in peril, and assures the good Sir John that Wallace's life will be spared. He is to be held in prison for 'King Edward would have him in subjection'. According to the poem, Menteith is offered Dumbarton Castle as a reward. In point of fact, however, Menteith was already Constable of Dumbarton, a position which he had held since 20 March 1304. He had not only submitted to Edward with alacrity but had been among the first of the Scottish collaborators to benefit from his submission.

Menteith, therefore, could have claimed, if it had ever been put to him, that he was merely doing his duty to his liege lord — in the weasel words of much more recent times, 'he was only obeying orders'. But it is an inescapable fact that he was a Scottish knight, previously high in the regard of the leadership of his country and an intimate friend of Wallace, who stood godfather to Menteith's two sons. For these reasons his treachery has always been regarded as more deeply dyed than that of his contemporaries. But what Harry hints at may have been pretty close to the truth. Menteith was a realist. Aside from the fact that he was of Norman blood and therefore no different from the vast majority of the English Establishment, he had probably realised the futility of continuing a struggle which, given the vastly superior resources of England, the Scots could never hope to win. Anglo-Norman rule, by men of his own class and origins, was inevitable. The sooner that Scotland and its peoples were subjugated and assimilated the better it would be all round. The only obstacle to this tidy, convenient and peaceful solution was that stiff-necked brigand Wallace. This, or something like it, must have been in Menteith's mind — and in the mind of almost everyone else who temporised, or passively accepted the situation, or enthusiastically worked for the new order.

Even so, according to Harry, Menteith was reluctant to act until he received a personal letter from King Edward exhorting him to get on with his mission. This can only be regarded as a flight of fancy; even two centuries later the treachery of Menteith seemed too horrible to contemplate unless it could be mitigated in some way. Harry claims that Menteith got his sister's son to attach himself to Wallace's band and keep his uncle informed of the guerrilla's movements, so that a fool-proof plan for his capture could be devised. The name of this youth is given improbably as Jack Short by Robert de Brunne, and Harry adds that his hostility to Wallace arose because the guerrilla had slain Jack's brother in some previous encounter. Whatever the truth of this allegation, it is a plain fact that Sir John de Menteith was the uncle of Sir John Stewart of Bonkill who fell at the Battle of Falkirk, and it has been suggested that Menteith harboured a grudge against Wallace for the manner in which Stewart was surrounded and killed by the English in that battle.

According to Harry, 'Wallace was happy on receiving Bruce's letter, and soon removed, with his personal attendants, to Glasgow'. He allegedly remained there for at least a month, waiting for Bruce to keep his appointment. Every night for a week, with only Kerly, the most trusted of his comrades, and his new page, Jack Short, Wallace rode out to Robroyston, northeast of the city, in the hope of meeting Bruce. On the eighth night Menteith is said to have received notice from his nephew, and 'with sixty sworn men, of his own kin and of kinsmen born', Sir John hastened to the scene. About midnight Wallace and Kerly both went to sleep — most unlikely and uncharacteristic in the circumstances. It may be that they had been drugged by the treacherous page before he stole their arms and gave the signal to Menteith. At any rate, around midnight, according to

Robert de Brunne, Menteith 'took him when he weened least, on night, his leman him by', implying that Wallace was in bed with his mistress when he was seized. This story has a parallel in the metrical chronicle of Peter of Langtoft who wrote, 'We have heard news among companions of William Wallace, the master of thieves; Sir John de Menteith followed him close at his heels; and took him in bed beside his strumpet.' Oddly enough, this colourful touch is ignored by the other chronicles, and the story that Wallace was accompanied by Kerly rests entirely with Blind Harry. Robroyston was no more than a farm steading — the modern name is but a corruption of Ralph Raa's toun — an isolated building in densely wooded country which was ideally suited to Wallace's purpose, but which must also have made the task of his captors much easier.

Kerly, who had served Wallace faithfully for many years and come through countless battles and skirmishes unscathed, was taken outside and put to the sword on the spot. The brutal slaying of his companion must have disabused Wallace of any illusions that he would be treated honourably by King Edward. He leapt out of bed and reached for his weapons, but finding them gone he fought off his attackers with his bare hands. There was a dreadful struggle and Wallace, with all the desperate strength at his command, broke the back of one of his assailants on the window-sill and knocked out the brains of another. 'Then as many as could, laying hands on him, seized hold of him to have him away by force; but the whole of them could not lead him one step out of the house, till he or they were dead.' Harry has Menteith call out to Wallace that the house is surrounded by a large force of English barons and knights and that further resistance is pointless. He assured Wallace that he would be safe under his protection at Dumbarton Castle. In view of their former close friendship, Wallace was inclined to believe him, but made him swear that this was the truth. As Harry remarks, 'That wanted wit; what should his oaths avail any more, seeing he had been long forsworn to him?' But Menteith gave his promise and Wallace naïvely consented to be taken. Then, and only then, was he securely bound hand and foot and led out of the house. When he saw that there were no English barons and knights, only Menteith's retainers, and beheld the corpse of Kerly, he realised that he had been duped. The manner in which Wallace was deceived into giving himself up strains our credulity to the limit; it is both derisory and a grave slight on his reputation.

Even as he was being conveyed south instead of to Dumbarton Castle as promised, Wallace probably comforted himself with the thought that the mighty King of England would treat him honourably, as a valiant foe who had never sworn fealty to him and who had fought well in times of war. Whether he was naïve enough to believe in Edward's chivalry towards a fallen enemy, Wallace must have known how leniently the King had treated those who *had* sworn fealty to him, yet broken their word. If he did so, however, then he had not reckoned with the vindictive paranoia of His Majesty.

The narrative given by Blind Harry and Brunne, and touched on briefly by Bower and Fordun, is amplified by documentary evidence. There is, for example, the record of a payment of forty marks made to *un vallet qui espia Will. le Waleys* (a servant who spied out William Wallace), and a further gratuity of sixty marks 'to be given to the others . . . who were at the taking of the said William, to be shared among them'.[8] Menteith's own reward is amply testified by the grant of land with an annual rental assessed variously as a hundred pounds or a hundred and fifty pounds, as well as other marks of royal favour. When the ten Scottish commissioners attended the English parliament in mid-September 1305 to negotiate the regulations for the government of their country, Sir John de Menteith was appointed by the King in place of the Earl of March. On 20 November Edward ordered his Chancellor to issue letters of protection in respect of certain burgesses of St Omer passing with their goods and merchandise through his dominions. The letters were drafted 'in such especial form as John de Menteith shall wish in reason, to last for two or three years as pleases him most'. Finally, on 16 June 1306, King Edward commanded Sir Aymer de Valence to deliver to Sir John Menteith the temporality or revenues of the bishopric of Glasgow, and on the very same day drew up a charter granting to Sir John the title and earldom of Lennox, 'as one to whom he is much beholden for his good service, as Sir Aymer tells him, and he hears from others'. Nothing that Menteith did, merely in his capacity as Constable of Dumbarton, could ever have justified such valuable rewards in Edward's eyes.

In view of the fact that Wallace was reviled by the contemporary English chroniclers as *ille latro* — 'that brigand' — it is surprising that he was not slain on the spot like his faithful squire Kerly. The elaborate plans for his capture — alive — and his subsequent treatment surely give the lie to the monkish propaganda which had tirelessly worked on Edward's behalf to diminish the fame of Wallace and cut the great patriot down to size. But Edward now had in his clutches no mere robber chieftain, and a quick despatch in the dead of night at Robroyston would be too merciful for the man who had stood up to Europe's most powerful monarch, routed one of his armies, resisted another commanded by the King himself, and maintained an obdurate and uncompromising campaign against his power for more than eight years. Now he must be taken all the way to London, to be humiliated and degraded publicly by the mockery of a trial at Westminster, and finally to be done to death in as sickening and fiendish a manner as human cruelty could devise.

Wallace was bound securely to a horse and escorted by a large band of turncoat Scots south to Carlisle. On the journey from Glasgow to the border Menteith's men went to great lengths to ride only by night and avoid passing through towns and villages where they might be observed in their treacherous work. There was always the possibility that Wallace's own men, once they realised what had happened, would follow in hot pursuit, or that the common people of Scotland, seeing their great hero in fetters, would rise up spontaneously and set him free. On the south side of the Solway sands Menteith handed over his prisoner to Sir Aymer de Valence and Sir Robert de Clifford, who conducted him as rapidly as possible to Carlisle where he was briefly lodged in a dungeon. Now Sir John de Segrave took over the custody of the important prisoner. To him fell the task of bringing Wallace down to London, a tortuous journey which lasted seventeen days.

News of the approach of Segrave and his entourage sped ahead of the column and as they progressed at a leisurely pace through the towns and villages of England, crowds turned out to gape at the young giant who had proved such a formidable enemy. English propaganda had painted a black picture of the bloodthirsty brigand who raped nuns and tortured priests, who burned women and children and mutilated the still-living bodies of English soldiers. As the cavalcade approached the capital, multitudes gathered to gaze with curiosity and hatred at this rebellious savage.

On the afternoon of Sunday, 22 August, Segrave's party finally reached London. The prisoner was lodged that night in the house of Alderman William de Leyre, a former Sheriff of London, at the end of Fenchurch Street in the parish of Allhallows Staining. It seems strange that such an important captive was not held in the Tower where, it has been suggested, Wallace might have made a formal submission to the King. It was stated in the *Scalacronica* that, at some point on the journey south, Wallace was brought before King Edward, but the statement is very vague and, being written a generation after the event, has tended to be discounted. Matthew of Westminster added that 'the King wished judgment to be done of himself' (*de ipso fieri judicium*). An anonymous, but apparently contemporary, writer says that Wallace 'was taken and presented to the King, but the King would not look at him, and commanded him to London for his trial'.[9] These accounts suggest that the two great adversaries did at least meet. Fergusson adds, 'It would be interesting to know if Edward turned from Wallace as Argyll, looking from the window of Moray House, turned away from the steady gaze of the captive Montrose.'[10]

The choice of a private house rather than the security of the Tower may have been dictated by sheer necessity. It is more probable that the jeering and abusive crowds that thronged the narrow streets and alleys leading towards the Tower made further progress by Segrave's cavalcade impossible, and in the end it seemed simpler to secure the prisoner under heavy guard in a house from which he could be taken the following morning to Westminster Hall. Certainly no time was lost in dealing with Wallace. Edward had already decided his fate but, ever the lawyer, he was determined to observe the judicial proprieties. He had decided to stage a show trial as a propaganda exercise, with the intention of impressing France and the Papacy as much as the peoples of England and Scotland. In the days between news of Wallace's capture and his arrival in the capital, Edward and his minions laid their plans with meticulous care.

Early on the morning of Monday, 23 August 1305, William

Wallace was led on horseback from the City to Westminster to take part in the farcical ritual which Edward had decreed. Sir John de Segrave and his brother Geoffrey commanded the escort, and were accompanied on horseback by the King's Justiciar, the Mayor, Sheriffs and Aldermen of London, followed by an enormous crowd on horseback or on foot. Wallace came to his trial like no common prisoner but with all the pageantry of a great monarch on a state visit. On arrival at Westminster Hall, he was placed on a bench on the south side. A wreath of laurel leaves, the traditional victor's crown, was placed on his brow, allegedly to bolster the English propaganda that the proud, vain bandit chief had once boasted that some day he would be crowned king at Westminster. Some twenty years earlier, however, the head of Llewelyn had been exposed on the Tower battlements crowned with an ivy wreath, said to be in fulfilment of a prophecy of Merlin. Llewelyn had been slain in battle in 1282 but had never sworn fealty to Edward either, and it may be that Wallace's derisory adornment was based on this precedent. The following year, Sir Simon Fraser, who was to meet a similar fate, was dragged through the streets of London 'with a garland of periwinkle on his head after the new guise'.[11] Langtoft, on the other hand, says that Fraser's head was impaled on London Bridge 'without chaplet of flowers' as if the omission were a notable breach of custom. It would therefore be a mistake to suppose that the laurel crown was a special insult to Wallace. It may have marked the satisfaction of victory over a noteworthy enemy. The biblical parallel with Christ's crown of thorns is obvious.

Five days earlier the commissioners to try Wallace were appointed by the King. They included Sir John de Segrave, Sir Peter Mallory, Ralph de Sandwich, John de Bacwell and Sir John le Blound, any three or four of whom could constitute the King's justices; in the event, however, all five turned up. According to one contemporary account, Segrave's brother Geoffrey was also included, though this seems unlikely.[12] Mallory (or Mallore as it is sometimes spelled) was Justiciar of England, the chief law officer of the crown, and his name is frequently encountered in important documents of the period. His sanguinary exploits were particularly notorious in the aftermath of Bruce's seizure of the throne the following year, and included the condemning of such notable figures as Christopher Seton, Alexander Scrymgeour and John de Strathbogie, the Earl of Atholl. Mallory was assisted by another experienced judge, Sandwich, who rendered great service in this and the succeeding reign. As Constable of the Tower, he had been responsible for the confinement of many Scottish notables taken prisoner at Dunbar, including the Earls of Atholl, Menteith and Ross and Sir Andrew de Moray of Petty. Within the year he would preside over the court that sentenced Sir Simon Fraser to death. Sir John le Blound or Blunt was present on this auspicious occasion in his capacity as Mayor and chief magistrate of London. The fourth judge, John de Bacwell or Banquelle, is remembered solely for the gruesome manner in which he met his own death two years later, when he was suffocated in the crush at the coronation of Edward II.

Last but not least, there was Sir John de Segrave, a professional soldier and therefore the only one among his judges whom Wallace could respect. Segrave had fought in France and the Welsh campaigns, had served with distinction at Falkirk, been briefly captured and badly wounded at Roslin, and had taken part in the sieges of Caerlaverock and Stirling. It is interesting to speculate that Wallace and Segrave might have come face to face before that ignominious handover at Carlisle, for Sir John had commanded the troops who defeated Wallace and Fraser at Happrew in 1304. Since his appointment as Warden in March that year, Segrave had devoted himself single-mindedly to extirpating the last of the rebel Scots, and it was a point of honour that he should personally escort Wallace through the length and breadth of England to face trial at Westminster. It may have been as a signal mark of the King's approval that Segrave was appointed to sit alongside the distinguished panel of judges.

The life and exploits of Sir William Wallace were shadowy at best, obscure most of the time; but the whole course of his trial, sentence and execution was well documented by an eye-witness.[13]

The indictment, read out by Mallory, was comprehensive, William Wallace, 'a Scot and of Scottish birth', being charged with sedition, homicide, spoliation and robbery, arson and sundry other felonies. The charge of sedition or treason was based on Edward's conquest of Scotland. On Balliol's forfeiture in 1296 Edward had reduced all the Scots to his lordship and royal power; he had publicly received the homage and fealty of the magnates, prelates and a multitude of other people; he had proclaimed his peace throughout the land and had appointed wardens and other officials to maintain the peace and do justice. Yet this Wallace, forgetful of his fealty and allegiance, had risen against his lord; had banded together a great number of felons and attacked the King's wardens and men. In particular he had attacked, wounded and slain William de Heselrig, Sheriff of Lanark, 'and, in contempt of the King, had cut the said Sheriff's body in pieces'. He had assailed towns, cities and castles in Scotland; had made his writs run throughout the land as if he were Lord Superior of that realm; and having driven out of Scotland all the wardens and servants of the Lord King, had set up and held parliaments and councils of his own.

Even worse, Wallace had treasonably urged the Scots to submit themselves to the fealty and lordship of the King of France, and to aid that sovereign to destroy the realm of England. As if these crimes were not heinous enough, he had had the temerity to invade the realm of England,

> entering the counties of Northumberland, Cumberland and Westmorland, and committing horrible enormities. He had feloniously slain all he had found in these places, liegemen of the King; he had not spared any person that spoke the English tongue, but put to death, with all the severities he could devise, all — old men and young, wives and widows, children and sucklings. He had slain the priests and the nuns, and burned down the churches, together with the bodies of the saints and other relics of them therein placed in honour.

How Edward, the destroyer of the Border abbeys and burner of Dunfermline with its holy relics, had the unmitigated gall to frame this last charge is beyond comprehension. The indictment continued:

> In such ways, day by day and hour by hour, he had seditiously and feloniously persevered, to the danger alike of the life and the crown of the Lord King. For all that, when the Lord King

261

invaded Scotland with his great army and defeated William, who opposed him in a pitched battle, and others his enemies, and granted his firm peace to all of that land, he had mercifully had the said William Wallace recalled to his peace. Yet William, persevering seditiously and feloniously in his wickedness, had rejected his overtures with indignant scorn, and refused to submit himself to the King's peace. Therefore, in the court of the Lord King, he had been publicly outlawed, according to the laws and customs of England and Scotland, as a misleader of the lieges, a robber, and a felon.

The whole matter was cut and dried, the case treated as a *fait accompli*. There was no pretence at an examination of witnesses, no elaborate pleading by learned counsel at the bar, no deliberation among the judges. The long and detailed bill of indictment, a mish-mash of fact and fantasy all served up with a fine legal garnish, left the defendant no room to manœuvre. As a declared outlaw, Wallace was apparently not even asked how he pleaded, but notwithstanding the tyrannical attempt entirely to shut the prisoner's mouth, at some point in the proceedings he loudly asserted, in tones that reverberated around the crowded hall, that he had never been a traitor to the King of England, although he conceded the other charges against him. They were tantamount to the unremitting war which he had waged for eight years, sometimes virtually single-handedly, and he might as well admit it, and with pride. This outburst seems to have been Wallace's sole contribution to the trial.

We can imagine the prisoner standing alone, a majestic figure despite his shabby appearance, surrounded by scowling faces and the barely concealed hatred of those who had already determined his death. Perhaps, as the sonorous cadences of the King's Justiciar reciting the indictment rolled on, Wallace cast his mind back over the past eight years, to his triumphs and moments of glory, the crushing disappointments and the thankless struggles. Probably he was already resigned to his fate and determined to die as he had lived, with dignity and nobility. Perhaps he could even look forward to a time when his own spectacularly violent death would prove to have been the necessary sacrifice on the altar of freedom.

There was no deliberation among the commissioners, no

withdrawal of a jury to consider the verdict. Immediately after the indictment had been read, Sir John de Segrave delivered sentence:

> That the said William, for the manifest sedition that he practised against the Lord King himself, by feloniously contriving and acting with a view to his death and to the abasement and subversion of his crown and royal dignity, by bearing a hostile banner against his liege lord in war to the death, shall be drawn from the Palace of Westminster to the Tower of London, and from the Tower to Aldgate, and so through the midst of the City to the Elms.
>
> And that for the robberies, homicides and felonies he committed in the realm of England and in the land of Scotland, he be there hanged, and afterwards taken down from the gallows. And that, inasmuch as he was an outlaw, and was not afterwards restored to the peace of the Lord King, he be decollated and decapitated.
>
> And that thereafter, for the measureless turpitude of his deeds towards God and Holy Church in burning down churches, with the vessels and litters wherein and whereon the body of Christ and the bodies of saints and other relics of these were placed, that the heart, the liver and lungs as well as all the other intestines of the said William, from which such perverted thoughts proceeded, be cast into the fire and burnt. And further, that inasmuch as it was not only against the Lord King himself, but against the whole Community of England and of Scotland, that he committed the aforesaid acts of sedition, spoliation, arson, and homicide, the body of the said William be cut up and divided into four parts, and that the head, so cut off, be set up on London Bridge, in the sight of such as pass by, whether by land or by water; and that one quarter be hung on a gibbet at Newcastle-upon-Tyne, another quarter at Berwick, a third quarter at Stirling, and the fourth at St Johnston, as a warning and a deterrent to all that pass by and behold them.

Contrary to widely held belief, this was not some special punishment devised by the 'feline brain' of King Edward; it was, in fact, the standard punishment for treason, from the eleventh till the nineteenth centuries, although the full severity was not always invoked. In 1814, for example, the law was modified and that part of the sentence relating to partial hanging followed by disembowelment of the still-living felon was altered to hanging until death supervened; but drawing to the place of execution, and beheading and quartering of the corpse after hanging, were not abolished until 1870. Until 1790 the Common Law stipulated that a woman should be drawn to the place of execution and there burned at the stake, but in that year hanging was substituted for burning in the case of female traitors. These punishments, barbarous in the extreme, applied only in England; in Scotland the law was content with beheading (often performed by surgeons) after death by hanging.

The sentence on William Wallace was carried out the very same day. Outside Westminster Hall he was stripped naked and bound to a hurdle, face upwards, head pointing towards the ground, and dragged through the streets at the tails of two horses. The four-mile journey through the fetid streets on a hot summer's day would have been extremely unpleasant at the best of times but the circuitous route was chosen with care to ensure maximum exposure to the London populace who jeered and gloated, who pelted their humbled enemy with offal and garbage and excrement, and struck him with their cudgels and whips as he bounced along the cobblestones. Thus reviled and mistreated by the mob, Wallace bore the pain, the insults and the humiliation with noble stoicism. His religious training would have reminded him forcibly of the sufferings of Jesus on His way to Calvary.

At length, this ghastly procession came to a halt at the Elms in Smoothfield (later Cow Lane and today King Street in Smithfield). Now barely conscious and smarting from the missiles and blows sustained along the way, Wallace was unshackled from the hurdle and dazedly hauled to his feet. At the foot of the gallows he is said to have asked for a priest in order to make confession. Harry seems confused in placing this incident before the procession to Westminster; and his representation of the Archbishop of Canterbury as shriving Wallace, in defiance of Edward's express prohibition, is at any rate highly coloured in the details. Harry further records that Wallace requested Clifford to let him have the psalter that he habitually carried with him;

and that, when this was brought forth, Wallace got a priest to hold it open before him 'till they to him had done all that they would'. Then, with his hands still bound securely behind him, the naked giant — a fine figure of a man despite the privations of the past eighteen days — was made to mount the ladder to a high scaffold, affording a splendid view to the vast crowd which had gathered to watch the fun. The execution of traitors was a triple business, designed to degrade and humiliate, to inflict unspeakable pain and suffering, and finally to cause death. The hanging, mutilation and disembowelling, and final beheading were also regarded as death three times over. Matthew of Westminster was an onlooker and described the spectacle with immense relish in his *Flores Historiarum*:

> About the feast of the assumption of the blessed Mary, a certain Scot, by name Wilhelmus Waleis, a man void of pity, a robber given to sacrilege, arson and homicide, more hardened in cruelty than Herod, more raging in madness than Nero, after committing aimless atrocities had assembled an army and opposed the King at Falkirk. This man of Belial, after numberless crimes, was seized by the King's agents, carried to London, condemned to a most cruel but justly deserved death, and suffered this, all in the manner prescribed by the sentence but with additional aggravations and indignities. He was drawn through the streets of London, at the tails of horses, until he reached a gallows of unusual height, specially prepared for him; there he was suspended by a halter, but afterwards let down half-living; next his genitals were cut off and his bowels torn out and burnt in a fire; then, and not till then, his head was cut off and his trunk cut into four pieces . . . Behold the end of the merciless man, who himself perishes without mercy.

Before the invention of the drop gallows, hanging was an excruciating death by strangulation, a process which could take twenty minutes or more before life was snuffed out of the twitching corpse, the neck stretched grotesquely, the tongue swollen obscenely, the eyes popping out of the head. Great care would be taken to ensure that the running noose was at the side, rather than the back of the neck, so that the neck would not be broken and cause death prematurely. Victims, writhing in their agony, invariably urinated and defecated during the process and men, as a final obscene touch, had a massive erection and involuntarily ejaculated, to the amusement and entertainment of onlookers. In this instance, however, the executioners judged matters finely, cutting the rope before Wallace went into his death throes. Fiendish care would be taken to revive him partially — a bucket of water would do the trick — so that he would be conscious of the next part of the execution. His penis and testicles would be neatly sliced off, not so much in allusion to the fate of Cressingham but as part of the routine punishment meted out to traitors since the time of William the Conqueror, and keenly regarded as the last dishonour that could be inflicted on manhood.

Then, what the bloodthirsty mob had been looking forward to most of all, the deep gash in the belly and the drawing out of the intestines, consigned to the bonfire before the agonised eyes of the yet-living felon. Life would only be extinguished when the executioner reached into the chest cavity and plucked out the pulsating heart which would be held aloft with a flourish for all to see. The removal of the liver, the lungs and the other internal organs, one by one, would be accompanied by the rousing cheers of the mob, but a special shout of acclaim would greet the striking off of the head which, likewise, would be brandished aloft. The final act of butchery, performed with a heavy cleaver, was the division of the mangled torso into four parts, each with a limb attached. This, then, was the capital punishment known as hanging, drawing and quartering, which remained on the statute books of England until well into the nineteenth century, although the full rigour of the sentence had been a dead letter long before that time.[14]

Wallace's noble head was spiked and placed on London Bridge. It was dipped in pitch beforehand to delay the process of putrefaction as long as possible. Segrave, to whom had fallen the task of conveying the Scottish hero to London, now had the odious responsibility of ensuring that the four quarters of his body were taken to their appointed destinations. The chroniclers differ as regards the names of these places, Dumfries and Aberdeen being specified by one or another instead of the towns mentioned in the sentence. Wallace's right arm was hung above the bridge at Newcastle-upon-Tyne, 'over the common sewers', his left arm at Stirling, his right leg at Berwick and his left at Perth. There still exist two documents connected with Wallace's execution and the disposal of his body. One of these is a memorandum of expenses taken from the Chancellor's Roll (now in the British Library), in which his offences were recapitulated, and the manner of his death described, the expenses amounting to sixty-one shillings and tenpence. The other document is the account from the Memoranda Roll of Edward I, presented by the Sheriffs of London on 1 December 1305 for

> fifteen shillings of like money paid by the Sheriffs of London to John de Segrave in the month of August in the 33rd year of the King's reign, for the carriage of the body of William le Waleys to different parts of Scotland, conform to the King's writ; and receipt by the said John.[15]

The record shows, however, that the sheriffs were short-changed, being paid only ten shillings from the Treasury. One would like to think that this was nothing more or less than a piece of bureaucratic pettiness — surely Edward Plantagenet would never have behaved so meanly in connection with the disposal of the noblest enemy he ever faced.

In life Wallace had had a brief moment of power and glory, followed by seven years in the political wilderness, discredited but never quite defeated. Wallace in adversity became a folk hero, a cross between King Arthur and Robin Hood, and the chronicler Wyntoun could write of him 'Of his gud dedis and manhad, gret gestis, I hard say, ar made.' His death, rather than any achievement in life, assured him of immortality. The spirit of Wallace, indeed, rallied the people of Scotland. Edward committed the supreme folly of giving the Scots a martyr — and that made them a nation more surely than a decade of oppression.

As the flesh rotted away from the right arm and shoulder of the martyred hero, and the sun-dried sinews tightened, the skeletal hand of Wallace seemed to rise on the gibbet of Newcastle and point longingly to the north. Wallace had been denied the opportunity to die on his native soil, his mighty sword in his hands; now, it seemed, his mortal remains were directing his spirit remains back to Scotland. Eventually the bones would fall from their appointed places, to be scattered to the four winds. There is no record of so much as a fingerbone having been preserved after the manner of the relics of saints. It is almost as if the people of Perth and Stirling did not venerate the man who had, so recently, been their hero. Perhaps in the short term, like the English, they saw his horrible death as the end of an era. With the much-vaunted peace settlement of September 1305, only three weeks after Wallace's execution, perhaps they could do no more than hope that everything would work out for the best.

But before long, the tarred and laureated head of Wallace would be joined by others: those of Sir Simon Fraser, William's own brother John (executed in 1307) and John de Strathbogie, Earl of Atholl, the first nobleman of his rank to suffer this dread punishment since William the Conqueror disposed of Earl Waltheof at Winchester in May 1076. For the time being, however, the noble head of Sir William Wallace, sometime General of the army and Guardian of the realm of Scotland, remained alone. The sightless eyes gazed down upon the wherries and barges going up and down the Thames, the jumble of warehouses and booths, the hustle and bustle of Londoners going about their daily business. The pitch-filled ears were deaf to the plaintive cries of the seabirds soaring and wheeling about his lofty spike, high above the massive wooden bridge. Eight years previously, seagulls had wheeled with the same artless grace, the same indifference to the bloody deeds of men, above the flimsy, narrow bulwarks of Stirling Bridge.

Exactly seven months later, Robert Bruce, Earl of Carrick, was crowned King of Scots at Scone.

NOTES

1. Origins and Boyhood

1. John Major, fol. lxviii, trans. Alexander Brunton (1881), p.96
2. 'Genealogy of the Illustrious and Ancient Family of Craigie Wallace', Appendix B in *Wallace Papers*
3. The *Scotichronicon* (Scottish chronicle) is the name given to a compilation produced in the fourteenth and fifteenth centuries. It was started by John of Fordun (*d.c.*1384) about 1370 to record the history of Scotland, which had been virtually destroyed by the removal or destruction of many national documents by King Edward III. Fordun's five books ended with the death of King David I in 1153, but he left notes and other materials later utilised by Walter Bower for a further eleven books, which brought the record up to 1437. The whole history thus compiled became known as the *Scotichronicon*. The passages pertaining to Wallace were therefore written by Bower, but using materials gathered by Fordun.
4. Walter Bower, *Scotichronicon*, XI, p.83 (1991)
5. D.J. Gray, *William Wallace, the King's Enemy* (1991), p.27, following J. Fergusson, *William Wallace, Guardian of Scotland* (1938), p.6
6. Blind Harry, Book XI, ll.1425–28
7. The Marquess of Bute, *The Early Life of William Wallace* (1876)
8. *DNB*, 1883
9. A.F. Murison, *Famous Scots: Sir William Wallace* (1898), p.153
10. *Scotichronicon*, XI, p.83
11. Bute, ibid.
12. John of Fordun, *Chronicle*, LXVII
13. R.L. Graeme Ritchie, *The Normans in Scotland* (1954)
14. *Historical Documents*, vol. 3, pp.105–29
15. *Foedera*, II, pp.487–91
16. *Cal. Pat. Rolls*, 1291–92, p.192
17. Ibid., p.328; *Cal. Doc. Scot.*, I, 107

2. Early Manhood

1. P.F. Tytler, *History of Scotland*, quoting Sir Walter Scott's *Waverley Annals*
2. Fergusson, pp.10–11
3. Thomas Rymer, *Foedera* (1745), II, p.589
4. Blind Harry, Book I, ll.320–25
5. *Wallace Papers*
6. Blind Harry, Book I, ll.339–40
7. Blind Harry, Book IV, l.341
8. Lord Hailes, *Annals*, vol. I (1776), p.299

3. Toom Tabard

1. Blind Harry, Book I, ll.132–33
2. See, for example, the interpolation in *Tales of Sir William Wallace* 'freely adapted by Tom Scott', p.11
3. *Wallace Papers*
4. Geoffrey Barrow, *Robert Bruce*, pp.107–9
5. *Scotichronicon*, XI, 83
6. *Scalacronica*, p.17

4. From Outlaw to Guerrilla

1. Blind Harry, Book I, ll.191–200
2. Murison, p.52
3. Andrew Fisher, *William Wallace* (1986), p.9
4. Joseph Bain, *Cal. Docs. Scot.* II, p.191
5. Murison, p.58
6. Barrow, *The Kingdom of the Scots*, Chapter 12
7. Blind Harry, Book III, ll.80–90
8. Blind Harry, Book IV, ll.65–70
9. Fergusson, p.35
10. Blind Harry, Book IV, ll.380–83
11. Montrose charters
12. Blind Harry, Book V, ll.600–9
13. Murison, p.54
14. Charles Rogers, *The Book of Wallace* (1879), vol. II

5. From Guerrilla to Commander

1. Blind Harry, Book VI, ll.45–49
2. Murison, p.74
3. Rymer, *Foedera*, II, p.471
4. *Scotichronicon*, II, 484; George Eyre-Todd, *The Book of Glasgow Cathedral*, p.182

5. See, for example, D.J. Gray, *William Wallace, the King's Enemy* (1991), p.68; for a more fanciful account see Nigel Tranter's novel *The Wallace*
6. Stevenson, *Docs. Illus. Hist. Scotland*, vol. II, p.228
7. Evan Barron, *The Scottish War of Independence* (1934), p.34; Barron takes the unusual line that Moray, rather than Wallace, was the main leader of the independence struggle
8. *Cal. Doc. Scot.*, vol. II, p.742
9. Hemingburgh, II, p.297
10. Ibid., p.127
11. *Hist. Doc. Scotland*, vol. II, pp.183–84
12. *Scalacronica*
13. Hemingburgh
14. J.R. Lumby, *Chronicon Henrici Knighton* (1895), vol. I
15. Blind Harry, Book VII, ll.545–52
16. Murison, p.81
17. Blind Harry, Book VII, ll.879–83
18. Barron, p.60

6. Stirling Bridge

1. Harleian MS
2. *Wallace Papers*, pp.34–48
3. Fergusson, pp.54–55
4. Ibid., p.57
5. Hemingburgh
6. Rishanger, p.180

7. · The Invasion of England

1. Tytler, vol. I, pp.141–42
2. Fergusson, pp.80–81. This letter was first published by Dr Lappenberg of Hamburg in 1829
3. *Cal. Hist. Docs. of Scotland*, vol. II, p.260
4. Hemingburgh
5. Hailes, vol. I, p.398; *Wallace Papers*, p.53
6. Printed as an appendix in Jamieson's edition of Blind Harry, *The Wallace*

8. Guardian of Scotland

1. McNair-Scott, p.241
2. *Wallace Papers*, No.XVI, p.161. A facsimile appears in Anderson's *Diplomata Scotiae*

3. *Scotichronicon*, XI, cap. 31; *Wallace Papers*, p.110
4. *Cal. Hist. Docs.*, vol. II, pp.247
5. Palgrave, vol. I, pp.331–32
6. Rymer, *Foedera*
7. Sir Robert Sibbald (ed.), *Relationes Arnaldi Blair* (1758)
8. Bain, p.987

9. Falkirk

1. *Wallace Papers*, p.37
2. British Library, Harleian MS, p.37; Hemingburgh, p.61
3. *Wallace Papers*, p.19
4. Fergusson, p.136. His argument is more fully set out in an Appendix, pp.221–26
5. *Wallace Papers*, p.10
6. Other variants include:
    Lo, I have brought you to the ring: revel (dance) the best that you know
       (Matthew of Westminster)
    I have put you into a game; hop if ye can (Wallace Papers, p.10)
    I haif brocht you to the ring, hap gif ye cun (Hailes, Annals, I, p.315)
    To the ring are ye brought, hop now if ye will (Robert de Brunne)
    It was said long after that William Wallace had brought them to the revel
    if they would have danced (Scalacronica)
7. Blind Harry, Book X, ll.90–210
8. Bain, 1007, 1011
9. *Wallace Papers*, pp.10–11
10. Hemingburgh, De Brunne, *Wallace Papers*, pp.146, 148

10. Diplomatic Manœuvres

1. Bain, 998, 1008, 1017, 1023
2. Murison, p.117
3. Rymer, *Foedera*
4. *Scalacronica*
5. *Scots Peerage*, vol. II, p.218
6. Ronald McNair-Scott, *Robert Bruce, King of Scots* (1982), p.241
7. Bain, 1301; Barron, pp.132–34
8. Sir Francis Palgrave (ed.), *Documents and Records Illustrating the History of Scotland*, vol. I (1837), p.333
9. Bain, 1081
10. Ibid., 1949
11. *Wallace Papers*, p.11
12. Rymer, *Foedera*, vol. II, p.176

13. *Wallace Papers*, p.11
14. Ibid., p.163. A facsimile appears in Rogers
15. *National Manuscripts*, Part I, lxxv, p.42
16. Blind Harry, Book IX, ll.427–520; X, ll.797–960; XI, ll.1–360
17. Tytler, vol. I, p.176

11. The Comyn Wars
1. Murison, p.125
2. Transcript in Murison, p.126
3. *Scotichronicon*, XII, p.299
4. *Wallace Papers*, p.167
5. Ibid., xviii
6. Bain, 1463
7. *Wallace Papers*, pp.179–80

12. Betrayal and Death
1. F.W. Maitland (ed.), *Memoranda de Parliamento*, 1305 (Rolls Series, 1893)
2. Murison, pp.139–40
3. Ibid., p.140
4. Bain, 1689
5. *Cal. Docs. Scotland*, vol. IV, p.477
6. Fergusson, p.194; Gray, p.138
7. Barron, p.172
8. *Wallace Papers*, p.169
9. Ibid., p.147
10. Fergusson, p.211
11. T.Wright, *Political Songs of England*, p.218
12. William Stubbs, *Chronicles of the Reigns of Edward I and II*, vol. I (1882), p.139
13. *Wallace Papers*, Arundel MS, pp.189–93
14. For a graphic description of this revolting punishment, still theoretically valid at the end of the eighteenth century, see Charles Dickens, *A Tale of Two Cities*, Book II, Chapter II
15. *Hist., Docs. Scotland*, vol. II, p.485

SELECT
BIBLIOGRAPHY

Bain, Joseph (ed.), *Calendar of Documents relating to Scotland, 1108–1509*, Edinburgh, 1881–84

Barron, Evan M., *The Scottish War of Independence*, Inverness, 1934

Barrow, Geoffrey W.S., *The Kingdom of the Scots*, London, 1973

Barrow, Geoffrey W.S., *Robert Bruce and the Community of the Realm of Scotland*, Edinburgh, 1976.

Barrow, Geoffrey W.S., *The Anglo-Norman Era in Scottish History*, Oxford, 1980

Barrow, Geoffrey W.S., *Kingship and Unity, Scotland 1100–1306*, London, 1981

Bellamy, J.G., Barrow, Geoffrey W.S., *The Law of Treason in England in the Later Middle Ages*, Cambridge, 1970

Brown, P. Hume, *History of Scotland*, 3 vols, Cambridge, 1901

Brunne, Robert de, *see* Stevenson, *Documents Illustrative of Sir William Wallace*

Brunton, Alexander, *The History of Sir William Wallace and Scottish Affairs*, Dunfermline, 1881

Burns, William, *The Scottish War of Independence*, 2 vols, London, 1875

Burton, J. Hill, *The History of Scotland*, Edinburgh, 1897

Bute, Marquess of, *The Early Life of William Wallace*, Glasgow, 1879

Calendar of Documents relating to Scotland, 1108–1509, *see* Bain, Joseph

Calendar of the Patent Rolls Preserved in the Public Record Office

Crawfurd, George, *General Description of the Shire of Renfrew*, Edinburgh, 1710

Dickinson, W.C., Donaldson, G., and Milne, I.A., *A Source Book of Scottish History*, vol I, London, 1952

Dictionary of National Biography

Donaldson, G., *Scottish Historical Documents*, Edinburgh, 1974

Ferguson, W., *Scotland's Relations with England: a Survey to 1707*, Edinburgh, 1977

Fergusson, J., *William Wallace, Guardian of Scotland*, London, 1938

Fisher, Andrew, *William Wallace*, Edinburgh, 1986

Gray, D.J., *William Wallace, the King's Enemy*, London, 1991

Hailes, David Dalrymple, Lord, *Annals of Scotland*, vol. I, Edinburgh, 1776

Hamilton of Gilbertfield, W., *The History of the Life and Adventures and Heroic Actions of the Renowned Sir William Wallace*, Edinburgh, 1816

Hemingburgh, *see* Rothwell, H. (ed.)

Hog, T., *Nicholas Trivet: Annales*, London, 1845

Jamieson, Revd John (ed.), *The Life and Acts of Sir William Wallace of Ellerslie by Henry the Minstrel*, Glasgow, 1869

Keen, M.H., *The Outlaws of Medieval Legend*, London, 1961

Kightly, C., *Folk Heroes of Britain*, London, 1982

Laing, David (ed.), *The Orygynale Cronykil of Scotland by Andrew of Wyntoun*, Edinburgh, 1879

Lang, Andrew, *History of Scotland*, 4 vols, Edinburgh, 1903–7

Lumby, J.R. (ed.), *Chronicon Henrici Knighton*, 2 vols, London, 1895

Matthew of Westminster, *Flores Historiarum*, 3 vols, London, 1890

McDiarmid, Matthew P. (ed.), *Blind Harry: Wallace*, 2 vols, Edinburgh, 1968–69

Mackay, James A., *Robert Bruce, King of Scots*, London, 1974

Mackenzie, Agnes Mure, *Robert Bruce, King of Scots*, Edinburgh, 1934

Mackenzie, W.M. (ed.), *John Barbour: The Bruce*, London, 1909

Macpherson, D. (ed.), *Rotuli Scotiae, 1291–1516*, 2 vols, London, 1814, 1819

Major, John, *Historia Majoris Britanniae, De Gestis Scotorum*, Edinburgh, 1740

Maxwell, Herbert (ed.), *Chronicle of Lanercost*, Glasgow, 1913

Maxwell, Herbert (ed.), *Sir Thomas Gray: Scalacronica*, Glasgow, 1907

Miller, J.F., *Blind Harry's 'Wallace'*, Glasgow, 1914

Murison, A.F., *Sir William Wallace*, London, 1898

Nicholson, R., *Scotland, the Later Middle Ages*, Edinburgh, 1974

Oman, Sir Charles, *The Art of War in the Middle Ages*, New York, 1960

Palgrave, Francis (ed.), *Parliamentary Writs and Writs of Summons, Edward I and Edward II*, 2 vols, London, 1827–34

Powicke, F.M., *The Thirteenth Century, 1216–1307*, Oxford, 1953

Prestwich, M., *Edward I*, London, 1988

Prestwich, M., *The Three Edwards, War and State in England, 1272–1377*, London, 1981

Riley, H.T. (ed.), *William Rishanger: Chronica et Annales*, London, 1865

Ritchie, R.L.G., *The Normans in Scotland*, Edinburgh, 1953

Rogers, Revd Charles, *The Book of Wallace*, 2 vols, Edinburgh, 1879

Rothwell, H. (ed.), *Chronicle of Walter of Guisborough*, London, 1957

Rymer, Thomas (ed.), *Foedera*, London, 1816–30

Salzman, F., *Edward I*, London, 1968

Scots Peerage

Scott, Tom, *Tales of Sir William Wallace*, Edinburgh, 1981

Shead, N.F., Stevenson, W.B., and Watt, D.E.R. (eds), *Scotichronicon by Walter Bower*, vol. 6 (Books XI and XII), Aberdeen, 1991

Sibbald, Sir Robert (ed.), *Relationes Arnaldi Blair*, Edinburgh, 1758

Skene, F.H.J. (ed.), *Liber Pluscardensis*, Edinburgh, 1880

Skene, W.F. (ed.), *John of Fordun: Scotichronicon*, 2 vols, Edinburgh, 1871–72

Stevenson, Revd J. (ed.), *Documents Illustrative of the History of Scotland, 1286–1306*, Edinburgh, 1870

Stevenson, Revd J. (ed.), *Documents Illustrative of Sir William Wallace, his Life and Times*, Edinburgh, 1841

Stones, E.L.G. (ed.), *Anglo-Scottish Relations, 1174–1328: Some Selected Documents*, Edinburgh, 1964

Stones, E.L.G., and Simpson, G. Grant, *Edward I and the Throne of Scotland, 1290–96*, 2 vols, Oxford, 1979

Stones, E.L.G., *Edward I*, Oxford, 1968

Stubbs, William (ed.), *Chronicles of the Reigns of Edward I and Edward II*, 2 vols, London, 1882–83

Tytler, Patrick Fraser, *History of Scotland*, Edinburgh (n.d.)

Vickers, K.H., *England in the Later Middle Ages*, London, 1961

Wallace Papers, see Stevenson, Joseph, *Documents Illustrative of Sir William Wallace, his Life and Times*

Wright, T. (ed.), *Peter of Langtoft: Metrical Chronicle*, London, 1866

Wright, T. (ed.), *Political Songs of England*, London, 1839

Wyntoun, see Laing, David (ed.), *The Orygynale Cronykil of Scotland*

INDEX